Praise for the First Edition of *The M̶̶̶̶̶ ̶̶̶̶ ̶̶̶̶ Roared*

"One of America's boldest critics. . . . Henry A. Giroux is a voice to which we would do well to listen."—*The Times Higher Education Supplement*

"Aims to expose the cultural manipulations of global corporate capitalism, as embodied by the Disney Corporation, and its allegedly malign effects on children and families. Giroux's contention is at once fecund and ironic, and deserves a thorough examination."—*The Times Literary Supplement*

"In this polemical, didactic work, Penn State education professor Giroux charges that Disney is in fact a powerful corporation whose ideology is far from innocent."—*Publishers Weekly*

"Disney is masterly at rewriting history to convey self-serving messages. . . . [Giroux] makes the link between the corporation's use of 'imagineering' and the broad way in which many big companies (through advertising and other promotional material) do all they can to distort either the past or the present in order to make it more likely that people will buy their goods or services."—**Peter Marsh,** *Financial Times*

"Giroux makes clear that Disney is an extremely important vehicle of education and deserves critical attention by parents, educators, consumers, and cultural critics alike."—*Cultural Studies*

"Henry Giroux doesn't deny Disney's ability to delight us, but he does debunk the notion that the entertainment offered by the 'world's most influential corporation' is just innocent fun. Analyzing the messages sent by Disney through its movies, merchandising, and attractions, he convincingly demonstrates how insidious the company's portrait of the United States—as white, suburban, middle class, and heterosexual—can be."—*St. Petersburg Times*

"Henry Giroux has long been known as one who relishes digging into the meaning behind everyday social phenomena. That's what makes his exploration of Disney Corp.'s influence—reported in his book *The Mouse That Roared*—so intriguing."—*Democrat and Chronicle*

"Giroux's book is a must for parents and teachers."—*Daily Item*

"Giroux's warning that Disney's main interest is in turning the younger generation into perfect little consumers remains alarmingly valid."—*European Journal of Cultural Studies*

"This book illuminates well the particularly important variety of cultural and pedagogical critique that Giroux has advanced during the past 15 years. . . . A work accessible to the general reader that models the kind of 'language of critique' for which he has made the case in the past. Giroux closely examines Disney's role in shaping consciousness through its animated children's films, its amusement parks, its intrusion into public schooling, its toy stores. . . . Because the current class of undergraduates was raised on this stuff, the book will necessarily resonate with them. Highly recommended for all levels."—*CHOICE*

"*The Mouse that Roared* . . . by the eminent cultural critic Henry Giroux . . . is unusually balanced, conceding that Disney's products can be viewed different ways and recognizing the company's occasional good deeds before lowering the boom with an extremely disturbing array of facts gathered from widely disparate sources. . . . Giroux provides invaluable documentation of the company's exploitative labor practices abroad, its censorship of specific authors, its killing of particular ABC news stories and, most troubling of all, its recent efforts to exert influence over public education both within its planned community (Celebration, FL) and beyond."—**Jonathan Kalb**, *New York Press*

"Readers awed by the broad power of Disney Company should read this critical examination. Ideal supplementary material for students examining the commercialism of American culture."—*Booklist*

"Henry Giroux's pioneering spirit of inquiry never ceases to impress. Here he opens our eyes to the messages that consumer mass culture sends to our children, our schools, our homes. What you see is not what you get—read this book and learn what that is."—**Homi Bhabha, Tripp Professor in the Humanities, University of Chicago**

"Henry Giroux has led the way in contemporary cultural studies in insisting on the need to address the critical question of the effects on children of cultural production and representation. Giroux links the cultural messages promoted by Disney Inc. to the corporate economy, exploitative, and exclusionary practices it at once represents and pushes. In doing so, he faces squarely and analyzes uncompromisingly the implication for democratic politics of culture and desire, education and entertainment, representation and responsibility that most critics fail to register, let alone face."—**David Theo Goldberg, Arizona State University**

"Lost in the vast wilderness of 'Disney studies' Henry Giroux's stunning meditation on what the Disney empire teaches children is like having a compass in the enchanted forest. Like all of his work, he never wanders from his ultimate course: a radical democratic vision. Anyone who hopes to challenge the Imagineering of America and the world and promote an educational culture free of corporate domination must read this book."—**Robin D. G. Kelley, author of *Yo Mama's Disfunktional!: Fighting the Culture Wars in Urban America***

"An absolutely fascinating book about our children and commercial culture! A brilliant, lively, and complex analysis by one of the most interesting public intellectuals in the United States—and one that is remarkably fair-minded. Giroux does not deny the real delight that Disney brings our children. What he questions, really, are the uses of delight—and, at a deeper level, the misuse of innocence. All in all, a freshly written, unusually invigorating book that even fans of Mickey Mouse will find compelling."—**Jonathan Kozol**

The Mouse that Roared

The Mouse that Roared

Disney and the End of Innocence

Henry A. Giroux and Grace Pollock

Updated and Expanded Edition

ROWMAN & LITTLEFIELD PUBLISHERS, INC.
Lanham • Boulder • New York • Toronto • Plymouth, UK

Published by Rowman & Littlefield Publishers, Inc.
A wholly owned subsidiary of The Rowman & Littlefield Publishing Group, Inc.
4501 Forbes Boulevard, Suite 200, Lanham, Maryland 20706
http://www.rowmanlittlefield.com

Estover Road, Plymouth PL6 7PY, United Kingdom

British Library Cataloguing in Publication Information Available

Library of Congress Cataloging-in-Publication Data
Giroux, Henry A.
  The mouse that roared : Disney and the end of innocence / Henry A. Giroux and
Grace Pollock. -- 2nd student ed.
      p. cm.
  Includes index.
  ISBN 978-1-4422-0143-9 (pbk. : alk. paper)— ISBN 978-1-4422-0144-6
(electronic)
  1. Walt Disney Company—History. 2. Popular culture—United States. I.
Pollock, Grace, 1976- II. Title.
  PN1999.W27G57 2010b
  384'.80979494—dc22

                                                          2009040898

⊗ ™ The paper used in this publication meets the minimum requirements of
American National Standard for Information Sciences—Permanence of Paper
for Printed Library Materials, ANSI/NISO Z39.48-1992

Printed in the United States of America

Henry A. Giroux:
To Susan, to whom I give my heart every day.

Grace Pollock:
To my parents, John and Heather Pollock,
whose care is unwavering.

Contents

Preface to the Second Edition

Within the last decade, corporate power has expanded into all aspects of everyday life by leaps and bounds. One of the most visible examples of such growth can be seen in the expanding role the Walt Disney Company plays in shaping popular culture and broader public discourse in the United States and abroad. Once a company that catered primarily to a three- to eight-year-old crowd with its animated films, theme parks, and television shows, Disney in the new millennium has been at the forefront of the multimedia conglomerates now aggressively marketing products for infants, toddlers, and tweens (kids age eight to twelve). Websites, video games, computer-generated animation, Disney TV, and pop music—developed around franchises like High School Musical, Hannah Montana, and the Jonas Brothers and accessible online with the touch of a button—are now sustaining Disney fans into their teenage and young-adult years. Allied with multimedia giant Apple, Inc. (Apple CEO Steve Jobs is the single-largest shareholder in Disney) and the cutting-edge animation studio Pixar, Disney is beyond doubt an exemplary model of the new face of corporate power at the beginning of the twenty-first century. Understanding Disney is neither a simple nor a trivial task. Like many other megacorporations, it focuses on popular culture and continually expands its products and services to reach every available media platform. What is unique about Disney, however, is its titanium-clad brand image—synonymous with a notion of childhood innocence and wholesome entertainment—that manages to deflect, if not completely trounce, criticism at every turn. As an icon of American culture and middle-class family values, Disney actively appeals to both conscientious parents and youthful fantasies as it works hard to transform every child into a lifetime consumer of Disney products and ideas. Put the Disney corporation under scrutiny, however, and a contradiction quickly appears between the company's cutthroat commercial ethos and a Disney culture that presents itself as the paragon of virtue and childlike innocence.

I, a cultural critic and concerned father of three children, first set out to explore the contradiction between Disney's public relations image as a purveyor of wholesome entertainment and the less visible reality of Disney as a political and economic power that promotes a largely conservative culture and ideology conducive to its own corporate interests. When the first edition of *The Mouse that Roared: Disney and the End of Innocence* came out in 1999, Disney was a $22 billion profit-making machine. Ten years later, Disney is generating over $37.8 billion per year and quickly expanding the market for its products in countries such as China, where the latest Disney theme park—Hong Kong Disneyland—opened in 2005, and another park is now slated for development in Shanghai. This newly expanded and revised edition of *The Mouse that Roared* addresses Disney's ongoing relationship with children's culture while also exploring Disney as a paradigmatic instance of globalizing capital. As a worldwide distributor of a particular kind of cultural politics, Disney is a teaching machine that not only exerts influence over consumers but also wages an aggressive campaign to peddle its political and cultural influence in the United States and overseas. Corporate-controlled culture is fundamentally driven toward exploiting public goods for private gain, if it does not also more boldly seek to privatize everything in the public realm. Among U.S. multimedia megacorporations, Disney appears one of the least daunted in attempting to dominate public discourse and undermine the social and political capacities necessary for individuals to sustain even the most basic institutions of democracy. For these reasons, Disney matters to everyone.

We do not believe that condemning or boycotting Disney is either an ingenuous or a very effective way to counter Disney's power and influence. After all, we live in a commodity-driven culture, and Disney provides countless hours of enjoyment for millions of people. Nor do we critique Disney's exploitation of innocence in order to restore some kind of precommercialized, carefree childhood identity. We aim to draw attention to the too-often hidden or forgotten contexts surrounding the production, distribution, and consumption of Disney culture and, in so doing, to equip parents, youth, educators, and others with tools that enable them to critically mediate the ways in which they encounter Disney. Moreover, it is important to understand how the Disney corporation in the twenty-first century represents the new face of neoliberal power, capable of not merely providing entertainment but also shaping the identities, desires, and subjectivities of millions of people across the globe as ardent consumers and deskilled citizens. Comprehending Disney both in terms of individual desires and as a multinational corporation suggests asking larger questions: How do I spend my time? What cultural objects do I encounter in any given day? How do my experiences inform my perspectives? How might my activities impact on others, particularly children? How does the power of a corporation like Disney affect my life and shape my values as a citizen, consumer, parent, and individual?

American children from birth to adulthood are exposed to a consumer blitz of advertising, marketing, and entertainment that has no historical precedent. A typical tween or teen consumes over eight hours of recreational media daily (television, computers, DVDs, video games), according to the Henry J. Kaiser Family Foundation, which also found that children under six years old spend an average of two hours with screen media every day.[1] While most parents will take time to think carefully about the schools their children attend and to advocate for their child's right to a quality education, they rarely consider the fact that average American youth spend nearly two-thirds more of their time watching television than being in school. A 2000 study by Nielsen Media Research uncovered the alarming fact that the average American parents spend only 38.5 minutes per week in meaningful conversation with their children. Too many parents have become mere shadows in the lives of their children, who spend endless hours absorbed by the visual imagery on a screen.

Under the tutelage of Disney and other megacorporations, children have become a captive audience to traditional forms of media, such as television and print, and even more so to new digital media such as mobile phones, portable media players, video games, and the Internet. By exposing them to a marketing pedagogical machinery eager and ready to transform them into full-fledged members of consumer society, the commercial world defined by Disney and a few other corporations conscripts children's time, and the amount of time they spend in this world is as breathtaking as it is disturbing. Typical children see about "40,000 ads a year on TV alone," and by the time they enter the fourth grade, they will have "memorized 300–400 brands."[2] Today's kids have more money to spend and more electronic toys to play with, but increasingly they are left on their own to navigate the virtual and visual worlds created by U.S. media corporations. Even if many of these kids do not end up developing obesity, attention deficit disorder, anxiety, and depression, to name just a few long-term effects of media consumption, they still lack the adequate nurturing, guidance, and support they need to feel secure and happy entering their adult lives.

Yet, parents often seem resigned, if not quite grateful, that their child is watching Disney television or playing the Cars video game rather than potentially being exposed to violent or sexually explicit adult fare. It may be the case that cynicism leading to obeisance is a more dangerous response to the structural and ideological dominance of corporate capitalism than informed consent. The point of critical discourse about Disney is not to pit "good" anti-Disney critics against "bad" Disney fans. It is possible for everyone to utilize encounters with the cultural images and narratives that constitute the Disney curriculum in order to learn about themselves and others. This book encourages readers to think about, and take control over, the ideas, feelings, and activities they experience in relation to their habits of consumption and to risk a defiant analysis of the way media messages shape their actions, hopes, and desires. It is as important to comprehend and mitigate what gives us pleasure as it is to examine what elicits our disapproval. Contesting Disney's cultural authority means becoming a responsible participant in a local and a global community, both of which can be shaped by the public interest rather than corporate interest. We believe megacorporations such as Disney should be held accountable, and arming people with the critical tools to defend individual agency, freedom, equality, corporate accountability, workers' rights, the environment, noncommodified culture, critical public spheres, and democratically motivated political activism is really only the first step, but it is a step that is absolutely essential to the realization of any viable democratic resistance.

Acknowledgments

HENRY A. GIROUX

I would like to thank Grace Pollock for agreeing to coauthor the second edition of this book. She has done a stunning job and in many ways has helped produce a book that is much better than the original. She has added at least 50 percent of new material for the book, and her contribution could not have been better. I could not have been more blessed in having her as a coauthor. I would also like to thank Susan Searls Giroux for the many conversations and hours spent watching all things Disney. My three boys—Jack, Chris, and Brett—even as they turned from teens into young men, were always helpful in talking about Disney culture and the influence it had on them. This book in its first edition would never have been written if Dean Birkenkamp, then my editor at Rowman & Littlefield, had not enticed me to write it while we were having lunch at a restaurant in State College. I am also grateful to McMaster University for giving me a home these past four years in which to teach, research, and write. David Clark has been an inspiring and outstanding colleague, always willing to read my work and give me the pleasure of reading his. And, of course, for this revision, I am grateful to Alan McClare for his persistent support in pushing us for a revision and his equally incredible patience in waiting for the final manuscript.

GRACE POLLOCK

I would like to thank Henry Giroux for having enough faith to invite my contribution to his brilliant and important original text. McMaster University, the University of Western Ontario (UWO), and the Social Sciences and Humanities Research Council of Canada provided resources and financial support during this project. I am very grateful to the colleagues and friends who have been so generous with their academic guidance and skillful mentoring over the years: Peter Walmsley, Grace Kehler, Susan Searls Giroux, Daniel Coleman, Imre Szeman, and Donald Goellnicht at McMaster University and Alison Conway at UWO. The professional assistance and personal support of Maya Stamenkovic, Antoinette Somo, Aurelia Gatto, and Mary O'Connor were also vital to the completion of this book. Without the compassion and engagement of steady companions, I would not have enjoyed my work nearly as much: thank you, Melanie, Ronn, Liz, Scott, Miranda, Clayton, Mike, and Deirdre. Finally, this book would not have been completed without the friendly enthusiasm, dedication, professionalism, and generosity of Alan McClare, whose passing during the final stages of manuscript production was an inexpressible tragedy.

Introduction

Disney's Troubled Utopia

The organization and regulation of culture by large corporations such
as Disney profoundly influence children's culture and their everyday
life. The concentration of control over the means of producing, cir-
culating, and exchanging information has been matched by the emergence of new technologies that have transformed culture, especially
popular culture, which is the primary way in which youth learn about
themselves, their relationship to others, and the larger world. The Hollywood film industry, television, satellite broadcasting technologies,
the Internet, magazines, billboards, newspapers, videos, video games,
and other media forms and technologies have transformed culture into
a pivotal force, "shaping human meaning and behavior and regulat[ing]
our social practices at every turn."[1] No longer simply a means of communication or entertainment, they are in the current historical moment
the primary sites at which education takes place for the vast majority
of young people and adults; they are what we call new forms of public
pedagogy.

Although the endlessly proliferating media sites seem to promise unlimited access to vast stores of information, such sites are increasingly
controlled by a handful of multinational corporations. Consider the Disney corporation's share of the communication industry. Disney owns or
holds a controlling share in the following media outlets: six motion picture studios, including three animation studios (Walt Disney, Pixar, and
DisneyToon), Hollywood Pictures, Touchstone Pictures, and Miramax
Films, which produce films for the theater; Walt Disney Studios Home

Entertainment, which distributes films for release on video; the ABC television network, with its 226 affiliated stations; two television production studios; cable television networks, including the Disney Channel, ESPN, and interest in at least six other channels; 227 radio stations; four music companies, including Buena Vista Music Group and Hollywood Records; five theme park resorts, located in California, Florida, Tokyo, Paris, and Hong Kong; three cruise lines and several smaller resorts; two theatrical production companies that produce Broadway and touring ice shows; several book publishing imprints within Disney Publishing Worldwide, including Hyperion Books for Children; fifteen magazine titles; five video game development studios; the ubiquitous Disney Stores; and the Walt Disney Internet Group, which claims "to provide a safe, secure environment for consumers to experience the Disney brand anytime and anywhere."[2] Besides Mickey Mouse, the current franchises include Baby Einstein, Winnie the Pooh, Disney Princesses, Disney Fairies, Cars, Toy Story, Pirates of the Caribbean, High School Musical, and Hannah Montana.[3] Disney's partnerships with Apple, Inc., and the Sony Corporation have also put Disney at the forefront of media companies expanding into digital technology and the Internet. For instance, in 2006, Disney became the first company to sell its films and television shows online for download from the Apple iTunes store to computers and portable media devices.[4]

As an integral part of a multinational apparatus that transmits dominant forms of public pedagogy, mass-produced images fill our daily lives and condition our most intimate perceptions and desires. At issue for parents, educators, and others is how culture, especially media culture, has become the primary educational force in regulating the meanings, values, and tastes that legitimate particular subject positions—what it means to claim an identity such as male, female, white, black, gay, straight, citizen, or noncitizen. Media culture defines childhood, national identity, history, beauty, truth, and individual agency.[5] The impact of new electronic technologies as teaching machines can be seen in some rather astounding statistics. It is estimated that the average American spends more than six hours a day watching video-based entertainment, and by 2013 the number of daily hours spent watching television and videos will match the number of hours spent sleeping.[6] The American Medical Association reports that the "number of hours spent in front of a television or video screen is the single biggest chunk of time in the waking life of an American child."[7] Such statistics warrant grave concern, given that the messages provided through such programming are shaped largely by a $263-billion-a-year U.S. advertising industry,[8] which sells not only its products but also values, images, and identities that are largely aimed at teaching young people to be consumers. Corporations such as Disney recognize the potential for lucrative profits to be made off the commodification of children's culture, and they stop at nothing to discover the buying habits of kids and ways through which kids can influence parental spending. For example, a 2009 front-page article in the *New York Times* reported that Disney is at the forefront of the corporate quest to capitalize on the $50 billion spent worldwide by boys ages six to fourteen.[9] One way in which Disney discovers "emotional hooks" that lure boys into the "wonderful world of Disney" is to hire child psychologists, anthropologists, and other researchers, such as Kelly Peña, also known as the "Kid Whisperer." Peña's research includes looking in kids' closets, going shopping with boys, and paying them $75 for an interview (without identifying Disney as the entity collecting the data).[10] One result of hiring armies of marketers and consultants to probe the minds of male youth is the Disney XD cable channel and website (www.disney.go.com/disneyxd), which features a lot of sports content and video games. Disney's strategy to tap into the male youth market is even more evident in its $4 billion purchase of Marvel Entertainment Inc.—which holds the license for superhero characters such as Spider-Man, Iron Man, and the Hulk—in 2009.[11] If Disney has its way, kids' culture will become not merely a new market for the accumulation of capital but a petri dish for producing new commodified subjects. Young people searching for purpose and hoping to establish independent identities are a particularly vulnerable group when faced with corporate giants such as Disney, which makes every effort to understand youth so as to develop marketing methods that are more camouflaged, seductive, and successful. A number of psychologists, especially Allen D. Kanner, have publicly criticized child psychologists who hire out their professional skills to corporations.[12] And one does have to wonder how such individuals can reconcile working for companies only interested in exploiting children for profit with their ethical responsibility to promote the physical and mental health of their clients. The fact that Disney's use of neuropsychological and field researchers to mine the inner lives and experiences of children gets covered without so much as a critical comment in the *New York Times* is notable not for pointing out that Disney is less reticent because it is "so proud of its new 'headquarters for boys'" than for indicating the reality of a widespread numbness, if not acceptance, regarding the commercialization of childhood among the broader public. If the turning of children into consumer research subjects does not cause alarm, then how will people react when Disney's recently established secret research facility in Austin, Texas, begins testing kids' biometric responses to Internet ads, as it does now with adults?[13] One would hope, if we are not yet living in Aldous Huxley's dystopian world of conscripted consumption, that such news would generate more than a sigh or a whisper.

As our lives become defined by deeper immersion in a new "marketing ecosystem" made possible by a deluge of digital technologies and viral marketing techniques,[14] we are losing the ability to recognize, let alone resist, the corporate control of time, space, bodies, and minds. Pixie-dust magic may appeal to the world of fantasy, but it offers no language for defining vital social institutions as a public good, even as it links all dreams to the logic of the market and harnesses the imagination to forces of unfettered consumerism. Of course, it would be reductionist not to recognize that there is also some excellent programming designed to encourage public participation and critical thought, but by and large much of what is produced on television and commercial websites and in the big Hollywood studios panders to the lowest common dominator, defining freedom exclusively as consumer choice and either debasing public discourse by reducing it to a spectacle or eliminating it altogether.[15] Whether we are talking about the United States or other parts of the globe, it is fair to argue that for the first time in human history, centralized, commercially driven conglomerates hold sway over the stories and narratives that shape children's lives.

Consider the enormous control that a handful of transnational corporations have over the diverse properties that shape popular and media culture. Not only are "51 of the largest 100 economies in the world . . . corporations,"[16] but the U.S. media is dominated by fewer than ten conglomerates, whose annual sales range from $10 to $170 billion. General Electric, AOL Time Warner, Disney, Viacom, News Corp., and Bertelsmann AG together control approximately 90 percent of the media holdings in the United States.[17] These major firms produce much of the content for the entertainment, news, and other sources of information that permeate our daily lives, and they also control the way it is consumed by developing "media software and [owning] distribution networks like television networks, cable channels and retail stores."[18] According to Mark Crispin Miller, "Just a few giant players [are] now co-directing all the nation's media," and this means that even professional journalism intended to inform the public becomes "yet another version of the entertainment that the cartel vends nonstop."[19] It has become increasingly clear that we need a new language to define the meaning and purpose of public culture, one that makes democracy a defining principle of both learning and everyday practices. This challenge requires alternative democratic conceptions of the meaning and purpose of education, organizations capable of mobilizing civic dialogue, and political movements that can influence legislation to challenge corporate power's ascendancy over the institutions and mechanisms of civil society.

This book focuses on the role that the Disney corporation in particular plays as an influential force in shaping American and global popular culture. It also makes clear on a general level that the cultural production of meaning, social practices, and desires is increasingly dominated by a consumer society. Yet, the relationships among consumption, individual agency, and social belonging are far more complex than can be accounted for by a simplistic theory of indoctrination. We believe these relationships require an understanding of the expanding and interrelated forces that contribute to the production, distribution, regulation, consumption, and globalization of corporate media culture. These crucially important relationships become more intelligible through models of learning: how learning occurs by providing the ideas and narratives that shape how people see the world and themselves; the impact of learning on people's lives and their ability to continue to learn; and the best strategies to turn learning into opportunities to resist authoritative narratives that constrict independent, critical thought or, for that matter, to create the conditions that enable people to connect learning to social change. Learning is constantly taking place, especially when educational sites are available through the mass media to large numbers of people at once. Young people more than adults are constantly engaged in learning, and, as suggested above, they are one of the primary targets of the corporate-mediated teaching apparatus that engages in public pedagogy, or what might be called the articulation of knowledge to the shaping of values and experience. Consequently, Disney's influence as a major participant in youth culture must be addressed both as an educational issue and as a matter of politics and institutional power. Although we focus on Disney's cultural politics and its attempt to mystify its corporate agenda with appeals to fun, innocence, and pure entertainment, the seriousness of the political and economic threat that Disney and other corporations present to democracy cannot be underestimated. As Crispin Miller makes clear, a "global superindustry" has emerged with the result that "the gigantic scale and thoroughness of the corporate concentration has made a world of difference, and has made this world a very different place."[20] We need to understand the full scope of the corporate monopoly of information and private industry's regulation of public culture if we want to loosen—let alone free ourselves from—the stranglehold such megacorporations have upon democratic forms of governance and social agency in the twenty-first century.

We are not suggesting that Disney is engaged in a conspiracy to undermine American youth or democracy around the world. Nor should Disney be characterized as an evil empire incapable of providing joy and pleasure to the millions of kids and adults who visit its theme parks, watch its videos and movies, or buy its products from stores or the Internet. For parents and educators who are helping youth to navigate a perilous cultural landscape, it is indeed tempting to fall back on the adage that Disney products are of "good quality," harmless to kids, and at least a better option than most other items on the market. But recognition of the pleasures that Disney provides should not blind us to the reality that Disney is about more than entertainment. Media conglomerates such as Disney are not merely producing harmless entertainment, disinterested news stories, or unlimited access to the information age. Indeed, it is impossible to imagine what might be meant by "pure" (apolitical) entertainment, given that we inhabit a society in which "the media becomes a critical site for the articulation of a major intellectual shift in the ground of public discourse . . . in which pricing systems are now brought to bear on any problem, anytime, anywhere."[21] Corporations like Disney are fully implicated in the realm of power, politics, and ideology as they engage in processes of commodification and exploitation that recognize profit as the sole determining factor in all their corporate decision making. And even if we choose not to consume Disney products ourselves, Disney should still concern us, as its represents both a major cultural influence and an exemplary case that can help us understand how corporate media conglomerates operate on a wider social scale, regardless of their impact on discrete individuals.

At the same time, it is equally important to acknowledge that the effects of Disney films, games, websites, theme parks, television shows, and other products are not the same for all who are exposed to them. Disney culture is not a self-contained system of unchanging formal conventions. Like all cultural formations, Disney is riddled with contradictions; rather than being a static and monolithic entity, Disney culture offers potentially subversive moments and pleasures within a range of contradictory and complex experiences. In fact, any approach to studying Disney must address the issue of why so many kids and adults love Disney and experience its resorts, websites, films, and consumer products as opportunities to venture beyond mundane, everyday experience while laying claim to unrealized dreams and hopes. We aim not to categorically reject Disney products but instead to appreciate and understand the cultural mechanisms that give a corporation like Disney enormous sway over the norms and values associated with U.S. and global popular culture.

For children, Disney is a wish landscape that combines fantasy, fun, and the opportunity to enter into a more vibrant and imaginary world. Its animated films usher children into exotic and provocative terrains—filled with fantasies of escape, adventure, and powerful emotional themes about survival, separation, courage, love, and loss—and provide sites of identification and the capacity to mediate and experience in the form of fantasy realities that children have not yet encountered. Disney's theme parks invoke a kind of education that escapes the discipline and regulation of school, while providing spectacular encounters with fascinating and grotesquely shaped Disney characters, the adventure of assuming multiple identities, and the visceral thrill of park rides. Disney offers children the opportunity to dream, vindicating the desire for fantasies that contain utopian traces and offering an antidote to the boredom, brutality, and emptiness of everyday life. But the dreams generated by Disney are not innocent and must be interrogated for the futures they envision, the values they promote, and the forms of identifications they offer, particularly with respect to children.

For adults, Disney's theme parks offer an invitation to adventure, a respite from the drudgery of work, and an opportunity to escape from the alienation and boredom of daily life. As Susan Willis points out, Disney invites adults to construct a new sense of agency founded on joy and happiness and to do so by actively pursuing their own pleasure, whether it be a Fairy Tale Wedding ceremony, a cruise ship adventure, or a weekend at the Disney Institute. Disney's appeal to the so-called child in all of us is also rooted in a history that encompasses the lives of many baby boomers. These adults have grown up with *The Wonderful World of Disney* and often "discover some nostalgic connection to [their] childhood" when they enter into the Disney cultural apparatus. In this sense, Disney theme parks can be thought of as an "immense nostalgia machine whose staging and specific attractions are generationally coded to strike a chord with the various age categories of [their] guests."[22] Disney's invitation to a world where "the fun always shines" does more than invoke utopian longing and the promise of the sun-drenched vacation. It also offers an acute sense of the extraordinary in the ordinary, which, under the right conditions, can become a powerful antidote to even the most radical forms of pessimism. That Disney parks evoke just such a sense can be seen in a recent travel article published in a Canadian newspaper. The journalist begins,

> I love the Mouse. . . . Walt Disney World makes me happy. It makes my children happy. It makes me want to pay nine bucks for a pair of Mickey Mouse ears for a young relative; makes me want to order Mickey waffles for breakfast, although I'm trying to avoid carbs and don't actually like waffles. . . . If you don't think you have it in you to love the Mouse, to believe in Tinker Bell and Peter Pan . . . to see grown-ups waddling by in duck costumes without wanting to shake them by the beak and demand to know where their dignity is, don't bother getting on a plane. Just don't come crying to me when you have lost your sense of wonder, your ability to scream in terror and to gasp in surprise, when you realize you haven't laughed until you were in tears in a very long time. Because that's what the Mouse gives you. That's the magic of Walt Disney.[23]

As this passage suggests, Disney's power lies, in part, in its ability to tap into the lost hopes, abortive dreams, and utopian potential of popular culture. A closer look at the journalist's impressions, however, reveals a clearly disturbing, and perhaps inadvertent, indicator of Disney's capacity to destroy individuality and to compel, even *control*, the will of individuals toward consumption ("I'm trying to avoid carbs and don't actually like waffles"). And the very fact that the article is positioned as a rebuttal to what are assumed to be prevailing negative attitudes among adults toward Disney speaks to the contemporary challenges faced by a corporation claiming to "make dreams come true." All this suggests that Disney's appeal to fantasy and dreams—occasioning a kind of psychological disavowal on the part of fans, as suggested by the journalist's admission to *knowing* about the darker implications of corporate Disney but still not *caring* to change her behavior—becomes paradoxically both more powerful and more dubious against a broader American landscape in which cynicism has become a permanent fixture.

But if the Disney invocation of nostalgia is losing some of its persuadability and cultural authority among adults, then Disney's popularity also appears in some contexts and with certain audiences to be on the ascendant. For non-Western cultures and for children today, Disney cannot embody nostalgia in the same way it does for Westerners and for baby boomers; instead, Disney offers access to a postmodern world of free-floating identity signifiers, as it unmoors a concept of selfhood from the stable social institutions and codes of an earlier generation (for instance, family, nation, and church) and replaces it with a performance-driven notion of the self as a brand that has the power to generate its own *global* social networks. In this context, self-actualization and empowerment—rather than a nostalgic sense of loss—come packaged as various self-enhancing commodities made available to those who have money to spend and the optimism to believe in them. Yet, both traditional and contemporary versions of the Disney utopia point beyond the given while remaining firmly within it. As philosopher Ernst Bloch points out, genuine wishes are felt at the start, but these are often siphoned off within constructions of consumer agency, careless fun, and childhood innocence that undercut the utopian dream of "something else"—that which extends beyond what the market and a commodity-crazed society can offer.[24]

As suggested above, the feeling of happy plenitude derived from Disney "magic" is more often than not revealed to be a mere "swindle of fulfillment"[25] through the varied and complex contradictions that emerge from the way adults and young people experience a Disney culture that simultaneously elicits both pleasure and irritation, subordination and resistance, passive identification and genuine affective involvement. For example, Disney's invitation to adult couples to

experience an erotic fling—an escape into a hoped-for rekindling of sen-
sual desire and pleasure by taking a vacation at one of Disney's theme
parks—is undermined by an environment that is generally antiseptic,
overly homogeneous, regulated, and controlled. Yet, this exoticizing of
the Disney landscape does contain a utopian element that exceeds the
reality of the Disney-produced commercialized spaces in which such
desires find their origins as well as their finale in the fraudulent promise
of satisfaction.

Of course, there are no passive dupes in this script. Disney's texts
are neither static nor universal, and some even present opportunities
for oppositional readings. For some cultural theorists, the strength of
Disney's texts lies in their potential to tap into viewers' desires and
in the multiple readings they provide for diverse audiences, although
most researchers find it necessary, as we do, to carefully balance the
discussion of the affirmative elements in Disney culture with acknowl-
edgment of its problems.[26] Granted that the importance of recognizing
that the mode of reception is constitutive of meaning and that the dif-
ferential meanings of a particular text are in part determined by how the
audience confers meaning, this insight does not eliminate the need to
take into account larger cultural, political, and economic contexts and,
in this case, the inordinate power of megacorporations such as Disney
to control the range of meanings that circulate within society. It would
be a political and pedagogical mistake to affirm only the "active and
critical element in popular cultural usages, [while] overlooking the
overwhelming historical realities of inequality and subordination that
condition [such responses]."[27] In other words, the potential for subversive readings, the complex interplay of agency and subordination, and
the mixture of alienation and pleasure promoted by the culture industry
do not cancel out the power of a corporation like Disney to monopolize
the media and saturate everyday life with its own ideologies. Although
it is true that people mediate what they see, buy, wear, and consume
and bring different meanings to the texts and products that companies
like Disney produce, it is crucial that any attempt to deal with the
relationship between culture and politics not stop with such a recognition but investigate both its limits and its strengths.[28] Although media
and popular culture are contested terrains, always subject to disruptive
translations and negotiations, the playing field is nowhere close to being
level. As Janet Wasko's work makes clear, most people share "similar

understandings of Disney," which unfortunately suggests that "there is little room for active or alternative readings of texts, like Disney's, which are carefully coded and controlled, and not polysemic and open."[29] Consequently, this book initiates a discussion about the ideas and values that people derive from their encounters with Disney culture by paying extensive attention to the commonsense narratives often encoded by Disney as an important step in the process of interrogating the historical, institutional, and political conditions that shape, limit, and condition the way people decode such narratives in an increasingly globalized, militarized, and market-oriented world.

This book aims to take seriously the cultural and political effects of the Walt Disney Company, to shatter commonplace assumptions that equate Disney with fun and games and childhood innocence, and to offer readers a set of tools that will enable them to inquire into what Disney represents, in a way that they might not have previously considered. In short, this book represents a critique of Disney that goes beyond studies that limit themselves to either close readings or populist interpretations of Disney texts or that fail to consider the diverse contexts that inform Disney culture.[30] At the same time, this book poses a challenge to anti-intellectual arguments that scholars who take a critical perspective of Disney have nothing better to offer than "self-righteous tirades against an endless litany of 'isms.'"[31] The issue at stake in Disney studies should not be the rhetoric employed by cultural critics or their neglect of the immense popularity of Disney's texts, but rather the problem of how to address and challenge the authority of an entity like the Walt Disney Company as it interacts with a whole assemblage of other cultural texts, ideologies, and practices. Within this perspective, accounting for why millions of people say they love Disney is not nearly as significant as posing the larger questions of how some ideas, meanings, and messages under certain political conditions become more credible as representations of reality than others and how these representations assume the force of ideology by making an appeal to common sense while at the same time shaping political policies and programs that serve very specific interests, such as the Telecommunications Act of 1996, the forging of school-business partnerships, and the U.S. invasion of Iraq as a post-9/11 response to terrorism.

Reading methods that remind us of the complex and indeterminate relationships between texts and their reception—but stop short of considering the effects of power on such relationships—may have "fallen into the trap of believing that method is sovereign and can be systematic without also acknowledging that method is always part of some larger ensemble of relationships headed and moved by authority and power."[32] For the late Edward Said, the forces of cultural production and reception were not equal, which suggests that we should always deal with the relationship among politics, power, and pedagogy when analyzing cultural phenomena. Focusing on how subjects interpret, mediate, or resist different messages, products, and social practices does not cancel out the concentrated assemblage of power that produces them; nor does it address the broader historical, cultural, and institutional affiliations that often privilege texts with specific intentions and meanings. Nor does such a limited approach to Disney enable the working out of a political project that takes a stand against particular forms of domination while struggling to expand democratic relations. There is no virtue, ideologically or politically, in either remaining on the level of theoretical abstraction or simply pronouncing what Disney means to various individuals and groups if such an approach also ignores the impact of corporate power and media monopolies on the larger culture and the ways in which resistance to their domination has resulted in revitalized and pluralized democratic public spheres.

This book approaches Disney by highlighting the pedagogical and the contextual and by raising questions about Disney, such as what role it plays in (1) shaping public memory, national identity, gender roles, and childhood values; (2) suggesting who and what qualifies as an agent; and (3) determining the role of consumerism in American culture and around the globe. These questions expand the scope of inquiry. Disney must be engaged as a public discourse, and doing so means offering an analysis that forces civic discourse and popular culture to be accountable to each other. Such an engagement represents both a pedagogical intervention on the terrain of cultural politics and a way of recognizing the multiple, shifting contexts in which any cultural phenomenon must be understood and engaged.

Each of the following chapters provides a different lens through which to examine Disney's influence as a cultural and corporate entity. Chapter 1 looks at the crisis that has emerged around the concept of childhood and the expanding role corporate culture plays in constructing new forms of childhood innocence. It explores the pedagogical practices that Disney employs in the attempt to substitute consumerism for democratic citizenship, first, in its tightly controlled themed spaces, which advance the ongoing privatization of public space, and, second, in its corporate work culture based on hierarchical rule and rituals. Chapter 2 discusses the expanding role that Disney plays in shaping education by producing learning materials for the very young that it claims are "educational" and by influencing older kids' attitudes toward schooling in its more recent television shows and films. Disney's partnership with the public education system in Celebration, Florida, is explored in detail since it represents a public relations venture that not only tried to affirm Disney's public image as a benevolent corporation invested in children's education but also exposed ways in which Disney is ultimately driven by market considerations rather than public interests. Chapter 3 provides contexts and readings for many of Disney's animated films, particularly ones made in the 1990s that served as the foundation for the radical expansion of Disney's corporate and cultural power during that decade. It proceeds to discuss how the Pixar Animation Studio's computer-generated imagery, or CGI, animated films have become the true heirs to both Walt Disney's artistic and creative legacy and the company's great nostalgia machine. Disney's authority in popular culture is so secure that it can withstand the self-critical and parodic elements of its more recent films—elements that expose the darker side of unchecked corporate power, for example, the commercialization of the children's toy industry (the *Toy Story* films) or the environmental impacts of hyperconsumption (*Wall-E*). Turning to politics, Chapter 4 explores the activities of the Disney corporation alongside the ominous expansion of neoliberal policies and ideologies in the United States and the implementation of a national security agenda after September 11, 2001. Two films, the ABC production *The Path to 9/11* and Disney/Pixar's *The Incredibles*, endorse a severely curtailed political agency that suggests a rapidly developing crisis in broader public discourse. Chapter 5 considers global contexts for approaching Disney: first, the market fundamentalism that underpins a vision of global expansion put forward by CEOs Michael Eisner (1984–2005) and Robert Iger (2005–present); second, the development of Disney theme parks in France, Japan, and China and the ways in which American models were adapted to local cultures; and third, the growing resistance among various groups around the globe to Disney's corporate policies and cultural influence, most especially to its use of sweatshops and other reprehensible labor practices. These various aspects of global Disney make clear that as the corporation grasps for more power—perhaps by eliminating healthy democratic public spheres or by increasing its control over the field of social meanings in more and more countries around the world—it will face a number of challenges arising from organized, informed protesters who refuse to be the passive consumers Disney needs to populate its global empire.

Questioning what and how Disney teaches through its corporate actions and its public pedagogy is part of a much broader inquiry regarding what parents, children, educators, and others need to know in order to critique and challenge, when necessary, antidemocratic institutional and cultural forces that have a direct impact on public life. Such inquiry is most important at a time when corporations hold an excessive amount of power in shaping children's culture as a largely commercial endeavor, using their various media technologies as teaching machines to commodify and homogenize all aspects of everyday life—in this sense posing a real threat to the freedoms associated with a substantive democracy. But questioning what megacorporations like Disney teach also means appropriating the most resistant and potentially subversive ideas, practices, and images at work in their various cultural productions and turning them into further opportunities to voice dissent.

This book does not purport to be *the* definitive study of Disney; rather, it aims to provide a framework for generating more dialogue, while also encouraging the use of public time and space to enter discussions about Disney both within and outside academic fields of study. It takes as its main tenet that what Disney teaches cannot be abstracted from a number of important larger issues: What does it mean to make corporations accountable to the public? How do we link public pedagogy to a critical democratic view of citizenship? How do we develop forms of critical education that enable young people and adults to become aware of and interrogate the media as a major political, pedagogical, and social force? How do we make education and culture central to any viable understanding of politics? How might we convince young people that while pleasure is central to any definition of popular culture, there is also another kind of pleasure, the pleasure of learning? At the very least, such a project suggests developing educational programs in both informal and formal schooling environments that offer students the opportunity to learn how to use and critically read the new media technologies and their cultural productions. Organizing to democratize the media and make it accountable to a participating citizenry also demands engaging in the hard political and pedagogical task of opening up corporations such as Disney to public interrogation and critical dialogue.[33]

Disney's overwhelming presence in the United States and abroad reminds us that the battle over culture is central to the struggle over meaning and institutional power. For learning to become meaningful, critical, and emancipatory, it must not be surrendered to the dictates of consumer choice or to a prohibition on critical engagements of how ideologies work within various cultural discourses. On the contrary, critical learning must be linked to the empowering demands of social responsibility, public accountability, and democratic citizenship. How we educate our children and youth is intimately connected to our collective future. We need to sustain the narratives that empower young people in the spheres of our public culture. As noncommodified public culture comes under assault, we are faced with a growing commercial sphere that profoundly limits the vocabulary and imagery available to youth and others for defining, defending, and reforming the self, the state, and various public spheres as centers for critical learning and citizenship. None of us is unaffected by the cultures of pleasure and entertainment that now hold sway over much of the Western world and are rapidly extending their influence to other countries, particularly Japan, India, and China. The test of these spreading culture industries cannot be based solely on whether they are capable of producing joy and merriment but must instead assess their capacity to offer narratives of pleasure without simultaneously undermining democratic movements and institutions. What we do not need is a global culture industry in which Disney imagineers and executives turn children's desires and dreams into fodder for advertisers and corporate-controlled media.

Chapter One

Disney and the Politics
of Public Culture

I think of a child's mind as a blank book. During the first years of his life, much will be written on the pages. The quality of that writing will affect his life profoundly.

—Walt Disney[1]

In the popular mind, Walt Disney, both the man and the company, is synonymous with the notion of childhood innocence. As suburban America witnesses urban violence invading its own schools, homes, and neighborhoods, Disney becomes a symbol for the security and romance of the small-town America of yesteryear—a pristine never-never land in which children's fantasies come true, happiness reigns, and innocence is kept safe through the magic of pixie dust.

Of course, Walt realized that innocence as a cultural metaphor had to be associated with a particular rendering of childhood as well as a specific view of the American past, present, and future. In other words, Disney's view of innocence had to be constructed within particular maps of meaning in which children and adults could define themselves through a cultural language that offered them both modest pleasure and a coherent sense of identity. Nicholas Sammond has written a brilliant account of how the Walt Disney Company created a market niche for children's entertainment alongside scientific discourses—mainly sociology and psychology—that were being popularized from the 1930s to the 1960s in an attempt to define the "normal" child. One result of children being seen as "the crucible of ideal American culture" was the proliferation of media that aimed to "correct the way children are raised" so as to "eliminate a number of social ills."[2] In particular, Sammond suggests that the paternalistic image Walt Disney promoted of himself was key to the corporation's being seen as an expert parental substitute whose products implemented new, cutting-edge ideas of what was best for children and society more generally. The fact that most of those ideas regarding the generic American child were largely aimed at reinforcing dominant assumptions about gender, race, religion, and class is yet another paradox lying at the heart of Disney culture. Indeed, Walt Disney quickly saw the advantages to linking childhood innocence with home entertainment, which became the pedagogical vehicle to promote a set of values and practices that associated the safeguarding of childhood with a strong investment in the nuclear family, middle-class Protestant values, and the market as a sphere of consumption. Refusing to separate entertainment from education, Disney challenged the assumption that entertainment has little educational value and is simply about leisure. Walt understood that education is not confined to schools but embedded in the broader realm of popular culture and its mechanisms for the production of knowledge and values. In creating his ideal democracy of consumers, he also knew that the Walt Disney Company had to make products that were lively and enjoyable.

Walt's fusing of entertainment and education blurred the boundaries between public culture and commercial interests and found expression both in the various attractions that came to characterize theme parks, such as Disneyland and Disney World, and in the extended range of cultural and media outlets that shape everyday life. For decades, Hollywood films, radio stations, television networks, sports franchises, book publishers, and numerous daily newspapers all provided Disney with sites from which to promote its cultural pedagogy. Among Walt Disney's more lucrative insights—one that continues to distinguish the Disney corporation—was the realization that the educational field could be reconstructed and transformed through the mastery of new spaces for leisure, new electronic technologies, and new global markets. Pedagogy, for Disney, was not restricted to schooling, and schooling did not strictly define the contexts in which children could learn, make affective investments, and reconstruct their identities.

If we imagine the Walt Disney Company as a teaching machine whose power and influence can, in part, be measured by the number of people who come in contact with its goods, messages, values, and ideas, it becomes clear that Disney has now wielded for decades an enormous effect on the cultural life of several nations, especially with regard to the culture of children. In 1995, "more than 200 million people a year watch[ed] a Disney film or home video, 395 million watch[ed] a Disney TV show every week; 212 million listen[ed] or dance[d] to Disney music, records, tapes or compact discs. . . . More than 50 million people a year from all lands pass[ed] through the turnstiles of Disney theme parks."[3] In the company's 1997 annual report, Michael Eisner, former chairman and chief executive officer of the Walt Disney Company, claimed that during the week of November 2 to 8, 1997, Disney culture attracted the attention of the following numbers of people, mostly children:

> During these seven days, 34.2 million people watched *The Wonderful World of Disney*, 3.3 million people turned on *One Saturday Morning*, 3.8 million subscribers viewed *The Disney Channel*, 2.8 million listened to *Radio Disney*, 793,000 visited Disney theme parks, 810,000 made a purchase at a Disney Store and nine million copies of *Beauty and the Beast: The Enchanted Christmas* were shipped to video stores across the country.[4]

Disney's success with brand licensing and cross-promotion of its hit television shows and films continues to exert a formidable influence on children and youth. In 2008, despite the economic recession, Disney had one of its most profitable years on record, generating $37.8 billion in sales.[5] The Disney website DisneyFairies.com, which helps very young computer users to generate fairy avatars, attracts more than 1 million daily visitors.[6] The tween franchises High School Musical and Hannah Montana helped to sell more than 33 million books.[7] The Disney Princess franchise, with its array of pink and gold items, is a "leading lifestyle brand" for six- to nine-year-old girls.[8] And Disney now claims to "fulfill the dreams of girls of any age, including brides-to-be," by selling bridal couture and home furnishings inspired by the "personality and style of each Disney Princess."[9] In 2007, Disney produced an estimated 40 percent of all the licensed merchandise in the United States and Canada.[10] Marketing analysts now report that consumers around the world spend about 13 billion "person-hours" per year in contact with Disney's various brands.[11]

Disney's commercial success testifies to the crucial role that culture and entertainment play "in the structure and organization of late-modern society, in the processes of development of the global environment and in the disposition of its economic and material resources."[12] Disney's success represents, in part, the power of the culture industries to mediate and influence almost every aspect of our lives.[13] Corporate culture uses its power as an educational force to redefine the relationships between childhood and innocence, citizenship and consumption, civic values and commercial values. Both how and what young people learn, in a society in which power is increasingly held by megacorporations, raises serious concerns about what noncommodified public spheres exist to safeguard youth from the ravages of a market logic that provides neither a context for moral considerations nor a language for defending vital social institutions and policies as a public good.

A vibrant democratic culture fulfills one of its most important functions when it views children as a social investment, whose worth and value cannot be measured exclusively in commercial and private terms. That is, a democratic culture provides the institutional and symbolic resources necessary for young people to develop their capacities to engage in critical thought, participate in power relations and policy decisions that affect their lives, and transform racial, social, and economic inequities that close down democratic social relations.[14]

The concept of democracy, when linked to the notion of social justice, refers to a society's obligation to create and maintain institutions that view education as a public asset and not merely a private good. The requirements of democratic citizenship necessitate vigilance in public affairs, criticism of public officials (and corporate interests), and participation in political decision making in the interest of expanding accountability, equality of opportunity, justice, and the public good. Such activity resists the privatizing impulses of corporations, which attempt to overshadow the demands of citizenship with the demands of commerce by replacing the notion of free and equal education as a right with the notion of restricted and income-based education as a commodity venture. The challenge democratic societies face with the rise of conglomerates such as Disney—with their profound interest in shaping all facets of youth culture—can be discerned in the crisis that has emerged around the very concept of childhood and the expanding role that corporate culture plays in shaping public education. The following section addresses this issue, before we turn to an examination of some of the pedagogical practices that Disney employs in its theme parks and its corporate work culture.

THE ECLIPSE OF CHILDHOOD INNOCENCE

The United States appears to be in the midst of a social and cultural upheaval regarding both how it views children and how it expresses its concerns for them. Tragedies involving young people are reported in the media every day. In addition to news stories about mental illness, drug and alcohol addiction, and bullying, more accounts of kidnapping, murder, rape, and enslavement seem to make the headlines all the time. There have been dozens of school shootings since the 1990s, with the massacres at Columbine High School in Littleton, Colorado; Red Lake High School in Cold Spring, Minnesota; and Virginia Tech in Blacksburg, Virginia (alone costing thirty-three lives) exacerbating the fear that childhood innocence is being eclipsed in contemporary American society.[15] Such fears mobilize public concerns about the growing threat to children's safety and well-being and fuel the emergence of a repressive security culture in schools.[16] The nation is also coping with the increasing, and even convenient, collapse of the boundaries between children and adults through the passage of state legislation that authorizes the prosecution and sentencing of kids as young as fourteen years old. Anger, confusion, and an eagerness to exonerate adults of responsibility toward youth have seeped into public consciousness, with one result being that kids are increasingly tried as adults in the criminal justice system. Children are now seen as both troubled and troubling, as the perspective of the country shifts from viewing children as a social investment to seeing them as threats to be contained or punished by expanding surveillance laws, enacting harsher criminal codes, imposing strict zero-tolerance laws in the schools, putting more young people into the criminal justice system, and dismantling traditional safety nets such as child welfare, health care, and school nutrition programs.[17]

James Wagoner, president of the social services organization Advocates for Youth, argues that this cynicism has less to do with public concern over the fate of the nation's children than with a trend toward blaming children for the very problems that society creates for them.

He writes, "Young people have been portrayed almost universally as a set of problems to be managed by society: juvenile crime, teen-age pregnancy, drug use. . . . That concept has taken such deep root that various institutions are permeated by it, and there's not enough of the other view, of youth as an asset, a group of people with their own perspectives on things who do pretty well."[18] The scapegoating of young people, especially those who are poor and belong to racial minorities, points to an increasing loss of childhood innocence, to a crisis in public discourse, and to a growing inability on the part of society to affirm and act on the principles of social justice, equity, and democratic community.[19] As the quality of public life diminishes, not only do the most vulnerable and powerless of our population suffer, such as children, the needy, and the elderly, but we lose, as a nation, a common vocabulary for defining and reforming those public spheres that are vital to the meaning and experience of democratic life.

When school shooter Kipland Kinkel of Springfield, Oregon, was asked in 1998 about a family trip to Disneyland, the youngster replied that he wanted to "punch Mickey Mouse in the nose." Although Kinkel appeared to be deeply disturbed, his comment begs consideration of the tensions that many youth must feel about, on the one hand, the cultural iconography of Disney as a purveyor of innocence and family fun and, on the other, the harsh realities of coming of age in a society that not only is weary of its youth but also repeatedly demonstrates that kids do not count for much—except as consumers. Kinkel's comment also suggests that we should consider whose hunger for innocence and absolution is given succor in the yearly family pilgrimage of middle-class America to the Magic Kingdom.

Thomas Hine recounts a story that suggests even further how Disney is concerned with associating its image with a particular kind of youth, not youth in general. In the summer of 1997, a group of suburban California teens dressed as goths in black clothes and white makeup began to frequent Disneyland. Their parents had given them yearly passes, and although Disneyland attractions did not hold much appeal for them, they were drawn to the benches of Tomorrowland as a place where they could hang out without feeling bothered. But that comfort did not last long. When the public began voicing complaints that they no longer felt safe in Disneyland because of the presence of the brooding teens, their sense of security was shattered, and the harassment began. Disney security forces announced a "zero-tolerance" policy and began arresting the teenagers "for even the tiniest infractions outside the park" and applying "quite restrictive rules of decorum within the park."[20] Hine draws attention to the fact that the theme park, as a private space, had the option to revoke the teen's passes, but instead it settled for "a stance of uneasy tolerance backed by coercion and force [that] seems symptomatic of the way Americans deal with young people now."[21] Hine offers several insights into what the teenage goths in Disneyland might signify, including the possibility that kids who are presented with only commercialized venues (which promise homogenization without a real sense of belonging) will find alternative outlets for expression that might seem extreme to adults but that actually speak to the failure of adult society and schools to provide youth with noncommercialized spaces in which to safely experiment with "the search for identity [and] assess their talents and desires in relation to the world." As Hine suggests, the discourse of innocence loses substantive meaning in a society in which young people—poor minority youth much more so than costumed white teens at Disneyland—"bear an inordinate share of the blame for society's failures, while they're given too little responsibility for its improvement."[22]

It is disturbing how public discussion of the problems facing youth in the past two decades seems limited to whether to provide our children with more stuff or to devise new, and often criminal, policies to contain them. If a kid does not end up facing extreme disciplinary measures and being shut away in the expanding "youth-control complex,"[23] then he or she ends up being bombarded with advertising. It is difficult to underestimate the enormous attention that children attract from corporate culture. Children and youth, especially those under age fourteen, have become a hot item for corporations because market analysts have recognized that the tween segment (ages eight to twelve) spends an estimated $170 billion per year on items such as mobile phones, video games, and music players.[24] Disney Consumer Products, eager to tap into such a market, fostered a partnership with Walmart in 2007 to sell merchandise based on the Hannah Montana, High School Musical, and other franchises, and expected its tween retail business to reach $400 million in sales in 2008. With respect to the collaboration, Disney spokesperson Ron Johnson indicated that the popular franchises will help Walmart "identify with this consumer," for the ostensible purpose of boosting sales for both corporations.[25]

The debate about children's loss of innocence signifies more than society's changing attitude toward young people; it also points to the rise of a corporate culture that reasserts the primacy of individualism and competitiveness and seduces young people into surrendering their capacity to become citizens in the fullest sense—possessed of the widest range of democratic skills and rights—replacing citizenship with a market-based notion of identity, one that suggests they should relinquish the role of critical subject for the passive role of consumer. Similarly, as corporate culture extends ever more deeply into the basic institutions of civil and political society, there is a simultaneous diminishment of noncommodified public spheres such as social service centers, churches, and recreational clubs, which offer the opportunity for people to engage in dialogues and practices that address the relationship of the self to public life, our responsibility to the demands of active citizenship, and a practical politics that connects our own interests to larger public problems.[26] As commercial culture replaces public culture and the language of the market becomes a substitute for the language of democracy, consumerism appears to be the only kind of citizenship on offer to children and adults alike.[27] Consumerism, corporatism, and technological progress become the central principles for constructing who we are and how we act. Democratic identities are replaced by consuming patterns, and the good life is constructed in terms of what we buy.

The eclipse of childhood innocence should be examined critically within the broader context of the decline of civic literacy and democracy and the ascendance of a market culture that takes over or eliminates the public spaces crucial to the education of young people and to the time needed for them to discover and experience democratic values, identities, and social relations. As corporate power extends its influence and reach over public schools, education is subordinated to the logic of the market and to the creation of corporate citizens, literacy is reduced to a consumer-oriented skill, and self-governance is reduced to the banality of market-based practices, such as learning name brands. The commercial spheres promoting such changes include Internet sites, shopping malls, and outlets like television, radio, cinema, and newspapers. They and other media are engaged in a cultural pedagogy marked by a struggle over meaning, identity, and desire. This struggle affirms the growing political and pedagogical force of culture "as a crucial site and weapon of power."[28] It also demonstrates how the education of desire by the mass media turns people away from striving for public voices and social betterment and toward individual acquisitiveness. Increasingly, large corporations work to confer a sense of meaning and purpose through a commercial logic that simultaneously constricts democratic identities, values, and citizenship skills.

Corporations like Disney use media culture as one of the most important vehicles through which they can express their commitment to middle-class family values, the welfare of children, and expansion into noncommercial spheres such as public schooling. But the public relations rhetoric represents more than the staged authenticity of the corporate swindle; it also works strategically to "celebrate innocence over politics and other forms of critical knowledge."[29] Corporate interest in the family also suggests the increasing recognition that youth hold the key to huge markets and profits in the twenty-first century and that such markets can be harnessed only if the identities and desires of children can be mobilized within the vastly influential educational spheres of both popular culture and public education.

DISNEY'S CORPORATE REACH

Within the past thirty years, corporate power, under the auspices of neoliberalism and multinational corporations, has grown by leaps and bounds.[30] One of the most visible examples of such growth can be seen in the expanding role that the Walt Disney Company plays in shaping popular culture and many aspects of everyday life in the United States and abroad. Allied with Apple, Inc., and the Sony Corporation, the Walt Disney Company is an important model of the multimedia conglomerate in the digital age as well as the new face of corporate power at the beginning of the new millennium. Like many other megacorporations, it focuses on popular culture and continually expands its reach to include not only theme parks but television networks, motion picture studios, music companies, radio stations, online entertainment, cruise lines, Broadway theater productions, publishing houses, and video game development studios.

In part, media conglomerates wield so much power because they pay to have their voices heard. Each year corporations spend millions of dollars to lobby government to ease regulations and shape legislation more favorable to media monopolies, bypassing the democratic constitutional processes. In 2000 alone, Disney along with the other parent companies of the big five broadcast networks (ABC, CBS, NBC, Fox, and CNN) paid almost $27 million to lobbying firms.[31] Besides sponsoring vacations for Federal Communications Commission regulators—a scandalous conflict of interest to say the least—media companies like Disney hire the same lobbyists as insurance agencies, pharmaceutical and tobacco companies, and weapons manufacturers. This could lead, as Alexander Lynch points out, to "a lobbyist taking a congressman on an all-expense-paid outing and arguing, for instance, the need to stop cheaper drugs from being imported from Canada (or demanding government and military contracts for his/her client) and then, and in the next breath, representing the interests of the media."[32] Mark Crispin Miller comments on an even more "fundamental conflict of interest afflicting American journalism. . . . On the one hand, the press has a tacit constitutional obligation to inform people. On the other, publicly traded corporations that own news are run by people who have a strict fiduciary obligation to shareholders. These two obligations are utterly opposed for many reasons."[33] The question then becomes, What kind of investigative coverage of corporate corruption is provided by a network like ABC if it uses the same lobbyists as the corporation that is the focus of the reporting or, even worse, if the coverage might implicate Disney, its own parent company? Apparently, the answer is none. In 1998, ABC's investigative program *20/20* was set to air a story on convicted pedophiles working at Disney theme parks and Disney's failure to screen its new employees or to aid investigators of crimes committed on Disney property.[34] The story never aired at the command of David Westin, the president of *ABC News*, despite the rule guiding journalistic integrity that management should not interfere in news coverage, which is a matter of the public trust. Although ABC cited "editorial standards" as a justification for killing the story,[35] the implications of such censorship were clear: investigative reporters and the news division cannot do stories critical of their boss, the Walt Disney Company, particularly when such a story would not only tarnish its pristine image as protector of childhood innocence but perhaps make parents think twice about taking their kids to Disneyland. As one veteran ABC correspondent, speaking on the condition of anonymity, stated in the *Philadelphia Inquirer*,

"The nightmare is that the news division and our ability to be reporters would appear to be compromised because of our ownership."[36] Disney, unlike other media conglomerates such as Time Warner or News Corporation, is uniquely situated as an icon of American culture and middle-class family values. It actively appeals to both parental concerns and children's fantasies as it works hard to transform every child into a lifetime consumer of Disney products and ideas. Under closer examination, however, a contradiction emerges between the reality of Disney's cutthroat commercial ethos and the Disney image, whereby the company presents itself as the paragon of virtue and childlike innocence. Disney has built its reputation on both profitability and wholesome entertainment, largely removed from issues of power, politics, and ideology. Yet, this is merely the calculated rhetoric of a corporate giant, whose annual revenues in 2008 exceeded $37.8 billion as a result of its ability to manufacture, sell, and distribute culture on a global scale, making it the world's most powerful leisure icon.[37]

The image of Disney as a political and economic power promoting a specific culture and ideology appears at odds with a public relations image that portrays the company as offering young people the promise of making their dreams come true through the pleasures of wholesome entertainment. The contradiction between the politics that shape Disney culture and its effort to construct and influence children's culture is disturbing. But holding Disney accountable for the way it shapes children's desires and identities becomes all the more important as the Disney corporation increasingly presents itself not only as a purveyor of entertainment and fun but also as a political force in developing models of instruction that influence how young people are educated in public schools, a sphere traditionally understood to offer children a space for critical and intellectual development uninhibited by the relentless fascinations of consumer culture.

Some critics suggest that the Walt Disney Company is tantamount to an "evil empire."[38] Although Disney is rife with contradictions, it is crucial to recognize that Disney culture is "simultaneously reactionary and progressive, nostalgic and challenging."[39] Such contradictions should not be taken as grounds for dismissing Disney as a cultural force but instead should be exposed and used for the potential spaces of resistance they provide and for the imaginative possibilities they might offer. Not only have some critics highlighted the more progressive

messages and elements in Disney,[40] but there is no question that Disney
also provides a certain measure of pleasure and happiness to the countless millions who buy its products, visit its theme parks, watch its media
broadcasts, play games on its websites, or see, for example, its outstanding Broadway production of *The Lion King*, which not only debuted in
South Africa in June 2007 but has drawn an audience of over 44 million
since the musical opened in theaters in 1997.[41] People will not necessarily stop enjoying Disney products because they are informed about
the implications of the corporate domination of public culture; rather,
there is pleasure to be gained from the more complex engagements with
Disney made possible by critical insight into the broader contexts in
which the company's products are designed, marketed, and sold around
the world.

Still, the enormous ideological and material power that Disney exercises over civic culture raises important questions about the fate of
democracy, given such unbridled corporate power. The company's
threat to democracy is not canceled out by its offering partner benefits
to its employees since 1996, supporting an unofficial "Gay Day" in late
spring at Disney World, and extending its Fairy Tale Wedding package
to include same-sex couples in 2007.[42] As Sean Griffin remarks about
Disney's liberal attitude toward homosexuality, "Profit margin and
corporate finances most definitely guided the studio's move towards
a 'family' image" earlier in the company's history; today "economic
pressures . . . have led Disney to recognize a 'gay market' for its
product."[43] Surely, Disney's global and domestic efforts to exercise
censorious power over the news, book, and electronic media industries
are not offset by the facts that various groups, subcultures, and audiences appropriate Disney goods for their own purposes and that they
do so as neither passive consumers nor dupes. These appropriations do
not neutralize the systemic attempts by the Walt Disney Company and
other massive corporations, such as Time Warner, PepsiCo, and Philip
Morris, to form powerful monopolies that wipe out competition, stifle
dissent, and exercise enormous influence over the shape and direction
of children's culture—and increasingly over public life.

As part of a handful of market-driven industries that control the
"country's media-cultural space,"[44] Disney represents the alarming
victory of structural power and commercial values over those important public spheres and value systems that are vital to a just society

and democracy itself. As corporate and consumer rights prevail over citizenship rights, the tension between corporate and civil society is either downplayed or displaced, and the commercialization of everyday life, along with the waning of democratic institutions and social relations, continues, although not without countervailing tendencies and organized resistance. The following sections address several of the dominant ideologies, values, and practices that define the boundaries of Disney's cultural politics as the company navigates the tension between corporate and public culture.

DISNEY ENTERTAINMENT AND POLITICAL POWER

Michael Eisner, former CEO of the Walt Disney Company, once suggested that the educational and political force of American entertainment was so profound that it was partly responsible for the fall of the Berlin Wall in 1989: "It may not be such an exaggeration to appreciate the role of the American entertainment industry in helping to change history. The Berlin Wall was destroyed not by the force of Western arms but by the force of Western ideas. And what was the delivery system for those ideas? It has to be admitted that to an important degree it was by American entertainment."[45] Eisner's comments are telling because they imply a number of assumptions about Disney's long-standing conception of entertainment and its educative force. First, as Eisner's remark suggests, the corporate executives at Disney acknowledge that popular culture does not merely reflect the world but actually plays a role in shaping it. Second, they understand that popular culture functions as an educational force in mobilizing people's interests and desires. And third, they recognize, though indirectly, that culture is about both ideology and power. How else could one understand or explain the conditions through which specific messages are produced, circulated, and distributed to diverse populations in vastly different parts of the globe? Surely, Eisner's remark indicates that popular culture can be used to constitute a political intervention, one in this case that connects knowledge, power, and free market ideology. Popular culture may be innocent in its shaping of childhood, but it is armed and weaponized in Eisner's view of Disney's alleged role in contributing to the fall of the Berlin Wall.

If the corporate executives at Disney are able to recognize larger forces at work in their own cultural productions, then the public ignores those same forces at its own peril. But even after we recognize that entertainment is always implicated as an educational force, the question still remains, What is being taught? If knowledge first has to be made meaningful in its form and content in order to become critical, what revelatory messages did American media deliver that inaugurated the fall of communism in Eastern Europe? Once again, Eisner was quite specific. He claimed that American entertainment, with Mickey Mouse serving as its ambassador of goodwill, imparted a "diversity of individual opportunity, individual choice, and individual expression [and reinforced the notion] for viewers around the world [that] America is the place where the individual has a chance to make a better life and to have political and economic freedom."[46] This was a remarkable statement because it presented Disney's corporate culture as synonymous with American-style democracy. But underlying Eisner's paean to the individual is an understanding of self-expression and individual choice constricted by a market rationality that, far from enabling the freedom of speech, turns democracy into the freedom to consume (as passive viewers). Such a conception eliminates the tension between corporate values and the values of a civil society, which cannot be measured in strictly commercial terms but are absolutely vital to democracy—specifically, justice, liberty, equality, pluralism, and human rights, including the rights to health care and education.

What kind of "diversity" is Disney's expansion going to produce? Certainly, Disney's ongoing attempts to turn the American landscape into a theme park for largely white, middle-class suburbanites (for a family of four visiting Walt Disney World, a week's admission to the park alone costs approximately $1,000) does not embody the diversity that would be central to a democratic culture. When Eisner mentioned individual choice and expression—perhaps an allusion to Disney's age-old celebration of entrepreneurial spirit—he must have been forgetting that the Disney corporation is run by a mere handful of people and that most media monopolies its size have little to do with expanding individual choices and a great deal more to do with eliminating them and meeting the bottom line. How else can one explain the so-called corporate commitment to "freedom" given the millions of Americans who have lost their jobs in the past thirty years as a result of corporate downsizing and outsourcing to sweatshops in the developing world?

It is easy for powerful corporations to celebrate freedom within the discourse of the unbridled power of the market. There is no recognition here (how could there be?) of either the limits that democracies must place on such power or the way that market fundamentalism and its narrow redefinition of freedom as a private good may actually present a threat to democracy equal to, if not greater than, that imagined under communism or any other totalitarian ideology. Benjamin Barber captures this sentiment in responding directly to Eisner's comments:

> How can anyone take seriously the claim that the market only gives people what they want when there is a quarter of a trillion dollar advertising industry? . . . The great myth of capitalism has been the idea that all markets do is license and legitimize choice; markets empower people to choose, to vote with their dollars, D-Marks or the yen. But, at the same time, they close down broader choices. The old example still stands: In many American cities you can choose from 25 models of automobiles, but you can't choose public transportation.[47]

In light of the current historical moment and the 2008 economic crisis, which exposed the unbridled greed and corruption of some of the major U.S. corporations, it is difficult to understand how Eisner's position continues to be embraced unproblematically today. The values that now shape the major financial and economic institutions that largely govern the United States appear increasingly less as a bastion of freedom than as holdovers from the now devalued Gilded Age—an age of rampant corruption, exploitation, inequality, greed, and unregulated activity by corporations, banks, and investment firms.

DISNEY AND THE POLITICS OF INNOCENCE

From its humble beginnings as an animation studio to its current reign as a global multimedia giant, the Walt Disney Company has nurtured a corporate image that equates the Disney brand with American patriotism. And it continues to be a central aspect of Disney's corporate agenda to give new meaning to the politics of innocence as a narrative for shaping public memory and producing a "general body of identifications"[48] that promote a sanitized version of American history—not to mention a utopian future based on elite technological dominance and capitalist acquisitiveness. Innocence serves primarily as a rhetorical device that cleanses the Disney image of the tainting influence of commerce, ideology, and power. In other words, Disney's strategic association with childhood, a world deemed free of contradictions and politics, not only represents the basic appeal of its theme parks and movies but also provides a model for defining corporate culture as separate from the influence of corporate power and corruption.

Despite recognizing that the dominant media use entertainment as an educational force to shape society in their own interests, corporate and advertising executives at Disney perennially refuse to acknowledge Disney's role in (1) harnessing children's identities and desires to an ever-expanding sphere of consumption, (2) editing public memory to foster nostalgia for a past unsullied by historical injustice, (3) marshalling reconstructed narratives of American history that serve Disney's corporate image, and (4) setting limits on democratic public life through the company's controlling influence on the media and its attempts to infiltrate schools. Education is never innocent because it always presupposes a particular view of citizenship, culture, and society. And yet, it is this very appeal to innocence, bleached of any semblance of politics, that has become a defining feature of Disney culture and pedagogy.

The Walt Disney Company's attachment to the idea of innocence provides a rationale for Disney both to reaffirm its commitment to children's pleasure and to downplay any critical assessments of the role Disney plays as a "benevolent" corporate power that sentimentalizes childhood innocence as it simultaneously commodifies it. Stripped of the historical and social constructions that give it meaning, innocence in the Disney universe becomes an atemporal, ahistorical, apolitical, and atheoretical space where children share a common bond free of the problems and conflicts of adult society. Disney markets this ideal, presenting itself as a corporate parent that safeguards this protective space for children by magically supplying the fantasies that nourish it.

Disney has long recognized the appeal to innocence as crucial to its success. Eisner and others have repeatedly affirmed the company's public relations position that innocence somehow exists outside the reach of adult society and that Disney alone provides the psychic economy through which kids can express their childlike fantasies. Eisner once commented, "The specific appeal of Disneyland, Disney films and products—family entertainment—comes from the contagious appeal of innocence. . . . Obviously, Disney characters strike a universal chord with children, all of whom share an innocence and openness before they become completely molded by their respective societies."[49] Eisner's claim is important because it suggests that Disney culture reflects, rather than shapes, a particular version of childhood innocence and subjectivity. When this remark is compared to Eisner's earlier statements about the fall of the Berlin Wall, it appears that corporate culture will adopt any view, however contradictory, most convenient to serve its ends at the time. During his tenure at Disney, Eisner commented that running the company "was like being left in a toy shop."[50] He never associated himself with the image of the corporate raider, fostering instead that of a man in touch with his "inner child." This should not really come as a surprise: Alan Bryman has argued that the childlike persona served Eisner and the company well as it allowed Eisner "to associate himself with the dream-like fantasy world and to deflect from himself a complete association with the world of business."[51] Eisner's portrayal of himself as just having fun was an updated version of Old Walt's desire to create a world of clean, well-lighted places, a world in which adult preoccupations with complexity and moral responsibility appear out of place or, perhaps, irrelevant.[52] In the context of children's culture, denying Disney's commercializing influence on kids makes its products less threatening to wary parents and consumers. But little in Eisner's comments suggests that Disney has always viewed children as an enormously productive market to fuel company profits and that old Walt Disney clearly understood the appeal to innocence as a useful alibi while mining the realm of childhood fantasies in a "relentless quest for new images to sell."[53]

Old Walt may have had the best of intentions when it came to making kids happy, but he had few doubts about the enormous commercial potential of youth. In fact, Disney was to become a pioneer in marketing not simply Disney toys but in licensing Mickey Mouse, Snow White, Mulan, and every other character turned out by the Disney imagineers to every conceivable advertising outlet. The historian Gary Cross points out that as early as the 1930s, the image of Mickey Mouse appeared on "blankets, watches, toothbrushes, lamp shades, radios, breakfast bowls, alarm clocks, Christmas tree lights, ties, and clothing of all kinds."[54]

Walt proved even more enterprising when he licensed the image of Snow White dolls a number of months before the release of *Snow White and the Seven Dwarfs*, the first Disney animated feature film: "No fewer than seventy corporate licenses were granted for dozens of items carrying the Snow White stamp."[55]

Michael Eisner took over the failing Walt Disney Company in 1983 and, following Walt's example, produced record revenues for the company through corporate expansion, aggressive advertising campaigns, and the creation of new licensing opportunities for Disney merchandise. Eisner established Disney as a major media outlet with the purchase of Capital Cities/ABC in 1995. As a consequence, Disney could not only use its media holdings to advertise its own branded products but also tap into the rapidly growing advertising industry, whose spending on marketing to children increased from $100 million in 1990 to $2 billion in 2000, climbing to an estimated $14.4 billion in 2004.[56] One of Eisner's goals was to make every person on the planet "a potential lifetime consumer of all things Disney, from stuffed animals to sitcoms, from Broadway musicals to three-bedroom tract homes."[57] Since Robert Iger took over from Eisner as CEO of Disney in 2005, the company has been colonizing the frontiers of new digital media. Its website, Disney .com, touted as giving children "easy access to all Disney businesses" while they watch videos or play games, has become the most popular entertainment Internet site among kids worldwide.[58] One part innocence and three parts corporate experience seems to be the formula for the Disney magic that makes cash registers ring in approximately 220 Disney Stores, not to mention thousands of Walmarts, in North America.[59] Global retail sales for Disney products totaled $11.5 billion in 2007.[60]

Innocence plays a complex role in the Walt Disney Company's attempt to market its self-image to the American public. Innocence not only registers Disney's association with a sentimentalized notion of childhood fantasy but also functions as a form of moral regulation and as part of a politics of historical erasure. In Disney's moral order, innocence is "presented as the deepest truth,"[61] which when left unexamined can be used with great force and influence to legitimate the spectacle of entertainment as escapist fantasy. In addition, innocence becomes the ideological and educational vehicle through which Disney promotes conservative ideas and values as the normative and taken-for-granted "premises of a particular and historical form of social order."[62] Recognizing that Disney has a stake in creating a particular moral and political order favorable to its commercial interests raises questions about what it teaches in order to produce the meanings, desires, and dreams through which it attempts to subscribe all of us to the Disney worldview. In addressing this issue, the following section explores Disney's theme parks as important pedagogical sites for rendering a version of public memory—a reading of how the past defines the present—and for articulating strategies of escapism and consumerism that reinforce an infantilized and utterly privatized notion of citizenship.

TURNING AMERICA INTO A THEME PARK

Amid much fanfare, Disneyland opened on July 17, 1955, and became an immediate hit. By 1960 the number of visitors it attracted had grown to around 5 million annually, and by the 1990s, the numbers had expanded to an astounding 30 million a year.[63] In 2008, attendance at all Disney-owned theme parks in the United States totaled around 70 million, a number that rises to 118 million when the rest of Disney's worldwide attractions are included.[64] Walt Disney set the tone for Disneyland as an embodiment of American idealism, an idealism that offered a mixture of fantasy, fun, curiosity, and optimism, on the one hand, and a strong affirmation and celebration of a mainstream view of American values and culture, on the other. Walt made this quite clear in his remarks celebrating the opening of Disneyland in 1955:

> The idea of Disneyland is a simple one. It will be a place for people to find happiness and knowledge. It will be a place for parents and children to share pleasant times in one another's company; a place for teachers and pupils to discover great ways of understanding and education. . . . Disneyland will be based upon and dedicated to the ideals, the dreams and the hard facts that have created America. . . . Disneyland will be something of a fair, an exhibition, a playground, a community center, a museum of living facts, and a showplace of beauty and magic.[65]

A couple of years later, in an interview, Walt was even more specific, arguing that "there's an American theme behind the whole park. I believe in emphasizing the story of what made America great and what will keep it great."[66] Steven Watts summarizes how the park was organized to promote an "unproblematic celebration of the American people and their experience":

> Main Street, USA, with its nostalgic images of turn-of-the-century small-town life, the heroic conquest of the West represented in Frontierland, the sturdiness of the heartland reflected in the Rivers of America, the Jungle Cruise in Adventureland with its playful pacification of the Third World, the promise of continued technological progress with Monsanto's House of the Future in Tomorrowland. The showcasing of sophisticated robot technology in the early 1960s—Audio-Animatronics, in Disney's parlance—enhanced Disneyland's celebration of the American people. The Enchanted Tiki Room, which initiated this technology in 1963, created a jovial melting-pot atmosphere as its brightly colored electronic birds comically represented French, German, Irish, and other stereotypes. But Great Moments with Mr. Lincoln was probably the culmination of the park's roboticized version of American values. In this attraction, an electronically controlled replica of the sixteenth president rose to his feet against a swelling backdrop of patriotic music and solemnly paid homage to the tradition of democratic constitutionalism in the United States.[67]

With its emphasis on safety, quality, cleanliness, and efficiency, the park provided the postwar generation an escape from the tensions of living in the atomic age. But Walt had more in mind than simply providing therapeutic relief for those anxious to flee, if only temporarily, the conflicts and traumas of modern society; he also insisted that the park provide entertainment-filled lessons that reaffirmed an unqualified patriotic enthusiasm for the American way of life as experienced through a powerful cultural matrix of sentiment, nostalgia, middle-class family values, unfettered consumerism, and an unadulterated celebration of technological advancement.

Walt both built upon the success of Disneyland and amplified its possibilities with the clandestine purchase in the 1960s of more than twenty-seven thousand acres of land around Orlando, Florida, for what would eventually become Disney World. The limited amount of land Walt had purchased in order to build Disneyland had always disturbed him. Purchasing land twice the size of Manhattan enabled him to isolate his new park from the grime and commercial incursions of the outside world. But Walt had more in mind than simply creating a theme park isolated from rival attractions and municipal oversight. He wanted to control the park's environment so that he could edit out negative aspects of reality and manage both the view the public had of the outside world and the imaginative possibilities open to them once they were met by Mickey Mouse at the gates of the Magic Kingdom.[68] (In a short time, Disney World would be surrounded by bars, motels, restaurants, and any number of commercial enterprises wanting to cash in on Disney's popularity, somewhat defeating Walt's plan.)

By the 1960s, Walt had become a staunch conservative and developed an enormous distrust of regulatory government, a distrust matched only by his trust in American industry's "capacity to solve social problems."[69] He envisioned Disney World as embodying his faith in the combined merits of entertainment, education, and corporatism. Not only would Disney World be a theme park, but it would also showcase the EPCOT (Experimental Prototype Community of Tomorrow) Center, a utopian model of modern urban life, replete with a celebration of technological rationality and the virtues of a corporate-designed future. EPCOT would provide a paradigm of how corporations would solve the problems of society through their technological wizardry: corporate culture, social engineering, and corporate control would banish the need for politics, broad-based intellectual inquiry, and a spirited citizenship based upon democratic values and social relations. Walt was determined to build a privatized, homogeneous, and risk-free city that represented his version of American virtues, a city politically autonomous and embodying a "born-again belief in the squeaky clean virtues of front-porch USA, and nostalgia for a supposedly uncomplicated, decent, hardworking, crime-free, rise up and salute the flag way of life."[70]

Waving the carrot of jobs and tourist revenue, Walt secured from Florida governor Haydon Burns assurances that the Disney World complex would be controlled almost entirely by the Disney organization. In 1967 the Florida legislature conceded to Disney special rights to set up the Reedy Creek Improvement District, which was not only exempt from many state laws but also granted the power to levy taxes, devise its own building codes, hire its own inspectors, run its own utilities, administer its own planning and zoning laws, and maintain its own fire protection.[71] By extracting enormous political and economic concessions from the state of Florida, Disney World matched its relative isolation from the outside world with a degree of governmental autonomy that allowed it to function as an independent municipality, if not a company town. Richard Foglesong, in his detailed study of Disney's evolving relationship with Orlando, likens the company's sovereign control of land in and around Walt Disney World to a "Vatican with mouse ears."[72] Michael Harrington commented in *Harper's* magazine in the late 1970s that control is the key to both Disney World and the type of future that it imagines. For Harrington, Disney World represented Walt Disney's version of a corporate utopia, if not a capitalist fairy tale, embodying the dream of American business to become "free of the pressures of democracy, [while treating] employees, customers, and children as so many pawns on the corporate board game."[73]

The ensemble of theme parks, including those opened in Tokyo, Paris, and Hong Kong in 1983, 1992, and 2005, respectively, is central to Disney's homage to white, middle-class, postwar America. The parks are a blend of "Taylorized" fun, patriotic populism, and consumerism dressed up as a childhood fantasy.[74] One employee of Walt Disney World explains the strict organization that underlies the management of rides: "At Big Thunder Mountain I'm supposed to handle 2,000 visitors an hour. It's just like a factory with assembly-line production, only this is a fun factory."[75] As Steven Watts rightly argues, Disneyland in particular "can be seen as the quintessential expression of the Disney culture industry machine in the postwar era."[76] While the parks vary in their sense of place and purpose, they share a number of assumptions essential to Disney's conservative worldview. Far from representing a benign cultural force, Disney's theme parks offer prepackaged, sanitized versions of America's past, place a strong emphasis on the virtues of the individual as an essentially consuming subject, transform the work of production into the consumption of prepackaged leisure, and ignore the exclusionary dynamics of class and race that permeate Disney culture.

But Disney's pedagogy has to do not only with the messages and values inscribed in the theme parks' attractions, social organization, and heritage displays but also with the manner and extent to which the ideologies that inform them are "connected to other projects in urban planning, ecological politics, product merchandising, United States domestic and global policy formation, technological innovation, and constructions of the national character."[77] Clearly, parents, educators, and others need to question how the ideologies that animate Disney's theme parks, its representation of particular values as universal values, its marketing strategies, and its global expansion shape the identities of today's children and youth, in part by constructing a close relationship between corporate culture and civil society. The following section turns to an analysis of the ideological and educational politics of Disney's theme parks, particularly Disneyland and Walt Disney World.

AMERICA, INC.: THE CULTURAL POLITICS OF DISNEY THEME PARKS

Commenting on a visit she made to Disney World in the 1990s, Elayne Rapping expressed shock at finding herself transported into a world that was totally "other" but at the same time "the most mundanely quintessential of American landscapes." Being from New York City, Rapping, a cultural critic, was ill-prepared to find herself in an entirely prepackaged and controlled environment. Shuffled through transportation systems with the utmost efficiency, met by an army of smiling, well-mannered "cast members," and presented with an endless array of prescribed tours, she found herself in a space where "nothing could possibly go wrong because nothing could possibly happen." As a simulacrum of society, now purged of conflicts, differences, and complexity, Disney World eliminates the need for people to utilize any of those capacities that mark them as social actors and critical agents. Instead, it positions them within a cultural landscape, as Rapping points out, "in which no trace of anything noncommodified, nonsimulated, nonregulated, non-smiley-faced, is visible or reachable."[78] And yet, it is precisely this editing out of conflict, this concern with control, this overdetermined emphasis on the familiar and the uniform that appeals to the white, middle-class families who make up most of the visitors to Disney World.

Films, rides, and a host of other Disney attractions are filled with Ozzie-and-Harriet-type images of what the family should be. Moreover, park presentations, such as the Carousel of Progress, provide the context for viewing not only history through the narrow lens of technological progress but also the nuclear family as anchoring society through changing patterns of history and industrial development. Alan Bryman, commenting on the predominance of traditional family values in Disney's theme parks, points out that "while waiting for the Michael Jackson science fiction rock fantasy, *Captain EO*, the assembled crowd is treated to a Kodak-sponsored series of photographs that depict the cycle of couple, babies, growing up, courtship, marriage, and back to babies. The implicit message of such presentations is clear: the conventional nuclear family is secure and will endure the vicissitudes that the future will bring to bear on it."[79]

Walt Disney and his successors recognized the importance of catering to families, but they were not interested in catering to all families. On the contrary, the primary appeal is to the normative, white, middle-class, heterosexual family. Such appeals are obvious in the way in which Disney stages commodified space as a suburban shopping mall, removed from the class and ethnic diversity of real cities. Disney's theme parks offer middle-class families an escape from crime, pollution, immigrants, the homeless, transportation problems, and work. Managed exoticism, security, the fantasy of consumption, and the packaged tour cancel out any regard for diversity, innovation, imagination, or the uncharted excursion.

But Disney's appeal to middle-class families provides more than the familiar safety of the suburban shopping mall. It also renders history as an affirmation of a Norman Rockwell painting. Disney theme parks have become the nostalgia machine par excellence and offer their visitors a very positive view of history, informed by what one imagineer terms "Disney realism, a sort of utopia in nature, where we carefully program out all of the negative unwanted elements and program in the positive ones."[80] Disney's same view of American history can be seen in its National Treasure films (directed by Jon Turteltaub) about a treasure hunter named Benjamin Franklin Gates (Nicolas Cage)—yes, offspring of the Founding Father himself—whose exploits include deciphering a hidden map on the back of the Declaration of Independence, decoding clues on a hunt for treasures hidden by Free Masons, and discovering a top-secret presidential diary at the Library of Congress. The films' appeal lies in their fast-paced action and the web of fantastic lore they spin around American history and monuments. But if unqualified patriotic sentiment seems a throwback to an earlier time, definitely more disturbing is the startlingly white, elitist, and patriarchal historical narrative that emerges. This Disneyfied Indiana Jones meets *The Da Vinci Code* paints a picture of the nation's founders as characterized by glory, honor, and self-sacrifice. There's no history of colonialism or evident discomfort with appropriating a Native American city of gold as the "greatest American treasure." And if one were to object to the striking absence of major historical elements in the films' narratives—such as any mention of slavery—then they could be referred to at least one detail: the spurious claim that Queen Victoria supported the Confederates during the Civil War. Disneyfied American history is not only mystified but also a means to direct blame for oppression toward the British Empire, leaving American righteousness and justice untarnished by historical truth—a revisionist technique that Disney has all but perfected at its theme parks.

The whitewashing of history at Disneyland and Disney World—embodied by Main Street USA, Adventureland, Frontierland, and even the retrofuturist Tomorrowland—reaffirms a past that appeals to the comfort of middle-class families, a past that is filled with optimism and implicitly proclaims the triumphalism of white culture. Eisner captured this sentiment when he described the now defunct plans for a new theme park in northern Virginia based on the Civil War era: "We see Disney's America as a place where people can celebrate America, her people, struggles, victories, courage, setbacks, diversity, heroism, dynamism, pluralism, inventiveness, playfulness, compassion, righteousness, tolerance. The park is being designed to create interest in our rich past."[81]

Bryman suggests that the Disney parks "reinforce the 'culture of comfort' and thereby the legitimacy of the lot of the relatively affluent middle class who are their patrons."[82] There are no historical records of labor strikes in Disneyland. There is no history of labor unrest. No history of attacks on immigrants. No history of slavery or segregation. No Red scare, no McCarthyism, no atom bomb.[83] Nor will one find in Disney's rewriting of public memory any mention of corporate monopolies, corporations' abuse of labor, the role of corporations in generating industrial pollution, or the dire effect of unemployment caused by corporate downsizing. Not in Disney's history. Walt Disney once announced, "Disneyland is a place where you can't get lost."[84] Disney's rewriting of public memory echoes that sentiment and offers its patrons a history that is sanitized, a history "without classes, conflict, or crime, a world of continuous consumption, a supermarket of fun."[85]

The historian Mike Wallace uses the term *Mickey Mouse history* to describe the merger of corporate culture and education witnessed in Disney's gross oversimplification and commercialization of the past. To provide a positive environment for consumption, the Walt Disney

Company makes history safe for its audiences, with the mythical Main
Street USA supplying the model for many of its attractions. According to Disney, the 1890s was one of the most optimistic periods in our
history, although this perspective requires glossing over or leaving out
actual historical events. Wallace writes,

> The decades before and after the turn of the century had their decidedly
> prosperous moments. But they also included depressions, strikes on the
> railroads, warfare in the minefields, squalor in the immigrant communi-
> ties, lynching, imperial wars, and the emergence of mass protests by
> populists and socialists. *This* history has been whited out, presumably
> because it would have distressed and repelled visitors. As [John] Hench
> noted, "Walt wanted to reassure people."[86]

NOSTALGIA AND CIVIC DUTY

Disney's theme parks are the result of corporate culture's growing
awareness of the tremendous marketing potential in the areas of family
life and civic education. To ensure that their children are not losers in
an increasingly globalized game of winner-take-all, parents strategize
about how to help their kids get ahead, but more often than not, bank-
rolling kids becomes the defining principle of responsible parenting, as
consumption becomes the unifying force through which families organize themselves and their relations to others. Disney theme parks know
exactly how to exploit this by providing resort guests over age three
with a room/park pass that doubles as a credit card. If parents are worried about letting their kids loose in the park with a charge card, they
can take their kids straight to EPCOT Center where The Great Piggy
Bank Adventure (sponsored by T. Rowe Price) uses interactive video
games to teach eight- to thirteen-year-olds basic lessons in personal
finance, including "setting goals, saving and spending wisely, staying
ahead of inflation and diversifying investments."[87] Despite the huge
expenses incurred by families during a visit to a Disney theme park,
the Disney myth-making machine can reconfigure such spending as
good parenting and even invest it with the significance of civic duty. As
Jane Kuenz points out, Disney's upbeat version of the American past
stresses that "what's important is the unity and equality we've ostensi-

bly achieved in the marketplace, which, as we've learned in EPCOT, is synonymous with history itself."[88]

Reflecting on her trip to Disney World, Elayne Rapping deplores how imagination is reduced to mindless routine. Encouraging spectatorship and passivity, Disney appropriates nostalgia to simply maximize consumption in the interest of fun and commerce. Main Street is developed primarily as a (disguised?) shopping mall, and attractions such as EPCOT and the World Showcase are transformed into advertisements for corporations. Rapping notes,

> Memory itself is what Disney has most ambitiously and arrogantly confiscated, transformed, patented and retailed. Walk out of any of the rides or events and you're on Main Street, 1900, as Norman Rockwell would have painted it, had he been able to imagine its many varieties of mass-produced useless objects, all linked to other Disney attractions. Buy a T-shirt and be lured toward the game, or movie, or ride of the same motif.[89]

Public memory, in Disney's worldview, is inseparable from commercial culture. And this equation raises serious questions about how history is written when it is sponsored by corporate interests. As a model for a corporate notion of utopia, Disney's theme parks collapse public and historical discourse into the language of entertainment and commercialism. In the name of "edutainment," Disney imagineers clean up the sullied aspects of history, just as they have cleaned up an unsavory rodent in the figure of Mickey Mouse—who now qualifies as the world's best-known icon of amusement. The parks, in conjunction with Disney's overwhelming brand presence in everything from toys to films to designer home furnishings, create audiences for advertisers. Put more succinctly, Disney educates and entertains in order to create corporate identities and to define citizens primarily as consumers and spectators. Given this goal, Disney realism raises serious questions regarding what the exercise of citizenship looks like within its environs, shaped as they are by the lure of profit and privilege. How is it possible to reconcile a critical reading of history, texts, and society with the interests of multi-billion-dollar corporations such as Disney? What constitutes social agency outside the logic of commercialism within the Disney worldview? Finally, what prevents the public from raising such questions, not to mention acting upon them?

Critics writing in the 1960s raised serious questions about Disney's cultural politics and the company's impact on the political and social landscape of America.[90] During the era of student demonstrations, political assassinations, and radical social reform, Richard Schickel accused Disney of fostering "unquestioning patriotism, bourgeois moral nostrums, gauche middle-class taste, racist exclusion, corporate profit mongering, [and] bland stands of social conformity."[91] If these criticisms were true in the 1960s, they became even apter as Disney grew more powerful under the control of Michael Eisner and Robert Iger. Schickel and other critics underestimated the degree of economic and political power the Walt Disney Company would wield in the twenty-first century and how it would use that power not only to continue to strip-mine the imagination but also to dampen dissent and narrow the possibilities for political and cultural democracy.[92] For instance, within a few weeks after the Walt Disney Company acquired ABC in 1996, it issued a formal apology to Philip Morris—a major television advertiser through Kraft foods—and paid millions of dollars to cover the bills of tobacco company lawyers. The tobacco company had initiated a suit against ABC before the Disney takeover in response to a broadcast of *Day One* documenting how Philip Morris attempted to "control levels of nicotine" in its cigarettes.[93] In light of the apology and settlement, the *New York Times* "reported that the lawsuit was part of a new tobacco industry strategy aimed at influencing news coverage."[94]

If there were any doubts about Disney's linkage of corporate power with the stifling of dissent, such doubts are disappearing. After taking over ABC, the Walt Disney Company fired popular, progressive talk show host Jim Hightower after he remarked on his show that he now "worked for a rodent." Lacking neither popular backing nor advertising revenue, Hightower was sacked because he denounced the Disney takeover of ABC and the passing at that time of the Telecommunications Act, which opened the door for media mergers and buyouts.[95] More recently, ABC/Disney intervened on behalf of the hosts at the KSFO radio station to stop an Internet blogger from posting recorded samples of violent rhetoric the conservative hosts used against Muslims, Democrat politicians, *New York Times* editors, and others. Intending to draw the attention of the station's advertisers to the hate speech being supported by and associated with their companies, the blog site, Spocko's Brain, documented such comments as "Indonesia is really just another Muslim nation. . . . You keep screwing around with stuff like this, we're going to kill a bunch of you. Millions of you."[96] Issued a letter by an ABC lawyer that argued the blog's use of recorded material violated copyright, the Internet service provider took down the site in 2007, although it has since reemerged (www.spockosbrain.com).

Disney's control of ABC has also been cited as the reason for the cancellation of a reality television show titled *Welcome to the Neighborhood*, which featured a homosexual couple and their son competing to win a house in Austin, Texas. Stephen Wright and his partner, John Wright, said they participated in the series in order "to show tens of millions of prime-time viewers that a real gay family might, over the course of six episodes, charm a neighborhood whose residents overwhelmingly identified themselves as white, Christian, and Republican."[97] ABC executives canceled the show ten days before it aired, explaining that they were concerned that homophobic comments in early episodes would offend viewers. However, the show ended with the homosexual couple winning the house and "Christians literally embracing their gay neighbors."[98] Both advocates of the show and members of the Southern Baptist Convention observed that the sudden cancellation coincided with the theater release of the Disney film *The Chronicles of Narnia: The Lion, the Witch, and the Wardrobe*. The Southern Baptist Convention had just lifted its eight-year boycott of Disney and was one of the major consumer groups expected to patronize the film version of C. S. Lewis's Christian moral allegory. An official from the convention commented that ABC's continuing with its original plans to broadcast the series "would have been a pretty stupid marketing move."[99]

Disney using its power to shut down websites or television shows — even those that offer important perspectives on tolerance, prejudice, family, and community — demonstrates that the allegedly "gay-friendly" company is willing to marginalize anti-oppressive views and appease the Christian Right if it means the dollars keep on rolling in. Disney has also shown few qualms about the repercussions of its expansion into foreign markets where there is profit to be made from selling its cultural goods. As a major producer and distributor of films, Disney has played a significant role in wiping out local production and distribution. It is bad enough that American films already have 90 percent of the German market, 65 percent of the French market, 85 percent of the Italian market, and nearly all of the British market.[100] Its policy for distributing and packaging its theater productions is one indication of Disney's greed:

> In the case of *The Lion King*, Disney has chosen to change the very rules by which the theatrical game is played. For producers who want to showcase *The Lion King* in other parts of the world, the rights are available only if they accept a package deal of five more productions. While packaging is common in the film industry, it is a rarity in theater, when even a hit show can operate in the red for years. Disney's extravagant productions thus far suggest that even one flop could sink a producer who accepts the deal. It's hardly surprising that there are grumblings of dissent among the rave reviews.[101]

Surprisingly, the Walt Disney Company's marketing tactics, coupled with its willingness to stifle dissent within its ranks and competition from the outside, have not undercut its self-proclaimed image as creator of the "happiest place on earth." On the contrary, it has fabricated a world in which corporate dreams and versions of history are manufactured with catchy dance tunes, glitzy movies, lifelike robots, and "the latest in special effects."[102] Or, as *The Nation* points out, the Walt Disney Company is its own "national entertainment state," for which issues of power and control clearly loom large.[103] The values that inform Disney culture become clearer upon an analysis of the pedagogical practices it uses to initiate its employees into Disney's version of corporate citizenship.

WORKING FOR A RODENT

Disney's corporate culture and the values that underlie its moral and political order are evident in the training programs the company provides for its employees, especially the programs incorporated into the curriculum at Walt Disney University in California and Disney University in Florida. Control, efficiency, predictability, and uniformity are the hallmarks of Disney's approach to people management, a style so successful that it is now marketed to other companies as an intensive three-day seminar. The secret to Disney's success, according to one seminar manager, can be found in its "pixie-dust philosophy":

The formula for pixie dust is simple: Training + Communication + Care = Pride. By carefully training and developing cast members, by making all cast communications timely and effective, and by encouraging a friendly and caring work environment, Disney creates a strong sense of pride in each cast member, which in turn inspires him or her to give first-rate service to all Disney guests. The participants in the people management seminar learn first-hand how the pixie-dust formula is applied to all aspects of the Disney World operation.[104]

Work culture in Disney is subject to the same control that permeates all other aspects of the company's organization. Fantasy mediates and subordinates issues of power, politics, and ethics in the Disney work culture through the intervention of what can be called Disney discourse. As if with the wave of a magic wand, a customer is transformed into a "guest," and an employee becomes a "host" or "hostess" or a "cast member." Hiring for a job becomes "casting," a uniform magically changes into a "costume," an accident is reduced to a mere "incident," and so it goes. Because the Disney organization considers itself a family, all cast members are on a first-name basis.[105] But, however light-hearted and fanciful it seems, Disney discourse does not displace the rigid and authoritarian nature of working for a cutthroat corporation.

"Casting" for new employees follows very strict rules, with Disney stipulating specific guidelines that job applicants must follow. In one instance, Disney held an on-campus "informational session" at Penn State University.[106] It seemed that Disney wanted a particular type of student to attend, as indicated by the detailed dress code a Disney memo provided for both men and women. The men were instructed to wear a suit with a color-coordinated shirt; the fabric of the suit was to be one "traditionally accepted for business." No necklaces, bracelets, or earrings were allowed for male students; nor were they permitted to have a mustache, beard, or hair extending "beyond or covering any part of the ears." No one was to show up with an "extreme look, including shav[ed] head or eyebrows." And, of course, no one would be admitted who had visible tattoos. Women were to wear a suit, a dress, or pants outfit (no jumpsuits, T-shirts, sleeveless dresses or blouses, and no clinging fabrics or suede leather). They could not wear more than two necklaces, and these could not exceed thirty inches in length. And in case these young women missed the point, they were not to wear more than one ring per hand.

These instructions suggest more than an old-fashioned prudishness; they impart an excessively regulating and authoritarian measure of control. Furthermore, Disney's selective hiring practices and treatment of its employees appear consistent with its construction of homogeneous, sanitized theme parks: each facet of the Disney experience is aimed at reassuring "guests," who increasingly experience the desire for social and spatial isolation so that they will not have to deal with differences that might upset the illusion of a carefully wrought fantasy world.

Disney's theme parks are designed, in part, to erase problems associated with low-skill, low-paying, and routinized labor. Happy, smiley faces are a mandatory part of "the costume" for "cast members" and service workers at Disney.[107] The reality of work has been excised both from the Disney discourse and from the public's view. As if modeled after Aldous Huxley's *Brave New World*, the dystopian world of work is banished, replaced with mantras not much different from "You can't consume much if you sit still and read books."[108] Utilities, power lines, storage pipes, workers' quarters, employee transportation, and all other signs of a labor force are relegated to a vast subterranean network of corridors and tunnels. The Seven Dwarfs' tune "Whistle While You Work" takes on surreal overtones as the difference between leisure and labor is obscured and hidden from view in the parks. Moreover, by undermining the reality of labor, the Walt Disney Company eliminates labor's resistance to Disney's social engineering and heavy-handed discipline. Securing employment in Disney's world means more than acquiring specific job skills; it means, as one employee put it, learning "a new way of life: the Disney Way."[109] Dick Nunis, a former vice president in charge of Disney theme parks, put it more bluntly: "When we hire a girl [as a hostess], we point out that we're not hiring her for a job, but casting her for a role in our show. And we give her a costume and a philosophy to go with it."[110]

The Disney philosophy preaches about everything from how employees should comport themselves (smile, use courteous phrases, and do not be stuffy) to how to dress, how to use Disney language, and even how to embrace Disney culture. Pedagogically, employees are drawn into a strong corporate culture through classroom training that emphasizes memorizing elaborate checklists of appearance standards. New employees are given written quizzes on Disney rules. One pedagogical strategy includes exposing workers to an endless chant of inane Disney mottos such as "We work while others play!" or "We never say no because we know the answers" or "We smile that extra mile."[111] Disney's emphasis on learning rules and mottos is matched also by attempts to influence its employees' emotional responses. As John Van Maanen, a former Disney worker, explains, "Employees are told repeatedly that if they are happy and cheerful at work, so, too, will be the guests at play. Inspirational films, hearty pep talks, family imagery, and exemplars of corporate performance are all representative of the strong symbolic stuff of these training rites."[112] Disney even provides its employees with a definition of Disney corporate culture to memorize, allegedly to help give them an emotional lift as they begin their workday.

> Dis-ney Cor-po-rate Cul-ture (diz'ne kor'pr'it kul'cher) n 1. Of or pertaining to the Disney organization, as a: philosophy underlying all business decisions; b: the commitment of top leadership and management to that philosophy; c: the actions taken by individual cast members that reinforce that image.[113]

Such efforts designed to reproduce Disney's corporate worldview come with a price. Job applicants are heavily screened and, once hired, enter a work culture characterized by strict rules, an authoritarian social structure, and constant surveillance.

A number of features characterize Disney's pedagogy for employees, but a few stand out. First, Disney's training programs expect workers to relinquish their individuality to be overwritten by Disney's corporate service model, which bestows "identity through a process carefully set up to strip away the job relevance of other sources of identity and learned response and to replace them with others of organizational relevance."[114] Second, there is little room for individuality and experimentation among the employees. Every behavior and action, from how one dresses to how one responds to questions raised by guests, is scripted by someone of higher authority. Innovation is viewed as a breach of policy, and anything resembling nonconformity is swiftly eliminated from Disney's technocratic utopia. For instance, it was reported that "when skippers on Disneyland's famous Jungle Cruise updated their standard shtick with mild jokes about Los Angeles and Rush Limbaugh, they were summarily dismissed despite positive guest reaction."[115]

Third, Disneyland employees work in a rigid pecking order: supervisors and foremen function less to offer advice and guidance than to monitor underlings in case they slip up or break a rule. In his study of Disney work culture in the early 1990s, Van Maanen claims that "supervisors in Tomorrowland are . . . famous for . . . hiding in the bushes above the submarine caves, timing the arrivals and departures of the supposedly fully loaded boats making the 8 1/2 minute cruise under the polar ice caps. . . . In short, supervisors . . . are regarded by ride operators as sneaks and tricksters out to get them and representative of the dark side of park life."[116] Finally, in a culture governed by such strict disciplinary procedures, it is not surprising that firings are frequent at the theme parks.

These features of Disney's labor policies clearly fly in the face of Disney's familial rhetoric and ideal of uncomplicated social harmony. Moreover, the reality of the Disney work culture is marked by enormous inequalities in power, income, and prestige. In fact, Van Maanen reports that while working at Disneyland, he was reprimanded more than once for growing hair over his ears. He did not anticipate, however, the form his eventual dismissal was to take.

> Dismissal began by being pulled off the ride after my work shift had begun by an area supervisor in full view of my cohorts. A forced march to the administration building followed, where my employee card was turned over and a short statement read to me by a personnel officer as to the formal cause of my termination. Security officers then walked me to the employee locker room where my work uniforms and equipment were collected and my personal belongings returned to me while an inspection of my locker was made. The next stop was the time shed, where my employee's time card was removed from its slot, marked "terminated" across the top in red ink, and replaced in its customary position (presumably for Disneylanders to see when clocking on or off the job over the next few days). As now an ex-ride operator, I was escorted to the parking lot, where two security officers scraped off the employee parking sticker attached to my car. All these little steps of status degradation in the Magic Kingdom were quite public.[117]

Van Maanen's experience raises serious questions about the corporate practices sanctioned by Disney's "pixie-dust" management philosophy. Unfortunately, Disney's reaction in this case appears in keeping with the sacrifices that the organization demands of its employees—unquestioned obedience, scripted responses, craven servility—coupled with the fact that most of its jobs are low paying.

As the above account suggests, those who work for Disney are under no illusion that the company has its employees' best interests at heart. The company has a notorious history of union bashing and labor disputes.[118] In 1991, a strike launched in protest of Disneyland's rules against employee facial hair ended with Disney's firing the strike leader rather than any amendment to the rule.[119] The fact that Disney's attitude toward workers has changed little since Old Walt was at the helm became more than apparent in 2008 when six hundred Disneyland hotel staff marched in protest near the entrance to the park. The workers, whose placards and slogans called on Disneyland to "provide better wages and benefits," were forced to move by police or arrested.[120] Disney is well known for staffing its service industries with new immigrants and foreign nationals who get stuck in minimum-wage jobs with high turnover rates. The labor dispute with hotel workers (whose contract expired in February 2008) provoked over fifteen protests while the workers' union tried to reach a contract agreement that would improve health benefits and the terms of what the union perceived as a "poverty job."[121] In July 2009, over eight hundred of the same Disneyland hotel workers, still without a contract, demonstrated once again. Meanwhile, Disney has withdrawn contributions to the union health care trust and tried to lure workers with $1,000 bonuses to sign on to Disney's latest contract offer.[122] And if being caught in the "low-wage trap of a tourist economy" was not already bad enough for Disneyland workers,[123] Disney sued the city of Anaheim in 2007 for attempting to build a low-cost housing project in the resort district that also includes the urban-renewal project called Downtown Disney, which consists of expensive restaurants and businesses open to the public but clearly designed for wealthy tourists. Instead of providing affordable housing to many of the people who work at its own parks, Disney would prefer "the 26-acre parcel at issue to be developed as an upscale hotel-condominium project."[124] These scenarios paint a picture of Disney as an employer patently uninterested in improving its employees' health and general welfare, let alone ameliorating the conditions under which they labor at the parks.

The profound routinization of work and discouragement of assertiveness among workers at Disney theme parks are matched only by the profound routinization of leisure and amusement there. In such contexts, both pleasure and work depend on apathy, intellectual laziness, and subservience. Disney offers "flight [not] from a wretched reality but from the last remaining thought of resistance."[125] The reduction of knowledge and citizenship to hierarchical control, consumerism, and the bottom line within the pedagogies at work in Disney culture appears to undermine any viable notion of critical agency, independent thought, and social responsibility.

Disney employees often find themselves working within a mythical discourse that prevents them from confronting the harsh realities—such as dangerous rides, crowd congestion, hours-long queues, and dehydration—that visitors sometimes face in the Disney theme parks. Although Disney never tires of spouting its commitment to ensuring the health and safety of both its employees and theme park visitors, the strict rules regarding how to deal with accidents contradict this public image. Accidents are labeled "incidents," and so as not to rupture Disneyland's trademark facade as the "happiest place on earth," injured people are transported to hospitals in low-profile vehicles rather than in ambulances. When serious injuries occur, the Disney corporation appears to make a systematic attempt to protect its corporate image by not informing the public in a responsible manner. For example, after the opening of the Indiana Jones Adventure ride on March 3, 1995, a lawsuit involving over one hundred people claiming to have been injured by the ride, including a Disney manager who suffered a disc injury in her back, was filed against Disney.[126] Many people had written letters complaining about the ride, and in one case, Zipora Jacob, a forty-four-year-old mother of two, claimed that after she got off the Indiana Jones ride on July 17, 1995, she vomited and collapsed. According to her suit claim, she eventually fell into a coma and suffered severe brain damage, including a tear in her brain, which required four major operations to repair.[127] Disney's response to this case is likewise disturbing: Disney not only made little effort to address several people's complaints about the rides and reported injuries but, according to Barry Novack, a lawyer who represented Zipora Jacob, "continually stalled the discovery process by refusing to produce documents regarding injury claims and safety related to the Indiana Jones ride."[128] Moreover, Disney tried to dismiss the Jacob lawsuit by claiming that a "head injury" was part of the "inherent risk" a Disney theme park visitor must assume on such a ride. Of course, Disney does not concede that the ride may have been unsafe or that brain damage is a high-risk trade-off for taking a theme park ride. In a brief to the Superior Court of the State of California for the county of Los Angeles, Novack argued,

Despite the fact that Disney employees and guests were being injured on the ride, the Disney defendants kept the ride at its injury-causing level and failed to heed the warnings of its injured guests. The Disney defendants acted in conscious disregard of the public safety by not adequately testing the ride before it was opened to the public and in keeping the ride at its injury-causing levels as of the time Zipora was injured.[129]

Disney then tried to dismiss the case, arguing that Jacob knowingly exposed herself to the possibility of a brain hemorrhage on the grounds that she knew about the ride's inherent dangers. Disney also tried to have a judge removed from the case, claiming he was prejudiced against the company's interests. Clearly, there is nothing innocent about a corporation like Disney when it comes to protecting its profits and its corporate image.

Disney eventually settled with Jacob out of court in June 2000, while the company was in the midst of a second lawsuit involving Deborah Bynum, who also claimed she suffered a brain hemorrhage after she rode the Indiana Jones Adventure ride in 1998. Disney settled with Bynum in 2001.[130] It seems Disney had not learned anything from these two publicized cases: in 2007, it once again settled a lawsuit before trial with the family of a woman from Barcelona, Spain, who died in 2000 from a brain aneurysm that the family claimed was triggered by her riding the Indiana Jones Adventure.[131]

In 2000, a four-year-old boy name Brandon Zucker was trapped beneath the Roger Rabbit's Car Toon Spin ride and suffered severe brain damage. A state investigation into the accident suggested that poor ride design and operator error had contributed to the accident.[132] Although Disney, ordered by the state, added improved safety mechanisms to the ride and then settled with the Zucker family for an undisclosed sum in 2002, the notorious shroud of secrecy with which Disney cloaks injuries and safety concerns was revealed by a fire captain involved in the response to a Space Mountain accident in 2000, when a roller coaster car derailed, injuring nine people. Apparently, Disney's security efforts to keep the incident quiet delayed the fire department's response time.[133] The state of California responded to Disney's subterfuge by passing tougher legislation in 2001 requiring Disney to report injuries sustained by theme park visitors and granting the state power to oversee ride safety by investigating accidents, shutting down rides, and ordering safety improvements. Disney's general compliance with such regulations, however, did not prevent Marcelos Torres, age twenty-two, from being thrown from the Big Thunder Mountain roller coaster and killed in 2003. A Disneyland spokesperson told the *Los Angeles Times* that the ride's mechanical failure was caused by "incorrectly performed maintenance tasks required by Disneyland policy and procedures," although Disney denied that there was a broader problem with safety maintenance stemming from budget cuts and department reorganization in the late 1990s.[134] A report by the California Division of Occupational Safety and Health recommended that "outside machinists be retrained and that Disney write new, clear guidelines instructing operators to take action if an unusual noise is heard."[135] Disney settled with the Torres family in 2005.

As these accounts suggest, the world of Disney—with its prioritizing of brand value over people's interests, silencing of protest and complaint, its squeaky-clean image of sanitized happiness, and its adherence to a cartoonish social imaginary—can exact a deadly price, in addition to incurring more general political and ethical costs. When we view Disney within the larger context of profit-seeking corporate culture, it becomes apparent that Disney hardly models self-reflection and social responsibility—two elements fundamental to quality education and democratic public life.

Theodor Adorno, writing about education in a post-Auschwitz world, raises a clarion call against pedagogies—such as those fostered by the Walt Disney Company—that destroy "the particular and the individual together with their power of resistance. With the loss of their identity and power of resistance, people also forfeit those qualities by virtue of which they are able to pit themselves against what at some moment might lure them again to commit atrocity."[136] Justice requires thinking citizenship. Action, to be meaningful, must be enabled by the exercise of thoughtfulness, critical judgment, and a willingness to take risks. While Disney's pedagogy should not be equated with the Nazi ideology that produced the atrocities committed at Auschwitz, we still need to examine whether Disney's corporate pedagogy might risk reproducing conditions that connect us to a barbarous unthinking past.

Disney's educational practices should be understood as part of a broader assault on public discourse that seeks to dispense with the principles of autonomy, critical self-reflection, and self-determination. Disney's pedagogy is not about harnessing the imagination to produce counternarratives capable of helping us to see beyond mundane reality. And it is certainly not about the power of the intellect to recognize the benefits and limitations of imagined realities in order to enter into critical dialogue with them and transform them when necessary. On the contrary, Disney offers a fantasy world grounded in a promotional culture and bought at the expense of citizens' sense of agency and resistance, as the past is purged of its subversive elements and translated into a nostalgic celebration of entrepreneurship and unending technological progress. Disney's trademarked version of fantasy has no language for imagining democratic public life outside consumption and, consequently, fails to be self-critical about the damaging effects of its cultural influence or even to acknowledge the real exigencies that confront people in their everyday lives. It is within the context of Disney's corporate pedagogy that the next chapter analyzes the Walt Disney Company's development of its own town in Celebration, Florida, and its move into public schooling, curriculum development, and educational materials.

Chapter Two

Learning with Disney

From Baby Einstein to High School Musical

It is time to recognize that the true tutors of our children are not schoolteachers or university professors but filmmakers, advertising executives, and pop culture purveyors. Disney does more than Duke, Spielberg outweighs Stanford, MTV trumps MIT.

—Benjamin Barber[1]

Public education has become one of the most contested public spheres as people across the globe, and particularly in the United States, witness democracy faltering alongside a growing militarization and corporatization of public life.[2] More than any other institution, public schools and universities serve as a reminder of both the promise and the shortcomings of the social, political, and economic forces that shape society. Public education provides a critical referent for measuring the degree to which modern society fulfills its obligation to equip all young people with the knowledge and skills necessary for critical citizenship and to offer them opportunities to engage democratic public life. Embodying the contradictions of the larger society, schools are often sites of intense struggle between various economic, political, and social forces; far from being affirmed as a crucial public good, they are often under attack from conservatives and liberals alike in their attempts to remove the language of critique from the discourse of learning and to reduce schooling itself to a largely privatized affair in which civic responsibilities are limited to the act of consuming. No longer viewed as institutions designed to benefit all members of the community, public schools are being refashioned in market terms, which are in the process of reshaping all public goods to serve the narrow interests of individual consumers and the economic policies of global megacorporations. Even under a liberal administration such as that of Barack Obama, federal policies are implemented that favor charter schools and expand the use of standardized testing to define what counts as knowledge and to measure and judge how teachers perform and students learn.[3] Under such circumstances, public schools promote training rather than critical pedagogy and become more aligned with privatized and corporate interests.

Corporate culture, by diminishing the role that schools might play as democratic public spheres, has redefined the meaning and purpose of schooling in accordance with the interests of global capitalism. As governmental support for public schools dries up, corporations attempt to harness all educational institutions to corporate control through calls for privatization, vouchers, so-called choice programs, and diverse forms of school-business partnerships. Reversing the tradition of schooling as a public good, corporations divorce questions of equity from excellence and subsume the social and political mission of schooling within the ideology and logic of the market. Public education is replaced by the call for privately funded educational institutions or school-business partnerships that ignore civil rights, exclude students who are poor and racially disenfranchised, and blur the lines between religion and the state.

The current assault against public schooling is part of a broader project to dismantle all public spheres that refuse to be strictly governed by the instrumental logic of the market. As such, the battle waged over education must be understood, more generally, as a battle for and against deepening and expanding democratic public life. At the same time, the struggle over public schooling should be addressed as part of a struggle over the educational force of a culture that has come to play an increasingly powerful and influential role in shaping the minds, desires, and identities of the young and the old alike. Such a struggle in favor of democracy suggests that public goods be defended from incursions of the market and that the political function of culture be linked to creating citizens who can challenge established conventions and reflect critically on pressing social and economic problems. More and more the absolutely crucial questions to raise in the age of the "national entertainment state"[4] should be, Who controls the production of culture? Who has access to the meanings produced by the culture industry? Whose interests do media monopolies represent? How do media monopolies produce and profit from the particular messages they circulate? And what might it mean to make public culture matter more than entertainment, spectacle, consumption, and tourism?

We can rescue democratic principles from the stranglehold of corporate culture by reasserting the primacy of a nondogmatic, progressive politics and by analyzing how culture as a force for resistance is related to power, education, and agency. Such an analysis suggests the need to understand how culture shapes our everyday lives. Culture constitutes a pivotal force in the struggle over meaning, identity, social practices, and institutional machineries of power. Reclaiming public education and cultural politics from the distortions of privatizing market agendas must be understood as both a political and a pedagogical project, one that expands the significance of the pedagogical by recognizing the "educational force of our whole social and cultural experience [as one] that actively and profoundly teaches."[5] Clearly, for such a project to take root, the implications of corporate encroachment into public and higher education must be fully understood and challenged. This means speaking out against not only Disney's role in shaping popular culture but also its strategic educational incursions into the domain of schooling through its development of educational products for babies and children, its production of curricular materials for schools, its partnership with the public school system in Osceola County, Florida, and its attempts to capitalize on the tumultuous experience of self-definition for teens and tweens while simultaneously reshaping the culture of schools in its promotion of the Hannah Montana and High School Musical franchises.

DISNEY IN THE NURSERY

The Disney brand has long been associated with the development of cultural products for children but has only recently been expanding the range of its products and services to appeal to the very youngest members of society. In 2000, Disney purchased the Baby Einstein Company from its founder, Julie Aigner-Clark, who had created a line of multimedia products and toys designed to entertain and educate toddlers and infants as young as three months old. The Baby Einstein DVDs and videos are known to mesmerize these youngest television watchers by displaying, for example, vibrant moving objects while playing a soundtrack of classical music selections. The marketing of the products suggests that parents can purchase toys and videos that will not only enable their children to develop great taste in music but also make them capable of great intellectual achievements, like the real Albert Einstein. (Disney/Pixar's 2004 film *The Incredibles* plugs Disney's Baby Einstein franchise shamelessly when the babysitter states, "Mozart makes babies smarter.") The videos' clever packaging implies that they are, at best, beneficial learning tools to be used in a child's most formative years and, at worst, harmless distractions for infant audiences. In fact, a 2007 survey by the Kaiser Family Foundation found that 48 percent of parents believe that baby videos have "a positive effect on early childhood development."[6] The Campaign for a Commercial-Free Childhood, increasingly disturbed by the marketing of baby videos as educational media, filed a complaint with the U.S. Federal Trade Commission for false advertising in 2006. The Baby Einstein Company avoided penalization by promising to remove from its website any claims about the educational and developmental value of the videos.

The idea that parents who want their kids to keep up in a highly competitive world must supply them with every available product that purports to nurture young minds can be linked to the pressure of living in a competition-ridden consumer society. The Baby Einstein videos' guilt-free legitimation of parenting practices that include having an infant stationed in front of a television set for extended periods also undoubtedly works in the product's favor. Screens filled with constant visual stimuli seem to be alluring and effective babysitters, but unfortunately for parents who hope to give their child a head start, scientists have shown that they are much less effective as teachers. University of Washington researchers, having discovered that 40 percent of three-month-olds and 90 percent of two-year-olds are regular watchers of television shows, DVDs, and videos, decided to study the effects of specific media on children less than two years old.[7] The news that baby DVDs and videos actually impair infants' cognitive development broke in 2007, when the University of Washington issued a press release about a study published in the prestigious *Journal of Pediatrics*, which concluded that infants eight to sixteen months old who were exposed to one hour of viewing baby DVDs and videos per day displayed slower language development: they understood on average six to eight fewer words for every hour of viewing than infants who did not watch the videos.[8] Among toddlers aged seventeen to twenty-four months, there was neither impairment nor improvement in language skills with exposure to baby videos, children's educational shows such as *Sesame Street*, and adult television programs. Reading to a child once a day, however, resulted in the largest increase in vocabulary.[9] Disney president and CEO Robert Iger responded to the publication of this data with the demand that the University of Washington immediately retract these statements on the grounds that the study's assessment methodology was faulty and the publication of the results was "misleading, irresponsible, and derogatory."[10] Disney's main objection was that the study did not differentiate between brands when it tested the effects of baby videos on language development.

The Baby Einstein website has since addressed some of the issues raised by the study, stating that the videos are designed to foster "parent-child interaction" by "allowing a parent to have two free hands while enjoying and experiencing the video with their little one." On a more cynical note, however, the website also cites a 2003 finding by the Kaiser Family Foundation that "in a typical day, 68% of all children under two use screen media."[11] The Baby Einstein Company does not characterize this statistic (surely an underestimate by 2009) as something that should alarm concerned parents and encourage different parenting practices; rather it becomes simple proof of "the reality of today's parents, families and households" and an indicator of how the American Academy of Pediatrics, which discourages television viewing for children under two years old, is simply stuck in the past.[12] Mark Emmert, president of the University of Washington, refused to comply with Iger's demand for a retraction and instead articulated a need for more "research aimed at helping parents and society enhance the lives of children."[13] Disney's logic, by contrast, suggests that parents should not only accept the ubiquitous presence of screen culture in their babies' lives but view it as an inevitable fact of life, one pointless to criticize and impossible to change.[14]

Perhaps equally disturbing, in 2007 Disney launched an educational website for parents, DisneyFamily.com, which offers parenting advice "in a manner that is compelling, comprehensive, entertaining and, most importantly, objective." Given Disney's attempt to refute work by leading researchers in children's health, it is unclear what the website intends to publish as "articles from experts in the parenting field." But if the expertise is not useful to parents, they can always turn to the "practical and reliable information on the editorial side of the site that is objective" or at least download a coupon from the "Family Tool Box."[15] The website also features the "Disney Family Learning Center," developed in collaboration with Sony Electronics and Powered, Inc., an online education provider that also happens to specialize in "social marketing." The website taps into the growing parenting industry, claiming to target "the more than 32 million moms that are online in the U.S."[16] Disney will undoubtedly find ways to promote its own products when advising parents on "family-relevant information" in its online courses, such as "Traveling Light with Kids and Technology." If Mom and Dad are not too annoyed with the barrage of product descriptions and buy buttons for Sony products, then "Capturing School Events on Video" apparently offers tips for child development, while entertainment suggestions can be found in the course "Contact Management for the Busy Mom and Dad"![17] The title of the latter course suggests that in its foray into online education for parents, Disney has no qualms about participating in the "professionalization of parenthood"—an approach that seeks to apply corporate "standards of efficiency and productivity" to the time parents spend with children. The American Academy of Pediatrics has identified this reconfiguration of a caring parent-child relationship to conform with a pressure-filled business approach to parenting as a serious problem in contemporary families.[18]

That corporate culture is rewriting the nature of children's culture becomes clear as the boundaries once maintained between the spheres of formal education and entertainment collapse. The scope and impact of electronic technologies as teaching machines cannot be underestimated. Disney's interest in capturing the attention of very young people has also involved the acquisition of Club Penguin, a web-based virtual world, in a $700 million deal in 2007. Disney's Club Penguin targets kids ages six to fourteen and provides each user with an animated penguin avatar that interacts in a snow-covered world, chats with other users, and earns virtual money to purchase items such as pets, clothing, and furnishings for an igloo home. Users can play for free but must pay

$5.95 per month for access to certain features of the game. As an interactive and "immersive environment," Club Penguin enables Disney to train children in the habits of consumption—merchandise, such as stuffed penguins, is advertised on the site—while making direct contact with its global consumer base through the online network. Harnessing the power of virtual space (Club Penguin had seven hundred thousand paying subscribers at the time of the Disney purchase) is a strategy openly championed by CEO Robert Iger, whose stated goal is for the company to establish "clear leadership in the kids and families online virtual worlds space around the globe."[19] Disney-branded online space also includes the Internet's first multiplayer game for kids, Toontown Online. As Sara Grimes points out, multiplayer online games "construct entire cultural experiences based around beloved characters, fantasy and play [but] entry into these worlds is only possible through a perpetual cycle of consumption."[20]

The Internet's commercial potential is certainly not lost on Disney; as Steve Wadsworth, president of the Walt Disney Internet Group, stated, "There is massive opportunity here."[21] Disney clearly sees online media as an opportunity not so much to enhance children's lives as to make money for shareholders, enjoy low overhead costs and quick growth, and keep the company's film and television franchises profitable. The Disney.com site, redesigned in 2007, includes video games, social networking, customized user content, and videos on demand. As of the summer of 2009, approximately 16 million users had designed customized fairy avatars that inhabit Pixie Hollow at DisneyFairies. com.[22] Internet sites offering cooperative games and social networking to children seem like a generally innocuous option in a media culture currently exploiting every imaginable angle to populate reality television's competitive worlds of winners and losers (think of The Learning Channel's repulsive docudrama *Toddlers and Tiaras*). It is far less innocuous, however, that these websites help Disney collect and use personal information to assail consumer groups with targeted, cross-promotional advertising. Web-based social media not only acculturate children to constant bombardment with advertising but give them the illusion of total control while they are being manipulated. Researchers have found that while children as young as three years old recognize brand logos, not until they are around eight years old do they understand advertising's intention to manipulate their desires.[23] Speculative benefits of online community and cooperative interaction aside, social media exemplify one of the widest-reaching and most insidious marketing tools to emerge from Internet development.

New media and technologies have transformed culture into a pivotal force for constituting, regulating, and altering meaning on a personal and social scale. In other words, media culture influences the content made available to help us define and understand broad cultural categories—for instance, gender, race, ethnicity, class, age, or sexuality—and what it means for each of us to claim an identity within these categories. The commercialization of the media and of culture, in general, limits the choices that children and adults can make in extending their sense of agency and selfhood beyond a commercial culture that enshrines an intensely myopic, narcissistic, and conservative sense of self and society. In particular, researchers have found that one of greatest costs associated with surrounding very young children with screen media is a reduction in the time they spend engaging in creative, unstructured play. In a 2007 report, the American Academy of Pediatrics lamented that "time for free play has been markedly reduced for some children."[24] For instance, there was a time when a family traveling in a car might entertain itself by singing or playing games. Now, however, many kids have their own laptop or cell phone, and many family vehicles come equipped with DVD players. Family members need not look to each other or the outside world for entertainment when a constant stream of media sources is at their fingertips. According to Susan Linn, a Boston psychologist and cofounder of the Campaign for a Commercial-Free Childhood, "Such unlimited access to miniaturized screens means that even when children are out and about, we are depriving them of opportunities to engage in the world and encouraging them to turn to screens instead."[25]

This redistribution of time can cause significant harm to children since creative play is widely recognized as a primary foundation for learning. According to Linn, "creative play" is linked to a child's interaction with others and to the capacity to learn and develop skills such as "critical thinking, initiative, curiosity, problem solving and creativity [along with] self-reflection, empathy, and the ability to find meaning in life."[26] Linn has also found that children's products based on media programs negatively affect the potential for creative play. By their very nature, predesigned imaginary worlds such as those proffered by Disney do not leave much room for children to use their own imaginations. Linn has found that passive entertainment (as well as Disney's propensity to generate multiple sequels and tie-in products for an original film) means children are "so locked into set characters and scripts that their play becomes quite constricted."[27] Furthermore, high-tech electronic toys provide a spectacle for children but do not require them to adapt the toy to their own make-believe ends.[28] (The popularity of faddish electronic gadgetry over traditional toys is, ironically, one of the nostalgia-generating themes in the Disney/Pixar film *Toy Story*.) Finally, Disney's perennial habit of taking popular children's books and rendering them on the big screen contributes as well to reducing opportunities for children to engage imaginatively with a text. What Jennifer Cypher and Eric Higgs call Disney's "colonization of the imagination"[29] (with reference to the way Disney theme parks manufacture encounters with "nature" and thereby erode people's capacity for unmediated experiences with the natural world) describes equally well Disney's relationship to the realm of books and reading. Josh Golin discusses the way in which children reading C. S. Lewis's *The Chronicles of Narnia*, after the onslaught of Disney marketing for its 2005 film adaptation, will likely visualize Disney imagery instead of conjuring their own images in order to envision the world described in the book.[30] And while they are picturing the digitally generated, Liam Neeson–esque version of the lion character, Aslan, they will undoubtedly be drawn to thoughts of the innumerable tie-in products (worth $150 million) that Disney marketers intended for them to associate subconsciously with the story, including junk food at fast-food outlets and cheap toys. In response to the excessive commercialism surrounding the Disney film, Josh Golin asks an incisive question: "Should definitions of 'family friendly' media be limited to discussions of sexual and violent content or should they be expanded to include the marketing and associated products as well?" The research discussed above suggests that parents, teachers, and others absolutely must pay attention to the impact of all kinds of commercial media in the lives of children.

Disney undeniably promotes the acquisition of lifelong consumer habits—such as brand loyalty, impulse buying, and dependency on consumption for pleasure (shopping as "retail therapy"). According to Linn, adults need to put more conscious effort into encouraging kids to "value their own creations above the things that corporations sell."[31] Perhaps even more significantly, psychologists have repeatedly linked children's exposure to screen media to long-term health issues, including the inability to form social bonds, a lack of emotional skills, anxiety, depression, sleep disturbances, obesity, and attention deficit disorders. Clearly, on an individual level, child-care providers need to intervene to limit the amount of screen time made available to kids. On a social level, parents, educators, and others must apply more pressure on the government and corporate media, ideally to advocate for stricter regulation of advertising directed at children. Corporations such as Disney should be held accountable and their intrusion into children's lives subject to federal regulation. At the very least, they should have to prove advertising claims that their products promote the educational development and happiness of children.

MICKEY GOES TO SCHOOL IN CELEBRATION, FLORIDA

Walt Disney once said, "I'd love to be part of building a school of to-morrow. . . . This might be a pilot operation for the teaching age—to go out across the country and across the world."[32] This desire has been realized in several ways, as the Walt Disney Company has a long history of involvement with public and higher education through partnerships, internships, and nontraditional programs. For instance, over five hundred third-grade students from eight different Maryland schools participated in a pilot program in 2006 called Comics in the Classroom, in which lesson plans based on classic Disney comic books were used to teach reading and writing skills. The vice president of Disney World-wide Publishing promoted the partnership, shoring up his case for the educational benefits of comic books with an unfortunate remark that clearly carries unintentional farcical implications: "Kids end up learning without even thinking about it."[33] Disney also offers high school graduates the CareerStart Program, which enables them to work for seven months at Disneyland or Walt Disney World and attend seminars to learn about the leisure and entertainment industries. They also get on-site, hands-on experience in such areas as engineering, marketing, and animation. Another program called Disney College invites college students to live in Disney housing complexes near Disney World or Disneyland, study topics such as hospitality and human resources, work as a cast member, and earn a certificate of completion, a "Mousters" degree or a "Ducktorate."[34]

Disney Studios also has a partnership with Monterey High School in Burbank, California, which includes hosting the graduation ceremony and providing scholarships for students. Disney also sends out volunteers to tutor elementary school children and employees to give talks at high schools and colleges about what it is like to work for Disney and how their own educations relate to the world of work.[35] Disney's involvement in these programs appears to be a mix of public service and self-interest, with the latter dominating. Disney's educational efforts are largely judged by how they affect the "organization's future labor pool." As one Disney supervisor put it, "We want the students [we hire] to be as skillful as possible."[36]

These educational ventures, although significant, provide neither high visibility for Disney's educational efforts nor a public relations opportunity to promote Disney's role in education on a national scale. As far back as 1993, the Walt Disney Company seriously considered getting involved in the business of education. It entered into negotiations with Chris Whittle to buy a controlling stake in the Edison Project and Channel One, both for-profit educational ventures. The deal fell through, undermining Disney's plans to build a private school system. But when Disney decided to build a new town called Celebration on its landholdings in Florida, it seized the opportunity to develop its own model school in partnership with the Osceola County School District and Stetson University. The Celebration School represents Disney's attempt to build "the school of the future," following what most educators would describe as a progressive curriculum. Such an institution, however, cannot help but be affected by the setting in which schooling takes place, the Disney-run town of Celebration.

Celebration began as Disney's version of a small town, a carefully marketed response to what the company called a "perceived lack of community in American life."[37] Celebration embodied the assumption that only a corporate-driven culture "can address the problems of the city with creativity and efficiency."[38] According to former Disney CEO Michael Eisner, "We looked at what made communities great in our past, added what we've learned from the best practices of today, and combined that with a vision and hope for strong communities in the future."[39] Designed according to the principles of New Urbanism—an architectural movement that views "suburban sprawl as a 'cancerous growth' and destructive of civic life"[40]—Celebration boasts pedestrian-friendly streets lined with porch-fronted houses that occupy tiny lots, offering inhabitants a proximity to each other that fosters neighborliness, conversation, and the pleasures of small-town life. Of course, the Walt Disney Company also looked to the booming security industry, capitalizing on the paranoid demands of a white middle-class imagination that is fed incessant images of the city as a space characterized by random street violence, drug trafficking, racial and ethnic tensions, homelessness, and joblessness. Lacking any firsthand knowledge of inner-city conditions, such an imagination feels besieged by a perceived expansion of urban conflict and marginalized groups, turning to the pastoral image of the residential enclave as a sanctuary offering both protection and security. "Security" in this sense has "less to do with personal safety than with the degree of personal insulation in resident, work, consumption and travel environments, from 'unsavory' groups and individuals, even crowds in general."[41]

Disney's nostalgia machine is premised on an appeal to a safer past and on the assumption that any "friendly" community is essentially middle-class and white. A promotional video for prospective home buyers relies upon a contrast between the Disney town and the implied chaos of real urban space. The video begins with a nostalgic and class-specific appeal: "There is a place that takes you back to that time of innocence. . . . A place of caramel apples and cotton candy, secret forts and hopscotch on the streets. That place is here again, in a new town called Celebration."[42] But the motivation behind building Celebration was far from innocent: it was driven by Disney's rush toward a postindustrial future of unregulated markets and profit making. In the 1960s, Disney purchased twenty-seven thousand acres of land from the state of Florida for approximately $200 an acre. Thirty years later, the company would diversify its holdings by developing quarter-acre lots on the former alligator-infested swampland and sell them to the public for over $80,000 apiece.[43] Embodied by a real-life community, all the trademarks associated with the Disney brand would take on a new meaningfulness and legitimacy. Innocence, playfulness, family life, and refuge from both the racial and the class anarchy of the city and the alienation of the suburb were now made available as commodified products for purchase.

The Walt Disney Company chose to open its $2.5 billion town on November 18, 1995, Mickey Mouse's birthday. Celebration—advertising "Health, Education, Place, Technology, and Community" for sale—would be a town where parents could provide their children with a safe place to play outdoors and where kids would have access to a model school based on the latest developments in educational theory.[44] Plus, homeowners could enjoy the benefits of small-town life without sacrificing modern conveniences. Each house, for instance, would be wired with a state-of-the-art fiber-optic cable system linking televisions, telephones, and computers. Celebration would strive to embody the principle that privatization and corporate control offer the best solutions to contemporary structural and social problems associated with city and suburban life. But as media coverage and personal accounts of life in the Disney town surfaced, Celebration would turn out to be far less utopian in reality than in its original design.

As Andrew Ross chronicles in his memoir about the early days of Celebration, problems plagued the town's corporate managers and residents from the very start. The promise of high-tech community life was never realized. The quality of the house construction was substandard, and the company contracted to build the homes faced numerous building-code violations.[45] A much-hyped diversity was certainly visible—albeit in the architecture of the houses, not in the inhabitants of the town, who were almost exclusively white. Diversity would not include housing affordable to low-wage earners, such as the majority of workers at the Disney parks, since Disney had paid Osceola County $300,000 for exemption from its affordable-housing mandate.[46] As Theresa Vargas reported in the *Washington Post*, Celebration became "a distant fantasy for many would-be-residents, a community where houses often sold for $1 million or more."[47] When it came to imagining the future, Disney took a lesson from Walt and the Disney imagineers and envisioned a place cloaked in nostalgia, merely obfuscating an overarching emphasis on corporate control, advertising hype, and profit-driven investment.

Celebration turned out to represent much more than a marriage of convenience between Norman Rockwell and Bill Gates: it also came to symbolize Disney's obsession with protecting its public image to the point of managing people's lives. Living in Celebration has a price. Safety and security are exchanged for a significant loss of control over a number of decisions that home owners make in most other communities. Much of Celebration, from its architecture to horticulture, is designed by the planners at Disney. Nobody can get lost in Celebration. The rules its residents must follow include such particulars as not hanging the wash out to dry, keeping the grass cut, not living elsewhere for more than three months at a time, holding only one garage sale in any twelve-month period, displaying only white or off-white window coverings, and using only approved house-paint colors. Disney even insisted on "social control over how many people [two, according to the rule book] slept in each bedroom."[48] Apparently Big Brother does not just come in the form of a totalitarian state; it can also come with a smiley face, masking the watchful eye of privatized government. When *New York Times* reporter Michael Pollan asked one Disney master planner about the excessive restrictions, he responded, "Regimentation can release you."[49] Despite Disney's sales pitch, life in Celebration closely aligns with the middle-class fear of freedom that not only feeds a growing hatred of urban spaces and diversity but also contributes to what Juliet Schor calls a "work-and-spend" culture and the "declining vitality of social life."[50] People get locked into a vicious cycle—aspiring to affluent lifestyles that require working longer days and accumulating more debt—leaving little time for meaningful community interaction other than in the roles of worker and consumer.

According to Bob Shinn, a former senior vice president of Walt Disney Imagineering, Celebration was conceptualized as fulfilling "Walt's ideal for a town of tomorrow. . . . With Celebration, we're giving something back, trying to blaze a trail to improve American family life, education and health."[51] But there is more at stake in Disney's venture than a simple enactment of Walt's vision for urban renewal: a carefully managed show of community, revolving around regulation, conformity, and security, is substituted for the unscripted nature of genuinely democratic relations. Disney leaves out of its upbeat promotional literature the rather tenuous notion of democracy that informs its view of municipal government, since Celebration is "premised upon citizens not having control over the people who plan for them and administer the policies of the city."[52] In Disney culture, community is about not self-rule but adhering to the rules laid down by a central authority—referred to in Disney language as "family-friendly planning"—and legitimated through an appeal to the rewards of the marketplace, all of which have a Disney copyright.[53] One such "reward" is decoupling political agency from the discourse of community. The community retailed by Disney has little to do with actively building democratic structures, fostering cultural diversity, or addressing pressing social problems and a great deal to do with the fantasy of social isolation—the luxury of not having to think about, or see, human suffering. Evan McKenzie argues that behind towns like Celebration is the notion that "I am going to leave America and go into this fantasy kingdom where there is no crime, with people only like me."[54] But people do not merely wake up one day with these sentiments in their heads: a yearning to return to a more comfortable place is generated by the powerful workings of a corporate culture that encourages individual self-interest as the basis for insatiable consumption. As Frank Furedi point outs, "Personal safety is a growth industry. . . . Passions that were once devoted to struggle to change the world (or keep it the same way) are now invested in trying to ensure that we are safe."[55] Although Celebration's earliest residents may have moved to the town hoping to fulfill a utopian longing (and banking on Disney's reputation for doing things correctly), they soon expressed dissatisfaction with the product sold to them, particularly with the "nontraditional" school system that the housing sales agents had lauded.

Recognizing that good schools attract home buyers, Disney invested heavily in the promotion of a quality school in Celebration. The Celebration School was initially advertised as a model educational institution because of its distinctive organization, curriculum, and cutting-edge technology. The school employed nongraded assessments and organized students into "neighborhoods," with approximately one hundred students and four teachers per neighborhood. The buildings housing these neighborhoods contained large open areas with computer workstations, teachers' offices, science labs, and water fountains. Instead of traditional school furniture, they featured cushioned window seats, brightly colored rugs, beanbag chairs, and a library with two beds on which kids could relax while reading. The cafeteria windows were fitted with computer hookups for students' laptops. Presenting itself as a state-of-the-art facility, the Celebration School's curriculum placed a strong emphasis on creative and lifelong learning, and evaluations focused less on testing than on student projects, portfolios, demonstrations, and exhibitions. In 1996 Leslie Postal, a newspaper reporter in Orlando, pointed out that Celebration School "is designed to be a showcase for high-tech and innovative instruction and is a drawing card for families building homes in the new town."[56]

But Disney was not using the school merely to sell expensive homes; the company's investment in public education also provided another route through which it could continue to legitimate its interest in children while expanding its control over them as a potential market. Not only do kids provide a captive audience open to the influence of a new electronic-media technology—aptly illustrated by the rising popularity of Disney. com—but Disney-sponsored schools provide the context for taking seriously both its role as a producer of cultural goods, texts, and entertainment and its claim that such commodities have educational value.

Although the K–12 school is owned and operated by the Osceola County School District, the Walt Disney Company donated the land, the design services, and up to $22 million to finance the project. Osceola initially spent $18 million in taxpayers' money for the school and continues to fund its day-to-day operations. Stetson University also played a major role in the school by contributing to its curriculum development and offering leadership programs to teachers. A three-member board, representing the Osceola County School Board, the Disney Celebration Company, and Stetson University, was set up to manage the school. The Disney public relations machine described the school as

> a unique public/private collaboration between the School District of Osceola Country, Disney, and Stetson University. Students are taught in multi-age groups focusing on personalized learning plans and portfolios that incorporate authentic measures of success. The school facility supports interactive learning and provides innovative technology linkages for communication throughout the community and the world. Celebration School was developed in collaboration with many of the nation's leading educational visionaries and institutions, and serves as a model for other school districts across the nation.[57]

Other public relations information included a list of fifteen educational principles, such as "accountability," "celebration," "communication," "cooperation," "equity," "human dignity," and "wellness." Although they sound progressive, these principles read less as elements of a specifically defined educational vision than as a grab bag of attributes that would have general appeal to conservative and liberal middle-class parents. The public relations campaign also listed leading educators who were instrumental in developing the school's curriculum, methods, and leadership principles. Included in the group were Howard Gardner, a Harvard University professor of educational psychology who specializes in the subject of multiple intelligences; William Glasser, author of *Schools without Failure* and a strong advocate of schools as therapeutic agencies; and University of Minnesota professors David Johnson and Roger Johnson, who are advocates of cooperative learning. According to one Disney source, the challenge that the group was to address was framed by the question, "What sort of school do we create to showcase the best ideas and practices in public education?" The answer published in a *Disney Magazine* article on Celebration School is suggestive: Gardner, Glasser, and the Johnsons "set to work researching the best practices in education—old and new. What emerged was a plan to help students find their most successful learning styles through, among other things, collaborative teaching, in which four to six teachers work together leading classes of 50 to 100 students, and collaborative learning, in which students work together, most often in teams of three or four."[58] The question challenging this group of educational theorists was provocative, but the answer appeared to go no further than simply sanctioning a set of methods. There was no attempt to understand teaching as a moral and political practice as opposed to simply a technical one. Nor was there any attempt to articulate a moral vision and social ethics that would provide a referent for justifying particular forms of pedagogical practice, teaching styles, and curricular choices. Questions of meaning and purpose in this context were treated as technical questions unrelated to issues of power, politics, and responsibility. There was no clarification of how Celebration School might contribute to the social imagination of particular communities or expand the capacities that its students need to exercise critical agency.

What was interesting about Disney's relationship with the school was that, on the surface, the school appeared progressive and quite at odds with the elements of Disney culture and pedagogy characteristic of Disney's other educational sites, but both in fact emphasized the acquisition of skills over critical, ethical thinking in order to produce students and workers trained to adapt to the world rather than to shape it. Although there were also hints of the other traditional Disney emphasis on turning the practical task of learning into the stuff of dreamy adventure, the claim to progressivism was founded largely on the school's use of sophisticated technologies, interactive learning, personalized learning plans, and portfolio-based forms of evaluation. But there was also the ideological underpinning, which is best understood through the experts Disney relied on for the school's design, resources, and methods.

The experts Disney called on to shape its curriculum were largely grounded in educational psychology, a field that has little or nothing to say about the relationship between schools and society or about how education works through the various processes in which knowledge and authority are constructed to produce power on an individual or social scale. But education empowers people only insofar as it fosters democratic identities, values, and relationships—that is, engaged citizens prepared to assume the moral, social, and political responsibilities of a substantive democracy. Howard Gardner is particularly interesting on this topic. As an educational reformer, he has become well-known for his lifelong focus on multiple intelligences. An advocate of the need for teachers to recognize students' different learning styles, he believes educators should organize subject matter according to models provided by disciplinary experts. Gardner has parlayed his approach into a virtual industry; one can find advertisements for his videos, teaching guides, and books in everything from standard educational magazines to airline travel guides. Gardner's student-as-disciplinary-expert fits in well with the emphasis on creating flexible, efficient, innovative, self-controlled, and collaborative workers. Understanding in this approach has less to do with critique than with problem solving, and the relationship between knowledge and power is addressed as a strategic issue rather than an ethical one. Knowledge means learning how to adapt to change; it emphasizes versatility, speed, and innovation, not how to challenge substantive injustices in a society founded on deep inequalities.[59]

Another "expert" that the Disney school relied upon, William Glasser, added a psychotherapeutic dimension to Gardner's emphasis on multiple intelligences and understandings. For Glasser, the key to successful schooling is "creating an environment of warm, personal involvement among the teachers."[60] Human relations become the stuff of good schooling in this discourse, which places strong emphasis on the importance of a school culture that promotes self-discovery and relevance. The problem with this approach is that it often reproduces a "me-centered politics in which the search for meaning replaces the search for justice."[61] In fact, Glasser has written books that integrate his psychological model with W. Edward Deming's account of Japanese corporate management styles in order to inform readers how to lead workers to produce "the quality work they know their companies need to be competitive" in the global marketplace.[62] Basically Glasser advocates a soft-style corporate management approach to classroom teaching, one that substitutes student self-direction for coercion and subtle manipulation for overt authoritarianism.[63] Effective teaching and learning in this discourse becomes simply experiential and has little to do with politics and systemic relations of power. Abstracted from considerations of politics, pedagogies such as Glasser's that fetishize "usefulness" and "relevance" tend to focus on deciphering students' needs so they can be redirected, monitored, and manipulated rather than considering what it means to educate students to become democratic subjects attentive to how the personal and the social interact as part of a larger network of power, governance, and critical agency.

Celebration School's staged philosophical emphasis on the cognitive and the therapeutic resonates with broader corporate pedagogies that encourage personal involvement, self-motivation, company loyalty, pride in one's work, and risk taking. While such an approach to leadership contrasts with Disney's heavy-handed efforts to control workers and shut down dissent in the spheres under its control, there is little doubt that the Celebration School's progressive classroom practices and curricular policies were fully compatible with contemporary theories of corporate leadership and power, particularly the "appeal to the 'new' industrial skills of cooperative problem-solving."[64] Addressing ways to meet students' stated needs, teachers were reduced to managers whose role was no longer to model critical thinking and learning but to cater to the students' "choice." In such a context that encourages students to work toward satisfying their own desires—quite fitting with a consumer model of education—it is unlikely that students will elect to interrogate media culture critically, engage in subversive readings of history, or dispute the role of people as mere spectators, consumers, and passive citizens. Would administrators and teachers at Celebration School ever show students *Mickey Mouse Goes to Haiti*, a twenty-eight-minute documentary "about the exploitation of workers in factories contracted to Disney"? Students at a Chicago school not only watched the film but protested Disney's practices in front of a local Disney Store—accompanied by teachers![65] Would Celebration take the issue of self-reflection, critique, and critical dialogue seriously by allowing its students to watch the video *Mickey Mouse Monopoly*, produced by the Media Education Foundation as a critique of Disney's corporate power and global cultural reach? With its corporate empire to protect, the question that looms large is, Would Disney ever provide an education that encourages students to develop the tools and citizenship skills to combat social problems that may not seem immediately "relevant" to their own self-interest?

Of course, Disney had little incentive, particularly in Celebration, to produce a body of civic-minded youth eager to participate in a wide range of social sites and speak to important social issues. But the company would still have to face a vocal group of parents who disliked the school's approach to learning and demanded "brisk consumer satisfaction."[66] Multiple levels of irony become evident in the narrative of the events that unfolded regarding the Celebration School: first, parents became very critical of the school and mobilized to actively resist the pedagogical practices informing their children's education, thus creating what Ross calls "some kind of provisional public sphere"[67]; second, the controversy over the school stemmed from the parents' desire for more traditional teaching methods and curricula. Disney was supporting a progressive school in a town that otherwise accepted strict adherence to the principles of obedience, conformity, and general passivity in the pursuit of a Disney utopia. And parents worried their children were not receiving the rigorous testing, scheduled classroom work, and grades that would enable them to get into college. When a group of parents demanded reforms to the school's progressive teaching methods, Disney's public representatives at first invalidated the parents' critique by stating the parents "had difficulty understanding the school's approach to teaching and grading."[68] In another instance, rather than taking seriously the parents' concerns about the perceived lack of curriculum structure and discipline, Disney officials claimed that many of the dissenting families were "just homesick for the towns they left."[69]

Brent Herrington, Celebration's community services manager, put out a newsletter soliciting contributions for the "positive parents fund," implying that those who did not support the progressive school curriculum were "negative parents."[70] All these efforts on the part of Disney to squelch dissent only added fuel to the fire. The controversy over the school led a number of families to move out of Celebration. The only catch was that they had signed a contract stating that they would not sell their house for a profit if they had lived in it for less than a year. Disney agreed to suspend the rule "only on condition of signing an agreement promising never to reveal their reasons for leaving Celebration."[71] For one dissenting family, the Walt Disney Company "offered to help in selling the house and other incentives in return for a promise 'not to disclose to any third party' their reasons for leaving."[72] It seems that a corporate-owned town such as Celebration could only respond to public debate as a danger to the community and, in typical Disney fashion, attempted to use its legal authority to squelch dissent. Despite the family's compliance with the gag order, Disney feared bad publicity from the remainder of Celebration's disgruntled clientele, and it removed its logo from billboards advertising the town and from the town's water tower less than two years after Celebration opened for business.[73] Disney did not have much to worry about, however, since Celebration residents were just as reluctant to publicize issues that might lower community property values.

Although insightful commentators have praised Celebration residents for having "developed their own modes of interpersonal civic action to address perceived injustices perpetrated by Disney," it becomes clear that if Celebration witnessed the birth of civil society, then it was formed along the lines of a consumer model of citizenship.[74] According to Ross, a survey showed that most teachers and students who responded were "fairly comfortable with the methods of instruction and assessment."[75] It was the parents in conjunction with the school administrators who transformed the school by shifting the pedagogical emphasis toward technical competencies. At the same time as the concerned parents saw through the flimsy corporate marketing gimmicks advanced by Disney, they maintained a position that Disney was a responsible, trustworthy corporation (unlike other corporations) and that they had rights as consumers to have their grievances addressed. Effective resistance on the part of the Celebration residents was launched within the language and framework of corporate culture; the parties involved in the debates accepted that public schooling could be treated as a commodity. The important lesson here is not to gain reassurance from the mere fact that such resistance is possible but to recognize the limits of resistance in the face of such an overwhelming corporate power as Disney. The parents' perspective on education was perhaps less imaginative than the Disney planners had envisioned, but ultimately (and ironically) it was more compatible with the typical corporate practices, such as bullying workers, employed by Disney. The supposed "civil society" that emerged in Celebration initiated a challenge to established authority to achieve its goals, but it sacrificed the participation of students and teachers in the process. Membership in the "democratic" community was based on a partnership between property owners and those in high-paid management positions. Three years after the school opened, only one teacher from the original development team remained at the school, and over twenty-five teachers had quit or been fired as a result of the battle with the parents, demonstrating a power imbalance as the outcome of the clash between private and public interests.[76] This is not good news if Celebration's debate over public education is to be used to teach students about the workings and effects of democracy.

There were other drawbacks to Disney's involvement with the Celebration School. The Osceola County School District invested millions of dollars in the school-business partnership with Disney, diverting funds from other schools in desperate need of improvement, schools that, for instance, "suffer[ed] from leaking roofs, faulty wiring, and cramped quarters."[77] What is more, the school intended to draw 80 percent of its students from Celebration itself, meaning that the school's expensive infrastructure would not benefit the vast majority of kids in Florida—many of whom already face obstacles to education such as racism and poverty, let alone the underfunding of their schools. That the town's affluent residents could overlook these deleterious effects of the school-business partnership on the larger community surrounding Celebration is somewhat surprising, although the fact that Celebrationites so readily entrusted their children's education to a corporation known primarily for "producing cartoons and simulations of historical and geographical clichés"[78] is more so. Also disturbing (and even less surprising) is that the relatively impoverished Osceola County School Board would agree to enter into a joint stewardship arrangement with

Disney, which repeatedly ignored the restrictions put in place to ensure equity among the schools in the district.[79] Genuine democracy recognizes individuals' responsibility to further a general interest in equality, justice, and freedom, not merely to advance their own narrow self-interest. Seen in this context, the victory of the Celebration parents in voicing their resistance to the school becomes as much a symptom of the creeping privatization and commercialization of public education as it was a triumph for corporate accountability. Disney, like most corporations, is used to catering to shareholders' demands, not the demands of consumers (after all, another customer is always waiting in line). But Disney is unlike other corporations in that it attempted to demonstrate in a very real fashion that it could be a responsible civic contributor. Disney's foray into public education made compliance with parents' demands necessary. Following corporate logic, Disney had decided to invest heavily in front-end design and infrastructure (and to disinvest in people and civic life) but could not prevent a host of problems from emerging later when policy was put into practice and forced a confrontation with the risk-filled dynamics of democracy. Building an urban utopia proved more difficult than Disney had originally anticipated, and the company will probably think twice before devising such an arrangement between the public and the private sector again.

HIGH SCHOOL, INC.

In 2006, Disney would finally realize its goal of creating the ideal school. It would be a high school in which all students were middle class, everyone approached life as a set of endless opportunities, and individuals resolved conflict by breaking into song and dance. Disney's efforts to design schools are apparently far more successful in the realm of fiction than in real life. The Emmy-winning Disney Channel original film *High School Musical* was a runaway hit. The story features a ridiculously talented group of clean-cut, acne-free teens who decide to all get along despite supposedly intractable differences: one math-oriented student loves hip-hop music, another dressed in skater garb plays the cello, and, most shockingly, a basketball jock loves to make crème brûlée. While the film's appeal to a harmonious multiracial community seems sincere, it can only parody toleration when it invariably reduces the question of difference to a set of personal preferences—some clearly connected to consumer culture. Significant issues of material and ideological difference involving gender, race, class, and sexuality are completely ignored in this Disney high school. Arguments like "Children are not ready to think about real differences" hardly seem accurate in a society in which children and teens daily confront racism, sexism, and poverty in their schools. But *High School Musical* is really intended to present a fantasy world for middle-class viewers in which individual talent cannot fail to win recognition, even if one chooses to be involved in community activities rather than to work alone. Although the main character, Troy Bolton (Zac Efron), risks compromising his jock identity if he performs in the high school musical, he begins and ends the story as the most popular kid in school. In this way, it is unclear when the protagonists sing about choosing not to "stick with the status quo" what could actually be meant by bucking the status quo other than finding diverse outlets for expressing one's endless store of talent. While his basketball teammates at first criticize rather than support Troy's singing endeavors, his divided loyalties are resolved for him when the team realizes that he's not playing very well and that their only hope for winning the championship is to help him make it to an audition where he can sing and dance with his girlfriend, Gabriella Montez (Vanessa Hudgens). Sharpay Evans (Ashley Tisdale), the film's antagonist and an ultrarich type clearly modeled on Paris Hilton, tries to prevent Troy and Gabriella from auditioning for the musical. In an upper-middle-class world of nice clothes, houses, cars, and resort vacations, the only true source of oppression seems to be the inability to express one's innate talent. While the romantic couple sings canned pop music of the kind first popularized by boy and girl bands of the 1990s, such as New Kids on the Block and the Spice Girls, the drama teacher, Miss Darbus (Alyson Reed), and longtime members of the drama club Sharpay and her twin brother, Ryan (Lucas Grabeel), are severely caricatured for their passion for colorful Broadway-type musicals. In this way, *High School Musical*, while claiming to challenge the boundaries between what is and is not "cool," simply endorses mainstream music and dance numbers (what Disney is marketing), further entrenching the perceived "uncoolness" of conventional musicals and high school drama classes.

A similar plot trajectory occurs in 2007's *High School Musical 2*, when the same group of Albuquerque, New Mexico, teens is hired to work at a ritzy country club resort owned by Sharpay's parents.

Sharpay, who has a crush on Troy, schemes to separate Troy and Gabriella by using her family's connections to introduce Troy to college basketball players and scouts, who represent Troy's hope for a college scholarship. As in the first film, Troy confronts divided loyalties, but this time he feels forced to choose between his friends, who feel betrayed by Troy's newfound sense of privilege and enjoyment of luxury, and his future educational goals. After accepting his friends' judgment that he has changed for the worse, he agrees to keep a promise to perform with Sharpay in the club's talent show, but only on the grounds that his friends also be allowed to participate. Troy's friends arrange it so that he can sing with Gabriella instead of Sharpay, and finally they all join together in an ensemble performance. In typical Disney fashion, Troy's decision to support his friends actually entails no sacrifice since the film implies that his talent is even better displayed by his duet with Gabriella, performed in front of representatives from the University of Albuquerque. If the film at first represents a middle-class family's struggle to pay for the high cost of postsecondary education, it ends up completely trivializing legitimate concerns regarding financial need by associating those concerns with self-interest, moral corruption, the favoritism allegedly displayed in college-admission procedures, unfair labor practices, and parental pressure. The utterly banal moral message is that you only need to be true to yourself (easier undoubtedly for those selves already defined as popular, talented, intelligent, fit, good-looking, white, suburban, heterosexual, male youths), and those around you will freely satisfy your every need and desire. No struggle required. In fact, the finale involves an ensemble performance of the song "All for One," a truncated version of the famous line from Dumas's *Three Musketeers* (1844)—all for one, one for all—suggesting that everyone is rallying behind Troy Bolton, the only developed character in the film whose minimal complexity contrasts with the homogeneity of the rest. In this gesture, the Disney "star machine" is working not only to bolster Zac Efron's teen idol status but also to train young viewers in the patterns of desire associated with celebrity culture.

While the film lamely attempts to invoke the warm fuzzy feelings of solidarity suggested by the ensemble dance number, the resulting uniformity is a movement away from diversity, except in the most superficial ways. Disney scholars have noted a similar contradictory effect in the visitor's experience at Disney theme parks, where the message imbibed is a celebration of liberty, individuality, and freedom—embodied by the figure of Walt Disney himself—in contrast to demands for guests' ready compliance due to "the outcomes of a large group environment, such as long lines, lack of privacy, and constant instructions . . . similar circumstances [that] outside the park would be perceived as infringements on freedom."[80] Elayne Rapping notes that Disney World, not unlike the world of the High School Musical films, is "uniform in its middle-American, asexual, uninflected sameness," all of which works to embody a "sense of classless luxury and unthreatening sameness . . . a synthetic spirit of democracy" that promises a kind of belonging free from the "stress of competition."[81] But, in its typical contradictory way, the park lures guests into experiences and commodities designed to celebrate "all the wonders of the world, all the culture, knowledge, and productivity that mark the greatest achievements of human civilization."[82] Consequently, at the same time as Disney consumers learn to believe in the power of individual genius—most recently on display in Disney's animated film *Meet the Robinsons* (2007), whose central theme, "Keep moving forward," quotes Walt Disney directly—they learn to belong to the adoring masses.

Despite the film's obvious weaknesses, audiences seem to love the depiction of an easy resolution to a conflict that arises from the teen protagonist's innocence rather than corruption. *High School Musical 2*'s first broadcast on the Disney Channel drew over 17.2 million viewers, receiving the highest ever ratings for a basic cable broadcast in U.S. history and becoming the most watched televised event by children six to eleven years old and the number one entertainment telecast for youth ages nine to fourteen.[83] *Variety* magazine reported that over 170 million people worldwide had seen the film, excluding sales of the DVD release.[84] Disney-ABC Television Group President Anne Sweeney emphasized that High School Musical was a "new important franchise for The Walt Disney Company, and a cultural touchstone for millions of kids and tweens around the world."[85] Although a *New York Times* review suggested that parents and kids liked the portrayal of high school life for the way it "allegedly sexes up schoolwork,"[86] the films clearly reinscribe traditional ideas about classroom learning as stuffy and boring in contrast to extracurricular life experiences. And while another reviewer loved a "standout number performed on a baseball field" as evidence of Disney's ability to "capture the generational Zeitgeist,"[87] no comment was made about the implications arising from the fact that all the players in the film's "staff baseball game" are male, while the female staff are reduced to cheerleading in the stands. The High School Musical films tell young people more or less directly that their identities should not be shaped by what they learn in the classroom but by the ways they circulate in other spaces that ostensibly allow for better modes of self-expression and interactions with peers. Disney does not say—but certainly enacts with its aggressive marketing of High School Musical merchandise and its creation of "cross-promotions with Major League Baseball, Wal-Mart, Sprint and Dannon yogurt, among others"[88]— that these supposedly alternative spaces of self-actualization are primarily mediated by one's degree of privilege and access to consumer goods. School only functions as a site of empowerment insofar as it is a space in which consumption is made visible and conspicuous. Consequently, it is unclear how the High School Musical films might expand and enliven children's view of schooling or teachers or, for that matter, their perspectives on selfhood. Instead of offering new and exciting learning experiences, the few scenes that take place in the classroom depict students eager to get out and on with their "real" lives, and their "real-life" scenes overtly reinforce stereotypes of gender and class behavior. In this way, Disney culture offers a certain notion of the past and the present that is not only safe and middle class but also largely indifferent to racial, class, and social conflict.

Disney's formulaic fantasy—reducing unpleasant and contradictory lived experiences to the "trials and tribulations" of well-off kids who "just want to fit in"—has obvious audience appeal, not least because, in a world increasingly defined by fragmentation and instability, Disney represents for youth a source of empowerment, however illusive. The wildly popular Hannah Montana franchise based on a Disney Channel sitcom that first aired in 2006 is another case in point. Following in the wake of the successful *Lizzie McGuire* television series (2001–2004) and feature film (2003) starring singer-actress Hilary Duff, Disney keeps on churning out young stars. *Hannah Montana* is the story of a teenage girl named Miley Stewart, played by Miley Cyrus (daughter of country singer Billy Ray Cyrus, who also plays her father on the show). Miley wants to lead a totally normal life at home and school and therefore decides to keep it a secret that she is also the superstar pop singer Hannah Montana. She achieves this goal by changing her clothing and hair color. On the show, then, the lead character, Miley Stewart, has a rock-star alter ego named Hannah Montana, and in real life Disney aggressively markets Miley Cyrus as a pop icon by producing music CDs and funding her 2007 concert tour, called *Hannah Montana/Miley Cyrus: Best of Both Worlds.* As one reporter for the *New York Times* commented, Disney's public relations' ingenuity ensures that consumers get "three girls for the price of one."[89] For one concert in New York, fans unable to get one of the coveted concert tickets were instead given the opportunity to buy Miley Cyrus merchandise at the Nassau Coliseum on Boxing Day.[90] The sold-out concert tour then appeared in select movie theaters as a Disney Digital three-dimensional musical documentary, grossing over $30 million on its opening weekend and breaking a record for the highest-ever average profit per theater for a limited-release film.[91]

Hannah Montana taps into the fantasy of celebrity, offering young people the lure of agency through an endless reinvention of the self. A tween girl watching the television show might identify with the family dynamics (brother-sister conflict, for example), but she can also transform herself among her classmates and achieve the chic look of a rock starlet merely by purchasing Hannah Montana clothing at Walmart. According to the Disney formula, self-expression is once again reduced to what a young person can afford to buy. The *Hannah Montana* television show also strengthens the identification between the show's main characters and its fans by blurring the line between fiction and reality as the television sitcom frames the real-life singing career of Miley Cyrus, which then frames and advertises the sitcom-turned-reality-television-show. Disney is expert at generating such cycles of reinforcement in the name of brand promotion. As Mike Budd explains, the company exhibits "highly developed corporate synergy in which every Disney product is both a commodity and an ad for every other Disney commodity."[92] What is more, the Disney Channel's cross-promotion of its various television shows upholds its simulated version of reality, which becomes a more compelling and coherent representation of actual celebrity lives when actors associated with one show make guest appearances on another. For instance, the cast of the High School Musical films appeared on *Hannah Montana*, and the Disney Channel combined its most popular shows in the three-part crossover special titled *That's So Suite Life of Hannah Montana* (2006). By connecting the casts of its television shows, Disney creates a whole hyperreal world defined primarily by its lack of conflict and opulent wealth, while simultaneously providing a crucial entry point for young people into that world through the acquisition of merchandise (including clothing and home decor). In one episode (titled "Achy Jakey Heart" in a parodic reference to Billy Ray Cyrus's hit song from 1992), the young fans surrounding Miley and her movie-star boyfriend, Jake Ryan, produce dozens of cell phones in order to snap photos of the couple. One of this scene's messages is that new media technologies such as cell phones are both necessary fan accessories and the route to instant fame and fortune. Another message is that social status depends on one's associates: successful self-branding means carefully selecting who and what will best reflect "you."[93] If young people exercise the creative (consumer) power to promote their own "brand" identities, they can at least achieve self-actualization, if not pass as ultrarich and talented. The glamorous model of multiple selves provided by *Hannah Montana* suggests that average kids can morph into the superstars they really are simply by acquiring the right accessories.

Childhood ideals increasingly give way to a market-driven politics in which young people are prepared for a life of objectification while simultaneously deprived of any viable sense of moral and political agency. In 2009, Disney enlisted the help of educators, anthropologists, and a former researcher with "a background in the casino industry" to study all aspects of youth culture—particularly the intimate lives of boys ages six to fourteen, who currently constitute one of the markets least accessible to Disney—in order to uncover the best "emotional hooks" to lure boys into the wonderful world of corporate Disney.[94] Given Disney's desire to expand into boys' culture, the company's 2009 announcement that it had purchased Marvel Entertainment Inc. came as no surprise. Marvel's comic book empire owns the licenses for approximately five thousand superhero characters. The *Wall Street Journal* remarked that by "bringing in macho types such as Iron Man, Thor, and Captain America, the Marvel deal would expand Disney's audience, adding properties that appeal to boys from their preteen years into young adulthood."[95] Another strategy to tap into the male youth market involved Disney spending $180 million on video game development in 2009. One product, the video game Epic Mickey, revamps the character of Mickey Mouse in an alleged effort to make him more appealing to today's generation of youth. With Mickey's popularity in decline in the United States, Disney's market-driven agenda is visible not only in its willingness to transform the hallowed icon upon which its corporate empire was built but also in the very way it has transformed Mickey Mouse's character. The mouse will no longer embody a childlike innocence and generosity but will instead be "cantankerous and cunning" and will exhibit "selfish, destructive behavior."[96] Although Disney's representatives suggest that this reimagining of Mickey Mouse merely reflects what is currently popular among young people, the question for concerned parents, educators, and others must remain, What kind of values and behaviors is Disney sanctioning, if not generating, in this new character of Mickey Mouse? Keeping in mind that corporate giants such as Disney express no scruples about their efforts to "expand 'inwardly' into the psyche and emotional life of the individual in order to utilize human potential" in the service of a market society,[97] these recent moves by the Walt Disney Company to darken the characters it incorporates into its cultural offerings should be seen as less a demystification of the brand image of Disneyfied innocence and more a signal of the company's awareness of a growing compatibility between the nature of Disney's public pedagogy and a commercial culture's ethos of egocentric narcissism, social aggression, and hypermasculinity.

The issues surrounding Disney culture as a source of identity for young people are complex. According to a *New York Times* article, for many people, but especially "parents unnerved by the spectacle of the Spears family," Miley Cyrus represents a relatively innocuous role model for "millions of girls still figuring out how they feel about boys."[98] However, consider the context of the show and what it teaches young girls in terms of their identities, values, and aspirations: Hannah Montana is not a superhero but merely a superstar whose only responsibility in life is to entertain her fans and make money; Miley Stewart's raison d'être is to deceive the people around her so that she can live her life unencumbered by the social responsibilities attendant on being a well-known public figure. Does such a role model not severely proscribe the imaginative possibilities for a generation of young women who are sadly being encouraged to think of shopping as "retail therapy"?

The comment from the *New York Times* about Miley Cyrus being a good role model also carries two further implications: first, that youth tend to identify strongly, perhaps even unthinkingly, with popular culture; second, that pleasure is intimately tied to identification rather than to a sense of difference. There are problems with both of these assumptions. To assume that young people are only capable of relating to culture through *identification* does them as much a disservice as assuming that all teens adopt the stance of alienated and angst-ridden outsiders. Although a dominant stereotype of preteens and teenagers tends to represent them as immature and incomplete people who flounder to shape their identities in ways that will continue to define their individuality throughout their adult lives, it is becoming more clear every day that adult existence, according to Zygmunt Bauman, increasingly involves "changing one's ego" through "an unending series of self-focused pursuits, each episode lived through as an overture to the next."[99] Whether or not this is a dramatic departure from the way life was lived in the past, it is nevertheless true that today virtually every aspect of one's life includes a constant negotiation of subjectivity that shifts in relation to others through processes that involve a constant engagement with educational sites throughout the culture. This is one reason why critical education and media literacy are so important. With the appropriate critical tools, children and young people are quite capable of critiquing the dominant culture around them; in fact, from their liminal position, they are perhaps even better able than adults (inured by a sense of agency that has been reduced to buying and selling) to recognize the "swindle of fulfillment" promised by rampant consumerism.[100]

It is equally mistaken to assume that pleasure can only be derived from unthinking identification with cultural messages and objects. Cannot critical thinking be viewed as a source of pleasure and as a kind of empowerment that produces sophistication and creativity rather than disillusionment and cynicism? Why does the perception still persist that the "happiness" and "innocence" of youth depend on a lack of critical engagement? Rather than understanding youth as a preadult state defined by an absence of self-awareness, we should see it as a pivotal time in which young people are learning the importance of an ethical act and taking responsibility for the choices they make and the places they occupy in their larger surroundings. In this context, defending childhood "innocence" does not mean defending the purity of a nonagent (the ideological basis for the Disney version of innocence). It means defending the "guiltless": securing young people's right to learn and think deeply about the effects of their actions within the complex network of human and animal life on this planet and thereby to remain as guilt free as possible in the way they live their lives. A critical education that explores the complexity of self and society is no guarantee that a person will live ethically, but it is the only way to equip youth with compelling reasons for why they should choose not to taint their innocence by inadvertently colluding in processes that further environmental destruction, the overwhelming power of multinational corporations, the exploitation of workers, militarization, a lack of health care and clean water, market deregulation, poverty, and genocide, to name only a few of the world's problems. Surely that parents, teachers, reporters, academics, and others project a simplistic notion of innocence onto children and associate childhood with an idealized state of stability and security says less about a realistic understanding of youth than about both the feelings of insecurity that prevail in contemporary society and the constantly shifting adult identities that are symptomatic of what Bauman calls an era of "endemic uncertainty."[101]

If imbibing the products of popular culture such as *Hannah Montana* were the only option, then young people's imaginations and thoughts would be limited to the kinds of choices that promise to create "a totally normal life" in this world of instability. But engaging in constant, habitual consumption is a far cry from achieving security or stability. If young people did happen to identify uncritically with television stars, then would it not be preferable for them to observe other young people engaged in complex life situations who must weigh the consequences of making difficult ethical choices? On the one hand, the desire for "normal" in the case of Disney's ultrarich characters seems to verge on the pathological, as any of the normal conflicts that affect youth each and every day—bullying, sexuality, alcoholism, violence, homophobia, drug use, poverty, censorship, and sexual abuse—are rendered completely invisible. On the other hand, there are examples of television shows pitched to young audiences that do address these issues. Two examples are the television series *Buffy the Vampire Slayer* (1997–2003) created by Joss Whedon and an earlier prototype for adolescent and youth programming, ABC's short-lived series *My So-called Life* (1994–1995). The latter series, despite critical acclaim, a devoted fan base, and the argument that the show was providing an important voice for underrepresented young women on network television, was canceled when Robert Iger was the head of ABC because of low ratings. But the mere existence of television shows in the mainstream media that combine a complex portrayal of youth with social critique is instructive. Disney chooses—because it is in its own corporate interests to do so—to represent critical agency and the transition to adulthood as an image makeover tantamount to learning to be a savvy consumer.

CONCLUSION

Corporate culture within the past decade has kindled the popular imagination with a discourse of reform that celebrates egoistic individualism, profits, and the culture of the market. Lost in this shift is the language of community, democracy, and public interest, a shift that undermines claims for public purpose, public service, and public education. As a result, we are witnessing a global decline of public culture and increased attacks on the most basic institutions of democratic public life. Public funding for the arts, backing for public schools, and support for social programs are on the wane. Accompanying such a decline is a shift from public action to private concern, social welfare to individual initiative, and public good to self-interest.

As the Walt Disney Company expands its corporate reach into everyday life, including its move into public schooling, it will not only undermine attempts to revitalize public education for all students but sanitize and trivialize any serious engagement with public memory, citizenship, and democracy. Disney's use of the new media technologies makes clear the danger that arises from corporate control of the new educational technologies that not only harness the powerful flow of information but intrude into children's lives in a way that was unimaginable twenty years ago. Disney's educational and political influence in all aspects of society raises important questions about turning over public culture—and civil society itself—to a totalizing corporate environment. The issue here is not whether people read Disney differently, or even enjoy the glut of entertainment and commodities that the company dumps into the culture, but whether a democratic society can safely allow an ever-expanding corporate culture to blur the distinction between public and private, entertainment and history, and critical citizenship and consumer identity.

What are the implications for a democratic society increasingly under the sway of corporations that subordinate politics, history, public discourse, and noncommodified forms of culture to consumerism, escapist entertainment, and corporate profits? We live at a time when it is crucial for young people to be educated critically so that they can understand the scope, severity, and range of problems that they face today. But there is more at stake here than confronting the challenge of what is to be done: there is the infinitely more serious issue of who is going to confront these challenges. Surely, corporations such as Disney are not going to take up that challenge; in fact, they are more likely to bury it in an ever-expanding culture of consumerist ideology, commodified objects, and modes of education in which the social collapses into the private and a market-driven rationality, hiding under the mantle of innocence, continues to produce the many serious problems facing young people today. Clearly, Disney as a register for corporate power and education must be relentlessly challenged, if we dare hope for a future that is better than the present.

Chapter Three

Children's Culture and Disney's Animated Films

Animation as a form of historical memory has entered real space. After all, any space or film that uses manipulated, interactive imagery must be called, by definition, a form of animation; and we are increasingly being submerged in life as a video game, even while our political crises deepen, and our class difference widens. . . . We act out stories inside cartoons now.

—Norman M. Klein[1]

Animated Hollywood films, particularly those produced by Disney, have been at the forefront of children's culture for decades. Such films are presented to audiences as exemplary forms of entertainment that stimulate the imagination, protect innocence, and create a healthy sense of adventure, all of which is assumed to be "good" for kids. In other words, in the absence of close scrutiny, such films appear to be wholesome vehicles of amusement, a highly regarded and sought after source of fun and joy for children. However, cultural critics are increasingly viewing these films as much more than entertainment.[2] Disney's animated films operate on many registers, but one of the most persuasive is their role as "teaching machines." The products associated with children's culture now garner at least as much cultural authority and legitimacy for teaching specific roles, values, and ideals as more traditional sites of learning, such as public schools, religious institutions, and the family. Disney films combine enchantment and innocence in narrating stories that help children understand who they are, what societies are about, and what it means to construct a world of play and fantasy in an adult environment. The authority of such films, in part, stems from their unique form of representation and their ever-growing presence within a media apparatus equipped with dazzling technology, sound effects, and imagery packaged as entertainment, spin-off commercial products, and "huggable" stories.

The significance of Disney's animated films as a site of learning is heightened by the widespread recognition that schools and other public sites are increasingly beset by a crisis of vision, purpose, and motivation. The mass media, especially the world of Hollywood films, constructs a dreamlike world of security, coherence, and childhood innocence in which kids find a place to situate themselves in their emotional lives. Unlike the often hard, joyless reality of schooling, children's films provide a high-tech visual space in which adventure and pleasure meet in a fantasy world of possibilities and a commercial sphere of consumerism and commodification. The educational relevance of animated films makes it all the more necessary to move beyond treating these films as transparent entertainment and to question the diverse, often contradictory, messages that constitute Disney's worldview. The sheer number of viewers of Disney/Pixar films alone would warrant exploration and critical understanding of the political messages they contain, but doing so is all the more critical because they captivate the imaginations of very young children.

TRADEMARKING INNOCENCE

Generations of children have learned from Disney films. Disney's teaching machine now shapes the identities of youth from infancy to the teenage years. It has become essential for parents and educators to pay close attention to what Disney culture and its products are saying, especially as Disney's brand image presents the company as one in which parents can place their unqualified trust. Given the glut of violence kids are viewing in Hollywood blockbusters, video games, and other commercial forms of entertainment, it may seem heretical to criticize the Walt Disney Company, a corporation that claims to share the major concerns of parents, particularly the need to protect children from witnessing and being influenced by social conflicts, sexuality, and the moral difficulties associated with adulthood. But while Disney films do not promote the extreme violence that has become central to many other forms of popular culture, they do carry cultural and social messages that require carefully scrutiny. After all, "the happiest place on earth" has traditionally protected itself from the interrogation of critics precisely by appealing to its trademark image of innocence.

The popular press often ignores criticisms of Disney. Yet, the charge by conservative Southern Baptists that Disney films promote a seditious, anti-Christian ideology received enormous publicity in the 1990s. As a consequence of this reporting of right-wing criticisms—a number of which appeared so extreme as to be comical—Disney, by contrast, appeared not only more moderate and tolerant of difference but also liberal in its political and social orientation. Mainstream reviews of Disney have perennially overlooked the racist, sexist, and antidemocratic ethos that permeates Disney films. For instance, *New York Times* critic Michiko Kakutani has argued that if anything is wrong with Disney's animated films it is that the characters are too preachy and promote "wholesome messages" that "only an ogre or bigot could hate."³ One cannot help but wonder what is "wholesome" about the overt racism Disney displays toward both African Americans in the notoriously racist *The Jungle Book* and Arabs in *Aladdin*, the retrograde gender roles at work in *The Little Mermaid* and *Beauty and the Beast*, the undisguised celebration of antidemocratic governments and racism (remember the hyenas, who sounded like poor blacks and Hispanics?) evident in *The Lion King*, or the nostalgic portrayal of gas-guzzling, humanoid automobiles who inhabit an asphalt world that could easily serve as an advertisement for ExxonMobil in *Cars*.

More is at work here than a successful public relations campaign intent on promoting Disney's fabled claim to goodness. There is also the reality of a powerful economic and political empire that in 2008 made over $37.8 billion in revenues from all of its divisions.⁴ Disney is more than a corporate giant; it is also a global cultural institution that fiercely struggles to protect its mythical status as a purveyor of innocence and moral virtue.

Quick to mobilize its monolith of legal representatives, public relations spokespersons, and professional cultural critics to safeguard the borders of its "magic kingdom," Disney has aggressively prosecuted violations of its copyrights and has a legendary reputation for bullying authors who use the Disney archives and refusing to approve their manuscripts for publication.[5] In its zeal to protect its image and extend its profits, Disney even threatened legal action against three South Florida day care centers for using Disney cartoon characters on their exterior walls. In this instance, Disney's aggressive endorsement of property rights and censorship undermined its usual role as a defender of conservative family values. While Disney's reputation as a moral authority on American values has been increasingly disputed since the first edition of this book was published in 1999, the ongoing power of Disney's mythological status should not be underestimated.

The penetration of the Disney empire into every aspect of social life consistently reinforces Disney's self-image as an icon of American culture. Disney's multi-billion-dollar global empire shapes young people's experiences through a maze of representations and products, including box office movies, home videos, theme parks, hotels, retail stores, classroom instructional films, popular music, radio programs, television shows, websites, and family restaurants.[6] Through the use of public visual space, Disney's network of power relations promotes the construction of an all-encompassing world of enchantment allegedly free from the dynamics of ideology, politics, and power.[7] At the same time, Disney goes to great lengths to boost its civic image. Defining itself as a vehicle for education and civic responsibility, Disney has sponsored teacher-of-the-year awards, provided Doer and Dreamer scholarships to students, and offered financial aid, internships, and other learning opportunities to disadvantaged urban youth through educational and work programs, such as an ice-skating program called Goals. Intent on defining itself as a purveyor of ideas and values rather than commodities, Disney aggressively develops its image as a public service industry.[8] No longer content to spread its message through media entertainment and theme parks, Disney has extended its reach into the growing lucrative market now enveloping educational institutions, from preschools to high schools.

Interesting here is that Disney does not simply dispense the fantasies through which childhood innocence and adventure are produced, experienced, and affirmed. Disney now actively seeks to provide prototypical models for families, schools, and communities. As discussed in chapter 2, Disney was a copartner in a business-school venture in Celebration, Florida, and continues to provide curricular materials to public school systems. From the seedy urban haunts of New York City to the spatial monuments of consumer tourism in Florida, Disney is refiguring the social and cultural landscape while spreading its corporate ideology through the inventiveness and marketing savvy of its imagineers. In the late 1990s, Disney transformed large sections of West Forty-second Street in New York City into an advertisement for a cleaned-up Disney version of America, featured in the Disney film *Enchanted* (2007) as the location of a magical portal between the two-dimensional land of Disney animation and the real-life ("live-action") equivalent of modern-day romance. Disney also designed the town of Celebration, according to Disney executives, after the "main streets of small-town America and reminiscent of Norman Rockwell images."[9] What Disney leaves out of its upbeat promotional literature is the rather tenuous notion of democracy that informs its view of municipal government, since Celebration is run by company managers rather than elected officials.[10]

But Disney does more than provide prototypes for upscale communities; it also makes a claim on the future through its nostalgic view of the past, which displaces a trenchant public memory with fantasies of simplicity, purity, and wholeness. The late French theorist Jean Baudrillard provides an interesting theoretical twist on the scope and power of Disney's influence, arguing that Disneyland is more "real" than fantasy because it now provides the images and narratives based on which America constructs itself and is perceived around the world. For Baudrillard, Disneyland functions as a "deterrent" designed to "rejuvenate in reverse the fiction of the real."

> Disneyland is there to conceal the fact that it is the "real" country, all of "real" America, which is Disneyland (just as prisons are there to conceal the fact that it is the social in its entirety, in its banal omnipresence, which is carceral). Disneyland is presented as imaginary in order to make us believe that the rest is real, when in fact all of Los Angeles and the America surrounding it are no longer real but of the order of the hyperreal and of simulation.[11]

In this principle of postmodern thinking—namely, that art provides the actual foundations for how we engage with life—we are alerted to the seriousness of the messages being presented by Disney culture.

Examples of the Disneyfication of America abound. For instance, the Houston airport modeled its monorail after the one at Disneyland. New housing developments throughout America appropriate a piece of nostalgia by imitating the early-twentieth-century architecture of Disneyland's Main Street USA. Moreover, throughout America, shopping malls imitate Disney's approach to retailing so "that shopping takes place in themed environments."[12] It seems that the most active political visionaries are those who reside not in Washington, D.C., but in California, and they call themselves the Disney imagineers. The boundaries between entertainment, education, governance, and commercialization collapse through Disney's sheer reach into everyday life. The scope of the Disney empire reveals both shrewd business practices as well as a sharp eye for providing dreams and products through forms of popular culture in which kids are willing to invest materially and emotionally.

Not only fans of Disney but most consumers of Disney media and products tend to reject any link between ideology and the prolific entertainment world of the Walt Disney Company. And yet, there are some critiques like ours that likewise argue that Disney's pretense to innocence is little more than a promotional mask veiling its aggressive marketing techniques and influence in educating children to become active consumers. Eric Smooden, editor of *Disney Discourse*, a book critical of Disney's role in American culture, suggests that "Disney constructs childhood so as to make it entirely compatible with consumerism."[13] Even more disturbing is the widespread belief that Disney's "innocence" renders it unaccountable for the way it shapes children's sense of reality through its sanitized notions of identity, difference, and history in the seemingly apolitical, cultural universe of the Magic Kingdom. Jon Wiener argues that Disneyland's version of Main Street America harkens back to an "image of small towns characterized by cheerful commerce, with barbershop quartets and ice cream sundaes and glorious parades." For Wiener, this view not only substitutes fiction for history while trivializing the real Main Streets at the turn of the twentieth century but also appropriates the past to legitimate a portrayal of the present world as "without tenements or poverty or urban class conflict. . . . It's a native white Protestant dream of a world without blacks or immigrants."[14]

CRITIQUING WHAT CHILDREN LEARN FROM DISNEY

The contradictory world of Disney is further evident in an analysis of some of its animated films produced since 1989. These films are important because they received enormous praise from the dominant press and achieved blockbuster status.[15] For many children they represent an entrance into the world of Disney. Moreover, the financial success and popularity of these films, which rival many adult features, do not engender the critical analyses often produced in response to adult films. In short, critics and audiences are more willing to suspend critical judgment about children's films. Animated films, promoted as fantasy and entertainment, appear to fall outside the world of values, meaning, and knowledge often associated with more pronounced educational forms such as documentaries, art films, or the news media. Elizabeth Bell, Lynda Haas, and Laura Sells capture this sentiment: "Disney audiences . . . legal institutions, film theorists, cultural critics, and popular audiences all guard the borders of Disney film as 'off limits' to the critical enterprise, constructing Disney as a metonym for 'America'—clean, decent, industrious—'the happiest place on earth.'"[16]

Given the influence that Disney products have on children, it is imperative that parents, teachers, and other adults understand how its animated films influence the values of the children who view them. As a producer of children's culture, Disney should not be given an easy pardon because it is defined as a universal citadel of fun and good cheer. On the contrary, as one of the primary institutions constructing childhood culture in the United States and around the globe, it warrants healthy suspicion and critical debate. Such a debate should not be limited to the home but included as a central feature of the school curriculum and other critical public sites of learning.

It is important to address Disney's animated films without condemning Disney out of hand as a reactionary corporation deceptively promoting a conservative worldview under the guise of entertainment. It is equally important not to celebrate Disney as an animated version of *Mr. Rogers' Neighborhood*, doing nothing more than providing sources of joy and happiness to children all over the world.[17] Clearly, Disney offers children and adults visual stimulation and joyful pleasure: dramatic thunderstorms, kaleidoscopic musical numbers, and fanciful transformations of real life into wondrous spectacles. Disney films offer children opportunities to locate themselves in a world that resonates with their desires and interests. Pleasure is one of the defining principles of what Disney produces, and children are both its subjects and objects. Hence, one can appreciate the trademark imaginative brilliance of Disney's animated films but at the same time interrogate and challenge the films as an important site for the production of children's culture. The fact is that Disney films are often filled with contradictory messages. Disney's influence and power must be situated within the broader understanding of the company's role as a corporate giant intent on spreading the commercial values that erode civil society while proclaiming to support and expand it.

Disney's role in shaping individual identities and controlling the fields of social meaning through which young people negotiate the world is far too complex to characterize simply as a form of reactionary politics. If educators and other cultural workers are to include the culture of children as an important site of contestation and struggle, then it is imperative to analyze how Disney's animated films powerfully influence the way America's cultural landscape is imagined. Disney's scripted view of childhood and society must be engaged and challenged as "a historically specific matter of social analysis and intervention."[18] This is particularly important since Disney's animated films work to provoke and inform children's imaginations, desires, roles, and dreams while simultaneously sedimenting affect and meaning.

The wide distribution and popular appeal of Disney's animated films provide diverse audiences the opportunity for critical viewing. Critically analyzing how Disney films work to construct meanings, induce pleasure, and reproduce ideologically loaded fantasies is not reducible to a mere exercise in film criticism. As with any educational institution, Disney's worldview must be discussed in terms of how it narrates children's culture and can be held accountable for what it contributes to a significant cultural public sphere in which ideas, values, audiences, markets, and opinions serve to create different publics and social formations. Of course, Disney's self-proclaimed innocence, its inflexibility in dealing with social criticism, and its paranoid attitude are now legendary and provide more reasons why Disney should be both challenged and engaged critically. Moreover, as a multi-billion-dollar company, Disney has corporate and cultural influence too enormous and far reaching to allow the company to define itself exclusively within the imaginary discourses of innocence and entertainment.[19]

The question of whether Disney's animated films are *good* for kids has no easy answer. It can be readily acknowledged, however, that such films will have *better* educational and entertainment value the more teachers, parents, and young people think about the conscious and unconscious messages and effects the films promote while resisting the temptation to view them as nonideological. The Disney animation studio demonstrated a profound ability to adapt to the changing expectations of a new generation of filmgoers in the 1990s. The series of feature-length films produced over the decade restored Disney's prominence as a purveyor of children's entertainment with *The Little Mermaid* (1989), *Beauty and the Beast* (1991), *Aladdin* (1992), *The Lion King* (1994), *Pocahontas* (1995), *The Hunchback of Notre Dame* (1996), *Hercules* (1997), and *Mulan* (1998). Each of these films continues to provide ample opportunities to address how Disney constructs a culture of joy and innocence for children out of the intersection of mass culture, pleasure, and consumerism.[20] All of these films were commercially successful in theaters and also generated a spate of brand franchises. Connecting the rituals of consumption and moviegoing, each of Disney's animated films establishes a "marketplace of culture," becoming a launch pad for endless numbers of spin-off products and merchandise that include DVDs, video games, Internet sites, soundtrack albums, children's clothing, furniture, stuffed toys, and new theme park rides.[21] As a commentator in *Newsweek* pointed out, "The merchandise—Mermaid dolls, Aladdin undies, and collectibles like a sculpture of Bambi's Field Mouse—account for a stunning 20 percent of Disney's operating income."[22]

In the 1990s, *The Little Mermaid* and *Beauty and the Beast* had combined sales of over 34 million videos. Aladdin earned over "$1 billion from box-office income, video sales, and such ancillary baubles as Princess Jasmine dresses and Genie cookie jars."[23] Moreover, the Aladdin video game sold over 3 million copies in 1993. When *The Lion King* was released in theaters in 1994, it became the highest-grossing hand-drawn animated film in history, making over $320 million in box office sales.[24] Disney sold over 3 million copies of the soundtrack.[25] In the first few weeks after *The Lion King* video appeared, it generated sales of more than 20 million, and Disney's stock soared by $2.25 a share based on first-week revenues of $350 million. Ranked as one of the most profitable films every made, *The Lion King* was projected to generate in the range of "$1 billion in profits for Disney over two or three years."[26]

At the launching of *The Hunchback of Notre Dame*, Disney Records shipped out 2 million sing-along home videos and seven audio products, including the soundtrack CD and a toddler-targeted *Hunchback of Notre Dame* My First Read Along book. Tie-in promotions for the film included products sold by Burger King, Payless Shoes, Nestle, and Mattel.[27] While *The Hunchback of Notre Dame* generated a disappointing $99 million in box office revenues in North America, signaling the beginning decline of the Disney two-dimensional animation renaissance, the combined sales of tickets and spin-off products, according to *Adweek* magazine, would generate as much as "$500 million in profit (not just revenues), after the other revenue streams are taken into account."[28]

One of Disney's biggest promotion campaigns began in the summer of 1995 with the release of *Pocahontas*. A record lineup of tie-in merchandise included stuffed animals, sheets, pillowcases, toothbrushes, games, moccasins, and over "40 different picture and activity books."[29] A consortium of corporations spent an estimated $125 million on cross-marketing *Pocahontas*. Two well-known examples included Burger King, which was basically converted into an advertisement for the film and gave away an estimated 50 million Pocahontas figurines, and the Mattel Corporation, which marketed over fifty different dolls and toys.

The Disney Princess franchise, featuring all the lead female characters in the animated films, along with classic Disney characters such as Mickey Mouse, Winnie-the-Pooh, and Tinker Bell, have become established prototypes for numerous toys, logos, games, and clothing that fill department stores all over the world. Disney theme parks, which made over $2.5 billion in revenues in 2007, made a sizable portion of their profits through the merchandising of products based on characters from the animated films.[30] Disney's culture of commercialism is big business, and Disney's animated films provide goods for hundreds of Disney Stores and other department stores worldwide.

But Disney's attempt to turn children into consumers and to make commodification a defining principle of children's culture does not diminish the aesthetic quality of its films. Disney has shown enormous inventiveness in its attempts to reconstruct the grounds on which popular culture is defined and shaped. For example, by defining popular culture as a hybridized sphere that combines diverse genres and styles and often collapses the boundary between high and low culture, Disney has challenged conventional ideas of aesthetic form and cultural legitimacy. For instance, when *Fantasia* appeared in the 1930s, it drew the wrath of music critics, who, holding to an elite view of classical music, were outraged that the musical score of the film drew from the canon of high culture. By combining high and low culture in the animated film, Disney opened up new cultural possibilities for artists and audiences alike. Moreover, as sites of entertainment, Disney's films succeed because they put both children and adults in touch with joy and adventure. They provide opportunities to experience pleasure, even when such pleasure must be purchased. Yet, Disney's brilliant use of aesthetic forms, musical scores, and inviting characters must be interpreted in light of the broader conceptions of reality shaped by these films within a wider system of dominant representations of gender roles, race, and agency that appear repeatedly in the visual worlds of television, Hollywood film, and other media.

A number of the films mentioned above draw upon the talents of songwriters Howard Ashman and Alan Menken, whose skillful arrangements provide the emotional glue of the animation experience. The rousing calypso number "Under the Sea" in *The Little Mermaid* and "Be Our Guest," a Busby Berkeley–inspired musical sequence in *Beauty and the Beast*, are indicative of the musical talent at work in Disney's animated films. Fantasy abounds, as Disney's animated films produce a host of exotic and stereotypical villains, heroes, and heroines. The Beast's enchanted castle in *Beauty and the Beast* becomes magical as household objects are transformed into dancing teacups and silverware and a talking teapot. But tied to the magical fantasy and lighthearted musical scores are themes and stereotypes characteristic of Disney's oversimplified worldview.

In *The Little Mermaid*, for example, the villainous Ursula, an obese black and purple squid, oozes with evil and irony, while the mermaid heroine, Ariel, appears as a cross between a typical rebellious teenager and a Southern California fashion model. Disney's representations of evil and good women appear to have been fashioned in the editorial office of *Vogue*. According to a 2001 study of nineteen Disney films, female characters are "adolescents and young adults more than expected."[31] The dearth of positive female role models in Disney films is a commonplace observation, and a 2007 study showed that when older women do appear, they are portrayed "in a particularly negative light, while older male characters tend to fill authority roles, such as that of clergyman, ruler, and mentor."[32] Negative stereotyping of the elderly includes their stigmatization as angry, senile, and overweight. The risk is that the quick and sweeping visual cues deployed by Disney films not only create strong associations (for example, between moral virtue and youthful beauty) but leave an indelible impression on children's consciousness. Minor characters, particularly ones that serve as sidekicks to the hero, are frequently shown to be of low intelligence, while workers are quite happy to "serve the rich and privileged, never questioning their subordinate position."[33] And male characters share a disproportionate number of villainous roles, prompting one researcher to suggest that this "preponderance . . . should be analyzed for its potential negative impact on children and their relationships with caring male adults."[34] Stereotyping also extends to ethnically coded speech accents. Rosina Lippi-Green observes that Disney films participate in the "sociolinguistic construction" of social dominance and inferiority in which characters who use mainstream American English tend to be associated with "strongly positive actions and motivations" and also to experience the widest variety of life choices.[35] The villainous uncle of *The Lion King*, Scar, masterfully voices scheming and betrayal using a British accent that contrasts with the all-American intonation of the ruddy-maned hero, Simba. All this suggests that the animated objects and animals in Disney films may be of the highest artistic standards, but clearly they do not exist in an ideology-free zone. The characters are tied to larger narratives about, for example, freedom, rites of passage, intolerance, self-determination, greed, and the brutalities of male chauvinism.

Enchantment comes at a high price if the audience is meant to suspend judgment of the films' ideological messages. Even though these messages can be read from a variety of viewpoints, the assumptions that structure these films restrict the number of cultural meanings that can be brought to bear on them, especially when the intended audience is mostly children. The role of the critic of Disney's animated films is not to reduce them to a single ideological reading but to identify the "preferred textual messages" they encode.[36] This includes analysis of the various themes and assumptions that inform these films, both within and outside the dominant institutional and ideological formations that attempt to limit a diversity of interpretations. Such analyses allow educators and others to broaden our understanding of how such films can become sites of contestation, translation, and critical exchange.

Beyond merely recognizing the plurality of readings such films might foster, there is also the pedagogical task of provoking audiences to reflect upon the ways in which Disney's themes function as part of a broader public discourse, privileging some definitions or interpretations over others. The conservative values that Disney films promote assume such force because of the contexts in which they are situated and because they resonate so powerfully with dominant perceptions and meanings (such as connecting how a character speaks to a particular racial stereotype). Pedagogically, this suggests the need for educators, parents, and others to analyze critically how the privileged dominant readings of Disney's animated films work to generate and affirm particular pleasures, desires, and subject positions that define for young people specific notions of agency and social possibility.

Texts shape their own interpretations, but also form a mutually constitutive relationship with the political, economic, and cultural contexts in which they are read. This means that the focus on Disney films must be supplemented with an analysis of the institutional practices, corporate ideologies, and social structures that work to produce such texts. Such analysis should suggest pedagogical strategies for understanding how dominant regimes of power restrict the range of views that children might bring to reading Disney's animated films. By making the relationship between power and knowledge visible, while simultaneously referencing what is often taken for granted, teachers, cultural workers, and critics can open up Disney's animated films so that students and others can read such films within, against, and outside the dominant codes that inform them.

There is a double pedagogical movement here. First, there is the need to read Disney's films in relation to their articulation with other dominant texts in order to assess their similarities in legitimating particular ideologies. Second, there is the need on the part of parents and others to use Disney's thematization of America and America's thematization of Disney as referents to make visible—and to disrupt—dominant codings and to do so in a space that invites dialogue, debate, and alternative readings. For instance, one major pedagogical challenge is to assess how dominant ideas that are repeated over time in these films and reinforced through other popular cultural texts can be examined in terms of how children define themselves within such representations. The task here is to generate readings of such films that might also serve as a theoretical foundation for engaging them in the contexts in which they are shaped, understood, or might be seen.[37] This means exploring pedagogically how we both construct and defend the readings we actually bring to such films, providing an opportunity to expand the dialogue regarding what Disney films mean while simultaneously challenging the assumptions underlying dominant readings of them. Taking a position on Disney films should not degenerate into a doctrinaire reading or legitimate a form of political or pedagogical indoctrination of children or anybody else. Rather, such an approach should address how any reading of these films is ideological and should be engaged in terms of the context, content, values, and social relations it endorses. Moreover, addressing Disney films and the readings they engender both politically and pedagogically establishes the basis for opening up the films to complex levels of inquiry rather than treating them superficially or accepting them uncritically, as mere entertainment.

READING GENDER, RACE, AND
HIERARCHY IN DISNEY FILMS OF THE 1990s

The construction of gender identity for girls and women represents one of the most controversial issues in Disney's animated films.[38] In both *The Little Mermaid* and *The Lion King*, the female characters are constructed within narrowly defined gender roles. All of the female characters in these films are ultimately subordinate to males and define their sense of power and desire almost exclusively in terms of dominant male narratives. For instance, modeled after a slightly anorexic Barbie Doll, Ariel, the mermaid in *The Little Mermaid*, at first glance appears to be engaged in a struggle against parental control, motivated by the desire to explore the human world, and willing to take a risk in defining the subject and object of her desires. But, in the end, both the struggle to gain independence from her father, Triton, and the desperate striving that motivates her dissolve when Ariel makes a Mephistophelean pact with the sea witch, Ursula. In this trade, Ariel gives away her voice to gain a pair of legs so that she can pursue the handsome prince, Eric.

Although girls might be delighted by Ariel's teenage rebelliousness, they are strongly positioned to believe, in the end, that desire, choice, and empowerment are closely linked to catching and loving a handsome man. Bonnie Leadbeater and Gloria Lodato Wilson explore succinctly the pedagogical message at work in the film:

> The 20th-century innocent and appealing video presents a high-spirited role for adolescent girls, but an ultimately subservient role for adult women. Disney's 'Little Mermaid' has been granted her wish to be part of the new world of men, but she is still flipping her fins and is not going too far. She stands to explore the world of men. She exhibits her new-found sexual desires. But the sexual ordering of women's roles is unchanged.[39]

Ariel becomes a metaphor for the traditional housewife in the making. Ursula's disclosure to Ariel that having her voice taken away is not so bad because men do not like women who talk is dramatized when the prince attempts to bestow the kiss of true love on Ariel even though she has never spoken to him. Within this rigid narrative, Ariel's maturity and identity are limited to her feminine attractability and embodied by heterosexual marriage. That Ariel's happiness is tied to the reward of marrying the right man and entails the renouncement of her former life under the sea is a telling cultural model for the values and choices presented to women in Disney's worldview.

The ideal of womanhood based on strict gender roles offered by *The Little Mermaid* does not represent an isolated moment in Disney's filmic universe; on the contrary, Disney's negative stereotypes of women and girls gain force through the way in which similar messages are circulated and reproduced, to varying degrees, in many of Disney's animated films. For example, in *Aladdin* the issues of agency and power center primarily on the young street tramp Aladdin. Jasmine, the princess he falls in love with, appears as an object of his desire as well as a social stepping-stone. Jasmine's life is almost completely defined by men, and, in the end, her happiness is ensured by Aladdin, who is finally given permission to marry her.

Disney's construction of gender roles becomes a bit more complicated in *Beauty and the Beast*, *Pocahontas*, and *Mulan*. Belle, the heroine of *Beauty and the Beast*, is portrayed as an independent woman stuck in a provincial village in eighteenth-century France. Seen as odd because she always has her nose in a book, she is pursued by Gaston, the vain, macho male typical of Hollywood films of the 1980s. To Belle's credit, she rejects him, but in the end she gives her love to the Beast, who holds her captive in the hope that she will fall in love with him and break the evil spell cast upon him when he was a young man. Belle not only falls in love with the Beast but also "civilizes" him by instructing him on how to eat properly, control his temper, and dance. Belle becomes a model of etiquette and style as she turns the narcissistic, muscle-bound tyrant into a "new" man, one who is sensitive, caring, and loving.

Disney promoters labeled Belle a feminist because she rejects and vilifies Gaston, the ultimate macho man. It is possible to interpret *Beauty and the Beast* as a rejection of hypermasculinity, but Belle's reformation of the Beast "implies that women are responsible for controlling male anger and violence. If a woman is only pretty and sweet enough, she can transform an abusive man into a prince—forever."[40] In this reading, Belle is less the focus of the film than a prop or "mechanism for solving the Beast's dilemma."[41] Whatever subversive qualities Belle initially personifies in the film, in the end she simply becomes another woman whose life is valued for how she can patiently solve a man's problems—and withstand emotional and physical abuse along the way.

Disney's next female lead, Pocahontas, appears both to challenge and to reproduce some of these stereotypes. Rather than portray the historical Pocahontas, who as a twelve-year-old once saved John Smith from execution, Disney remakes the Powhatan princess in the image of a shapely, contemporary, high-fashion supermodel. Although Disney's "buckskin Barbie"[42] is articulate, courageous, and politically progressive—challenging negative stereotypes of Native Americans in Hollywood films—her character is still, like most of Disney's other female protagonists, drawn primarily in relation to the men who surround her. Initially, her identity is defined by resistance to her father's attempts to marry her off to one of the bravest warriors in the tribe. But her coming-of-age identity crisis is largely propelled by her struggle to save John Smith, a blond colonialist who looks like he belongs in a Southern California pinup magazine of male surfers, and their subsequent love affair. Pocahontas exudes a soppy romanticism that even convinces the crew of a British ship to rebel against its greedy captain and return to England. If only the emissaries of historical colonialism were that easily put off!

Of course, this is a Hollywood rewrite of history that bleaches colonialism of its genocidal legacy. No mention is made of the fact that John Smith's countrymen would ultimately steal Pocahontas's land; bring disease, murder, and poverty to her people; and eventually destroy their religion, economic livelihood, and way of life. In the Disney version of history, colonialism never happened, and the meeting between the Old and New Worlds is simply fodder for another "love-conquers-all" narrative. One wonders how the public would have viewed this film had it portrayed a Jewish woman who falls in love with a blond Aryan Nazi while ignoring any references to the Holocaust.

The issue of female subordination hits with a vengeance in *The Lion King*. All of the rulers of the kingdom are men, reinforcing the assumption that independence and leadership are tied to patriarchal entitlement and high social standing. The dependency that the beloved lion king, Mufasa, engenders in the women of Pride Rock is unaltered after his death, when the evil Scar assumes control of the kingdom. Lacking any sense of outrage, independence, or resistance, the female felines hang around to do his bidding.

Gender stereotyping is somewhat modified in *Mulan*. The eponymous lead character is presented as a bold female warrior who challenges traditional gender stereotypes of young women. But for all of her independence, in the end, the movie is, as film critic Janet Maslin points out, "still enough of a fairy tale to need a Mr. Right."[43] Mulan may be an independent, strong-willed young woman, but the ultimate payoff for her bravery comes in the form of attracting the handsome son of a general. And if the point is missed, when the heroine's grandmother first sees the young man as he enters Mulan's house, she affirms what she (the audience?) sees as Mulan's real victory—catching a man—and yells out, "Sign me up for the next war!" And there is another disturbing side to Mulan's characterization as an allegedly strong woman. Rather than aligning herself against the patriarchal celebration of war, violence, and militarism, Mulan becomes a cross-dresser who proves that when it comes to war, she can perform as well as any male. By temporarily donning the guise of masculinity and embracing a traditional view of war, Mulan cancels out any radical rupturing of stereotypical gender roles. She simply becomes one of the boys. But lest the fantasy be taken too far, Disney reminds us at the conclusion of the film that Mulan is still just a girl in search of a man, and as in so many other

Disney animated films, Mulan becomes an exoticized version of the all-American girl who manages to catch the most handsome boy on the block, square jaw and all.

Given Disney's long-standing obsession with family values, especially the middle-class family's position at the center of consumer culture, it is curious that with the exception of *Mulan,* very few of the Disney films produced in the 1990s portray strong mothers or fathers.[44] Not only are powerful mothers absent, but Jasmine's father is outwitted by his aides, and Belle's father is an airhead. Only the Little Mermaid has a domineering father in King Triton, whose protectiveness stems from his inherent benevolence as the true patriarch heading a natural hierarchical order (it is those illegitimate usurpers one needs to watch out for!). But Disney's construction of weak or stupid fathers only works to make patriarchy appear unthreatening, if also sometimes foolish and preoccupied with business. Meanwhile, the absence of involved familial figures has the structural effect of thrusting the protagonist into character-testing situations unaided by a social support network. Most problematically, instead of exploring how the family's influence upon identity formation can be at once a source of security and confinement, Disney films conclude that each and every female protagonist, left to her own devices, will naturally discover her "true" feminine, heterosexual self, apparently with no prompting needed from external familial and cultural forces.

Jack Zipes, a leading theorist on fairy tales, claims that Disney's animated films celebrate gender stereotyping and "have an adverse effect on children in contrast to what parents think. . . . Parents think they're essentially harmless—and they're not harmless."[45] Disney films are seen by enormous numbers of children in both the United States and abroad. As far as the issue of gender is concerned, Disney's view of women's agency and empowerment is more than simply limited: it reproduces the idea that a child born female can only realize a gendered incarnation of adulthood and is destined to fulfill her selfhood by becoming the appendage, if not the property, of a man.

Racial stereotyping is another major issue in many Disney animated films. A long history of racism associated with Disney can be traced back to denigrating images of people of color in films such as *Song of the South*, released in 1946, and *The Jungle Book*, which appeared in 1967.[46] Originally, the main restaurant in Disneyland's Frontierland featured the real-life figure of a former slave, Aunt Jemima, who would sign autographs for the tourists outside her "Pancake House." And in the 1950s Frontierland also featured racist representations of Native Americans as violent "redskins."[47] Eventually Disney executives eliminated the exhibits and the Native Americans running them because the "Indian" canoe guides wanted to unionize. They were displaced by robotic dancing bears. Complaints from civil rights groups got rid of the degrading Aunt Jemima spectacle.[48]

One of the most controversial examples of racist stereotyping emanating from the Disney publicity machine occurred with the release of *Aladdin* in 1992, although such stereotyping later reappeared in 1994 with the release of *The Lion King. Aladdin* is a particularly important example because it was a high-profile release, the winner of two Academy Awards, and one of the most successful Disney films ever produced. Playing to massive audiences of children, the film's opening song, "Arabian Nights," begins its depiction of Arab culture with a decidedly racist tone. The lyrics of the offending stanza state, "Oh I come from a land/From a faraway place/Where the caravan camels roam./Where they cut off your ear/If they don't like your face./It's barbaric, but hey, it's home." This characterization plays right into Western stereotypes of a backward and demonic Arab culture and, at the time of the film's release, served to magnify the racist stereotypes deployed by the media coverage of the first Persian Gulf war. The racist attitude toward Arab culture primed by the American media and reinforced in the lyrics introducing *Aladdin* is later confirmed by several of the film's supporting characters, who are portrayed as grotesque, violent, and cruel.

Yousef Salem, a former spokesperson for the South Bay Islamic Association, characterized the film as follows:

> All of the bad guys have beards and large, bulbous noses, sinister eyes and heavy accents, and they're wielding swords constantly. Aladdin doesn't have a big nose; he has a small nose. He doesn't have a beard or a turban. He doesn't have an accent. What makes him nice is they've given him this American character. . . . I have a daughter who says she's ashamed to call herself an Arab, and it's because of things like this.[49]

As Salem suggests, racism in Disney's animated films appears not only in negative imagery but also in racially coded language and accents. *Aladdin* clearly portrays the "bad" Arabs with thick, foreign accents, while the anglicized Jasmine and Aladdin speak in standard American English.

Jack Shaheen, then a professor of broadcast journalism at Southern Illinois University, Edwardsville, along with radio personality Casey Kasem, mobilized a public relations campaign protesting the anti-Arab themes in *Aladdin*. At first, Disney executives ignored the protest, but responding to the rising tide of public outrage eventually agreed to change one line of the stanza in the subsequent videocassette and worldwide film release. Disney did not change the lyrics on its popular CD release of *Aladdin*.[50] Disney executives were not unaware of the racist implications of the lyrics when they were first proposed. Howard Ashman, who wrote the song, submitted an alternative set of lyrics when he delivered the original lines. The alternative lyrics, "Where it's flat and immense/And the heat is intense," eventually replaced the original lines, "Where they cut off your ear/If they don't like your face." Though the new lyrics appeared in the *Aladdin* video, many protest groups were disappointed because the line "It's barbaric, but hey it's home" was not altered. Equally significant, the mispronunciation of Arab names in the film, the racial coding of accents, and the use of nonsensical scrawl as a substitute for written Arabic language were not removed.[51]

Racially coded representations and language are also evident in *The Lion King*. Scar, the icon of evil, is physically darker than the good lions. Shenzi and Banzai, the despicable hyena storm troopers (voiced by Whoopi Goldberg and Cheech Marin), speak in the jive accents of decidedly urban black or Hispanic youth. Disney falls back upon the same racialized low-comedy formula in *Mulan*. Not far removed from the *Amos 'n' Andy* crows in *Dumbo* is Mushu, a tiny red dragon with a black voice (Eddie Murphy). Mushu is a servile and boastful clown who seems unsuited to a mythic fable about China. He is the stereotype of the craven, backward, Southern American, chitlin-circuit character that appears to feed the popular racist imagination. The use of racially coded language can also be found in an early version of *The Three Little Pigs*, in *Song of the South*, and in *The Jungle Book*.[52] It is astonishing that these films produce a host of representations and codes through which children are taught to laugh at or deride, rather than respect, difference and to think that anyone who does not bear the imprint of white, middle-class ethnicity is likely to be inferior and unintelligent at best, if not also deviant and potentially threatening.

The racism in these films is defined by both the presence of negative stereotypes and the absence of complex representations of African Americans and other people of color. Whiteness is simultaneously universalized through the privileged representation of dominant middle-class social relations, values, and linguistic practices. Moreover, Disney's rendering of history, progress, and Western culture bears a colonial legacy that seems perfectly captured by Edward Said's notion of Orientalism—a particular form of Western imperialism that shapes dominant thinking about the East—and its dependency on new images and exotic narratives in order to affirm and sanction the centrality of Western culture and its ongoing domination of others.[53] Cultural differences are either trivialized or expressed through a "naturalized" racial hierarchy, which is antithetical to any viable democratic society. There is nothing innocent in what kids learn about race as portrayed in the "magical world" of Disney. So even while *Pocahontas* portrays racial differences more positively—viewing the relationship between Pocahontas and John Smith as a respectful partnership of equals—the film's supposedly enlightened perspective on race still upholds Western ethnocentrism when viewed in a larger context. Unlike the other animated films, *Pocahontas* is based on a true story, which means that Disney's metaphorical reduction of actual colonial relations to a fictitious interracial love affair and the film's conclusion of peaceful coexistence between the Powhatan Nation and the colonialists completely erase the historical reality of European racist attitudes about, injustice toward, and oppression of Native Americans (not to mention the tragic plight of the historical Pocahontas herself, who was "kidnapped, held hostage, forcibly 'civilized,' and converted to Christianity, then married off to a colonist who viewed her origins as 'accursed,'" and died by the age of twenty-two).[54]

Another central feature common to all of Disney's animated films is the celebration of deeply antidemocratic social relations. Nature and the animal kingdom provide the mechanism for presenting and legitimating caste systems, hierarchies of gender and race, and structural inequality as part of the natural order. The seemingly benign presentation of fairy tale narratives in which men rule, strict discipline is imposed through fixed social barriers, and leadership capacities are derived from one's inbred social status suggests a yearning for a return to a more rigidly stratified society based on a neofeudal model, if not an absolute dictatorship. In Disney's animated films, "harmony is bought at the price of domination. . . . No power or authority is implied except for the natural ordering mechanisms" of nature.[55] For children, the messages suggest that social problems such as the history of racism, the genocide of Native Americans, the prevalence of sexism, and democracy in crisis are simply willed by the laws of nature.

DIGITAL DISNEY

At the end of the 1990s, after a decade of the company's producing wildly popular hand-drawn animated films, Disney's revenues waned. The success of competing animation studios, such as Pixar and DreamWorks, which were developing computer-generated imagery (CGI) films, spurred Disney into a collaborative partnership with Pixar Animation Studios. CGI technology enabled Pixar filmmakers to produce realistic three-dimensional images for *Toy Story* (1995), the first entirely computer-generated film, which was received with resounding critical acclaim, not to mention huge commercial success, and proceeded to set the industry standard for visual effects and animation. Under a contractual agreement, Disney helped produce and distribute *Toy Story* and Pixar's next five films, the box office blockbusters *A Bug's Life* (1998), *Toy Story 2* (1999), *Monsters, Inc.* (2001), *Finding Nemo* (2003), and *The Incredibles* (2004). But Disney's relations with Pixar remained stormy, and news stories emerged in 2004 of a falling out between Pixar owner and CEO Steve Jobs and then CEO of Disney Michael Eisner.[56] When Robert Iger took over from Eisner in 2005, he recognized Pixar's value to Disney and sought to mend the rift, working out a deal to purchase Pixar from Jobs in 2006 for a staggering $7.4 billion in an all-stock transfer that made Jobs the largest single shareholder of Disney and gave him a seat on the board of directors.[57] The deal also allowed Pixar Studios to maintain its creative autonomy, including regarding decisions about the making of film sequels. As a result, Pixar might not be producing "authentic" Disney fare, but through the deal Disney would at least be able to retain its dominance in the field that first guaranteed its cultural prominence and corporate profitability: the world of animated feature films.

Disney/Pixar films—which include, in addition to those listed above, *Cars* (2006), *Ratatouille* (2007), and *WALL-E* (2008)—diverge from the classic Disney formula, which focuses on archetypal narratives, budding romance, and evil villains. Instead, Pixar films typically explore complex friendships between nonhuman characters, rarely dividing the animated worlds into clear-cut realms of good and evil (one exception to this pattern is *The Incredibles*, discussed in detail in chapter 4). In this way, Pixar's technology and creative story lines revitalized a Disney whose plot formula had worn thin. By depicting mostly animals, monsters, and machines, Pixar also avoids many of the offensive gender, race, and class representations for which classic Disney has been justly criticized. But this does not mean that Pixar's productions are any less traditional than Disney's classic films. Walt Disney's idealization of the simple joys of a small-town American life of yesteryear is carried on quite successfully in Disney/Pixar films like *Toy Story* and *Cars*, whose clever self-reflexivity positions the values of the more authentic, "vintage" characters against glitzy, high-tech consumer culture. Even a postapocalyptic film like *WALL-E*, about a garbage-collecting robot that is the last remaining inhabitant of an ecologically devastated, corporate-controlled planet Earth, manages to incorporate an homage to show tunes through black-and-white clips from the 1969 film *Hello, Dolly!* Indeed, most Pixar films evoke a nostalgia reminiscent of Disney by developing a parody of consumer culture that contrasts an idyllic past with a vulgar, mass-marketed present. For instance, in *Toy Story* the old-fashioned cowboy doll, Woody, struggles to maintain the affection of his owner, Andy, who has just been given the trendy plasticized action figure Buzz Lightyear. In the end, Woody sacrifices his personal interest in order to stage a rescue mission to save Buzz from the next-door neighbor, a kid named Sid who takes sadistic delight in destroying toys. The film, reminiscent of Disney's *Pinocchio* (1940), in which a hand-carved wooden puppet comes to life, considers the theme of obsolescence in the age of mass production from the point of view of the toys, while also pointing more ambivalently to the transformation of imaginative play in a world replete with electronic gadgetry. The larger context of the CGI film's own technological sophistication and its status as a mass-marketed medium produce a cleverly ironic level of meaning (typical of Pixar) that would not be lost on adult viewers. For children, *Toy Story* brings to life a magical world surrounding what emerges as the unique personalities of otherwise inanimate objects. This mystification of the commodity nature of toys might be harmless enough if the corporate imperatives of Disney had not turned the film into a perfect marketing trope for the company's consumer-products division: following the film's popular success, Disney churned out *Toy Story* merchandise, including toys, bedding, video games, and other "collectible" items, which form a mutually reinforcing pattern of consumption with the film and sadly reduce the opportunities for actual children to engage in the kind of unscripted play enjoyed by the film's human child, Andy.[58]

It is accurate to say that in some cases, as Lee Artz has argued, "Digital Disney advances the same ideological content" as classic Disney films.[59] Manohla Dargis, for example, suggests that the choice of "ethnic" voices for certain characters in *Cars* follows the standard animated film formula.[60] *A Bug's Life* is one Pixar film that seems to stick close to the Disney formula. The film's central character is an ant named Flik who exhibits a highly independent mind-set within the rigidly organized but peacefully agrarian ant commune. Flik's hyperindividualism is reflected not only in his inventiveness (he makes equipment to make the ants' harvesting more efficient) but also in his fearless journey outside the community to find warrior bugs who can destroy the ants' enemies—vicious grasshoppers who expropriate the ants' food stores every year. The film ends with the ants' victory and the conventional heterosexual (albeit entomologically improbable) resolution of Flik's pairing off with the courageous Princess Atta, who is made queen of the colony. Although Artz views *A Bug's Life* as sanctioning "subservience to hierarchy," the film's romantic yoking of the two heroes seems to show a distinct preference for the more egalitarian nuclear family.

Annalee Ward has carefully documented the moral ambiguity and contradictions generated by classic Disney films,[61] and Pixar films can be opened up to multiple readings in a similar way. In fact, the medium of animation—although lacking the photographic realism of live-action films—seems even more suited to the layering of allegorical meanings. The cartoonish representations may seem more "simplified" with their big, bold lines and bright colors, as might the archetypal characters and plots that seem to rely more on cultural shorthand to generate meaning than on any intrinsically complex development. But it is precisely the films' carefully streamlined construction and their reliance on external iconic cultural references to establish their "universality" that end up producing a multilayered text, particularly rich as a repository for allegorical meaning. For example, Eleanor Byrne and Martin McQuillan interpret the militaristic themes in *Toy Story* and *A Bug's Life* as allegories that legitimate Western humanitarian intervention in Third World conflicts.[62] Alan Ackerman, by contrast, suggests that the dramatization in *Toy Story* and *Toy Story 2* of the toys' commodification opens up for viewers the possibility of recognizing their own commodification, even as the toys become themselves aware of their place in a global exchange network.[63] The film indeed encourages the viewers' identification not with Andy, Sid, or the toy collector Al from the sequel, but rather with the toys whose identity and agency are conferred upon them by an elaborate commercial machine. Despite Woody's efforts in the first film to dispel Buzz's belief that he is a real space ranger and to convince him that he cannot actually fly, Buzz only acknowledges his origins when he see an advertisement on television for himself as an action figure and then lifts the arm flap on his space suit to find "Made in Taiwan" embossed in the plastic. Woody then tries to cheer up a depressed Buzz by suggesting that his value comes from being loved by a particular human child despite his being a mass-produced commodity. Aside from the sentimentality, the film's message is that one's identity is not overdetermined by structural forces but instead takes on meaning through human relations, particularly others' recognition of one's humanity (even if you're a toy).[64] This moral lesson, which recognizes the humanization of commodities, also implies the darker reality of the commodification of humans, as suggested by Ackerman. The fact that viewers are drawn into the toys' world, not the world of Andy and Sid, suggests that an underlying shared reality already exists between the viewers and the toys: both are objects of global capitalism. From Disney's perspective, after all, the collective viewership of its films gets turned into a statistic that is then "sold" to financiers and advertisers as a "target market." If capitalism mystifies objects sold as commodities by erasing the conditions of their production (as products of human labor), then *Toy Story*'s awareness of social relations hiding within the toy-as-commodity reverberates back to the processes of production involving workers in a toy factory in Taiwan. (Lee Artz points to *Monster, Inc.* as another film that, despite affirming "proper corporate order" in the end, still refuses to "[rid] the animated environment of work and its necessary social relations."[65]) Buzz Lightyear's consciousness emerges from the realization that he is a toy because he has been made by humans, a reality that, instead of destroying his authenticity by shattering his self-conception as a "strange thing, abounding in metaphysical subtleties and theological niceties," actually makes him more real by forcing him to derive his own unique subjecthood from the particulars of his existence.[66] All this suggests the possibility of reading the *Toy Story* films as more than mere propaganda for American cultural imperialism. The films may not verge on political radicalism, but they do show how toys and other commodities circulate as part of a globalized circuit of production and consumption—and they should make us aware of the fact that we too, as consumers of the films, are products and producers within a larger network of cultural and material exchange.

While it is important to critique Disney and Pixar films for their shortcomings, especially their prejudicial representations of race, gender, and class, it is perhaps equally important to recognize, as Laurie Frankel does, when a particular film "avoids these pitfalls, not just incidentally but purposefully and interestingly, offering young viewers, and the rest of us, important messages about alternative families and alternative heroines."[67] For instance, the *Toy Story* films focus on friendship rather than sexual love and romantic coupling. As buddy films, they emphasize cooperation and empathy more than individualistic displays of heroism. *Finding Nemo*, as Frankel observes, represents a single-parent family in which an overprotective father learns that his son is able to handle the dangers of the ocean: patriarchy is still well-meaning but not infallible. And, unlike in classic Disney narratives, in which nontraditional families "are either nonexistent or unhappy," Nemo ends the adventure happily reunited with his single father, and both accept a new member into their family, female tang fish Dory, who has a severe memory-loss condition. The film does not rely on villains who must be vanquished, and a triumphant hero whose destiny is to win the love of a beautiful woman is nowhere in sight. Instead, as Frankel notes, the film's characters must struggle to overcome internal "demons," fears that "are scarier than any wicked stepmother or oversized octopus" and must eventually be displaced by "trust and loyalty."[68] *Finding Nemo* tells the story of the young clown fish Nemo, who wants to prove his independence to his father, Marlin, and so leaves the protective cover of their home to swim into the open ocean where he is promptly scooped up by a scuba diver and transferred to a fish tank. Marlin's search for Nemo takes him and Dory to the harbor off the coast of Sydney, Australia. Meanwhile, Nemo escapes the aquarium by falling down a sink drain, swimming through the Sydney sewer system, and being ejected out into the ocean. Although the film takes many liberties—some clearly for comic effect—by representing a typically predatory natural world as benign and harmonious (an ecocritic's nightmare: an anthropomorphic ocean playground in which seabirds and sharks frolic with, rather than devour, their number one food source), it positions humans by contrast as the greatest threat to the ocean and its inhabitants. The film's message that "all drains lead to the ocean" resonates more deeply than within the film's limited context as a simple affirmation of the idea that there's always an escape route from one's present condition (if you're a fish). Rather, the ecological consciousness embedded in the film is profound in its simple warning for humans to be aware of what they put into, and take out of, the thriving underwater world that surrounds a landscape already much altered to serve human existence.

David Whitley confirms that *Finding Nemo* "does not attempt to establish a picture of a pristine natural world, free from all negative signs of human intervention, as many earlier [Disney] animations involving wild nature had sought to do."[69] Nemo might have made it back to the ocean, but unfortunately the film could not escape being caught up in Disney's commercial juggernaut, which demonstrates the power of Disney/Pixar to immerse viewers in a commodity-driven culture that only requires them to buy, not to think. *Finding Nemo* not only spawned video games, theme park rides, and a flood of merchandise but also produced an upsurge in eager parents wanting to purchase ocellaris clown fish like Nemo for their kids' aquariums—and this despite the film's pedagogy, which suggested that fish do not enjoy being trapped in glass containers for the sole purpose of providing eye candy for onlooking humans. The film's ecological concerns seemed to get lost amid the enormous corporate apparatus that sought to connect the pleasure of film viewing with firmly entrenched habits of consumption—with this "Disney effect" eventually leading to concerns that the fish stocks on the Great Barrier Reef and especially in less regulated marine zones (where fish collectors use chemicals such as cyanide to stun and catch fish) would be totally plundered to satisfy market demand.[70]

If *Finding Nemo* could elicit from seasoned Disney critics statements such as "It seems not just fair, but also important, to note progress and offer praise where it is due,"[71] then *Ratatouille* succeeded in drawing uniformly positive critical approval that only perhaps *Toy Story* could rival.[72] Disney/Pixar filmmakers chose again to devise their own story rather than rely on popular fairy tales or legends. The film does not privilege romantic love or even family relationships; nor does it recall the familiar but tired formula of a coming-of-age tale. In *Ratatouille*, a young rat named Remy arrives in Paris with the hope of becoming a chef at the restaurant made famous by deceased culinary idol Auguste Gusteau, author of *Anyone Can Cook*. Remy's family is not unloving or dysfunctional, although his father is gravely concerned that a rat working in a restaurant kitchen has much less chance of survival than one living in the sewers. The restaurant, now reduced by food critics from a five-star to a three-star venue, is managed by a chef named Skinner whose ambition is to market low-quality, prepared frozen foods under the Gusteau brand. Despite the disapproval of Remy's father and attacks from rat-hating humans, Remy realizes his artistic dream by secretly guiding the restaurant's garbage boy, Linguini, through the motions of creating fabulous dishes based on Gusteau's recipes. Upon learning that Linguini is working with a rat, the entire staff of the restaurant walks out. One female chef, Colette, who has been dating Linguini, decides to stay after remembering Gusteau's adage, "Anyone can cook!" Remy, along with his rat family, succeeds in impressing a notorious food critic, Anton Ego, with a ratatouille (traditional peasant fare, not haute cuisine). Ego then declares the chef at Gusteau's to be the greatest in all of France. Although Gusteau's is promptly closed by the health inspector, Remy continues to prepare food with Linguini and Colette in a new bistro called La Ratatouille. Unlike the kind of unabashed consumer-culture pastiche showcased in *Hercules*, *Ratatouille* pays homage to the elite world of fine dining and good taste at the same time that it critiques its exclusivity by asserting the moral that "a great artist can come from anywhere." More importantly, while so many Disney films have been severely criticized for stereotypical and inappropriate representations of other cultures, *Ratatouille* was well received in France, breaking records during its debut week as the most popular animated feature film ever released in theaters.[73] The film works as a contemporary fable that celebrates the acceptance of all kinds of difference, as Remy's innate talents and desires run counter to normative rat behavior. Without a single female rat in the pack, the film might get around the issue of offensive gender stereotyping, but the pleasant homosocial worlds of

Ratatouille open the film up to reading Remy's unusual preference (for cooking) as an allegory of a young gay man's coming out.[74] The film at least leaves itself tantalizingly open to the proliferating queer readings of Disney films documented by Sean Griffin in *Tinker Belles and Evil Queens*.[75] On a general level, the film suggests that attempting to be normal stifles creativity, but the kind of individual creativity the film promotes allows for collaboration. Expressing one's creativity does not require being the entrepreneurial outcast threatened by mindless and exploitative collectivism (*A Bug's Life*) or the angst-ridden superhero who needs to prove his greatness by not letting anyone hone in on his bid for celebrity (*The Incredibles*). Nor do we have a hero who simply follows the inevitable trajectory established as his elite destiny à la classic Disney. As film critic David Denby suggests, the concept of achievement developed by Pixar more closely approximates "something like self-willed, even civic, passion."[76] Linguini and Colette join Remy in a collective effort that shows compassion and responsibility to others, and close bonds need not be cemented by biological closeness. But the fact that the film's complex story and character development are neither high-tech nor so easily reducible to a quick, easy moral lesson as other Disney/Pixar films is perhaps best reflected in Disney's decision not to build a commercial franchise around *Ratatouille*. Aesthetic achievement seems to warrant a greater respect, which one would hope even the Disney corporate branding machine recognized. Instead, Robert Iger simply remarked that the film "wouldn't be one we would consider a true franchise in terms of its leveragability across multiple businesses or its ability to drive huge value over a long period of time."[77]

There is little doubt that Pixar Studios is the true heir to Walt Disney's legacy of creative ingenuity and artistry (even if CGI animation overtakes the art form pioneered by Old Walt himself). But Pixar's relationship with its corporate parent does not necessarily follow the standard Disney script of submission to a benevolent authority. In fact, without a healthy dose of cynicism of the kind provided by Pixar, animated films might be far less appealing to a new generation of kids and adults. Pixar's ambivalence toward Disney corporatism is most evident in the film *WALL-E*, in which unrestrained human consumption turns Earth into a giant garbage dump that cannot sustain life, and a megacorporation (named Buy n Large [BnL]) suggests that its spaceships can host the humans on a five-year cruise while robots clean up the planet.

The film reveals that corporate power has so successfully maintained its customers' dependency that humans have been living in space for seven hundred years and have grown lazy and obese inhabiting a luxurious starliner that is a totally controlled corporate environment (Disney Cruise Line vacation anyone?). The human captain of the ship does not know his job because the ship runs on an autopilot program directed by the first CEO of the Buy n Large Corporation to keep the humans in space. The film's satire of corporate culture's mercenary profit motives and unscrupulous surveillance of its customers was extended further by a fictitious BnL website (no longer available) that inundated browsers with spoof ads for the company and presented a cleverly disturbing disclaimer that users of the website automatically authorized BnL to "share your personal information with third parties whenever it deems such sharing to be advantageous to it, including when you engage in certain activities on our site such as using a menu, viewing, clicking your mouse or breathing" (www.buynlarge.com/disclaimer/disclaimer.html). Although *WALL-E* was received with critical and popular acclaim, how many viewers likely connected BnL with the Walt Disney Company or with Walmart, one of Disney's corporate partners? The film is explicit about the dangers of a corporate structure becoming so entrenched that humans lose all sense of agency and responsibility. But it seems even a Disney film cannot taint Disney's image or dampen the consumer impulse to buy *WALL-E* merchandise. And this is perhaps the most disturbing of all the film's implications: the sheer power of Disney to lull audiences into complacency about (if not disavowal of) an underlying corporate reality and to maintain such a strong association of its brand with purely imaginative entertainment makes the corporation all but impervious to criticism, even when such criticism appears in products of its own making.

Criticism about the gender and racial politics in classic Disney animation has so far resulted in far fewer clever responses from Walt Disney Pictures—certainly as far as can be deduced from the film *Enchanted* (2007). Despite a promising beginning, the film does not sustain the kind of postmodern self-reflexivity familiar to a generation raised on *The Simpsons* and brilliantly applied to fairy tales in *Shrek* (2001). Despite many intertextual references to classic Disney animation that self-consciously expose its reliance on stock characters and formulaic plots, *Enchanted* basically leaves the romance trajectory unaltered. In fact, the film is a slightly updated, partially animated, and fully Disney-fied version of the corporation's 1990 hit film *Pretty Woman*. Both films borrow from the Pygmalion myth, depicting young women who find themselves in unfamiliar places and out of their comfort zones, but who win the hearts of their male companions after going through classy makeovers and experiencing a sudden awareness of their own desires, which had been to that point overwritten by the desires of others. Although Giselle (Amy Adams) is a sexually inexperienced fairy tale maiden and *Pretty Woman*'s Vivian (Julia Roberts) is a prostitute, both lack the appropriate mannerisms and designer dresses to attract the male leads. Even though Vivian has been hardened by poverty and sexual exploitation, this does not alter the similar trajectory of the heroines. Both charm their male companions, despite the mild embarrassments caused by their uncouth behavior. They win admiration for their gutsy resilience and fierce loyalty. Their beauty bespeaks their internal goodness. A growing love for their men is symbolized in the almighty kiss. And the assertion of newly gained self-knowledge culminates in shopping sprees that provide visual imagery for the metaphorical transformation from caterpillar to butterfly. Disney's version of how women become agents of their own desires is to expand the agency of women into the public sphere of the marketplace. This could not be exemplified more clearly than by *Enchanted*'s ending when Giselle opens her own clothing boutique, called Andalasia Fashions, which outfits little girls with princess gowns (Disney has its own version of such a store/salon called Bibbidi Bobbidi Boutique). All these similarities show that *Enchanted*, despite the initial gesture toward postmodern irony, falls back on tired clichés without so much as debunking a single one.

The film begins in hand-drawn two-dimensional animation with Andalasia's Prince Edward vanquishing an ogre who is threatening the innocent, beautiful country maid named Giselle. Both characters instantly recognize their "true love" and assume they will be married the next day. The prince's jealous stepmother, Queen Narissa, attempts to keep her crown by thwarting their wedding plans. She casts a spell on Giselle that sends her to a place where "there are no happily ever afters." Giselle subsequently emerges alive and no longer animated from a manhole in the middle of Times Square. Giselle's naïveté drives the romantic and comic elements of the plot, as she tumbles into the arms of a jaded and single divorce lawyer named Robert (Patrick Dempsey) and quickly transforms his domestic space into one full of cleanliness, delightful song, and more authentic-looking computer-generated animal assistants, while waiting for her prince to arrive and take her back to Andalasia. In the meantime, we see Giselle ostensibly transition from a two-dimensional cartoon into a three-dimensional human being when she develops an awareness of herself outside the classic Disney script. The childlike Giselle is eternally optimistic, but she eventually becomes articulate enough (with Robert's coaching) to identify her feelings and state them to others—in this case, her anger and her lust (both toward Robert) signal her emergence as a more assertive female and a better partner for the Manhattan lawyer, who not only has a career-minded girlfriend he respects but who also presents his daughter with a book titled *Important Women of the World.* Giselle's lesson for the too-severe Robert, then, is to convince him that respect in a relationship is less important than romance (and it is the man's duty to direct the courtship) and that his daughter would prefer to be treated as a princess (she's missing the pixie dust from her childhood). Perhaps the most disturbing element of the film is how it provides a point of entry for child viewers by drawing Robert's six-year-old daughter into a commercial web: she presents Giselle with daddy's credit card and then treats her to a shopping spree and salon makeover. And Disney does not shy away from reconstructing good parenting as taking a child on retail adventures. Giselle's quality bonding time with Robert's daughter ends with the little girl's plaintive query, "Is this what it's like to go shopping with your mother?" Film critic Dana Stevens remarks that her disappointment with the film stems not so much from its "retrograde affirmation of true love and happy endings" but from "the movie's solemn celebration of a ritual even more sacred than holy matrimony: shopping."[78]

Despite the film's surface critique of classic Disney, its carries the strong message that every woman's fantasy—no matter how mature and intelligent she may be—is still the Disney princess fantasy. If there remains any ambiguity as to the film's message that heterosexual union is the culmination of every woman's life, then it is fully dispelled in the end: first, by having Robert awaken Giselle with "true love's kiss" and, second, by having Robert's now ex-girlfriend give up her hard-won success and independence (she tosses away her cell phone, a symbol of her career) in favor of jumping into the cartoon world to marry the prince. Just as the film blurs animated fantasy with real life, Disney's clear preference is for women and girls to be colonized by "enchant-ment." For those who want to emulate the brides of *Enchanted*, Disney has developed a line of bridal gowns, including one called "Giselle" (www.disneybridal.com). And, of course, Disney also has over forty thousand ready-made Princess items available for young girls, along with the optimistic message that faith in commodities will solve their problems and help define who they want to be, namely, pretty enough to win a man on whom they can depend financially.[79]

Given Disney's reluctance to change the script, it remains to be seen if Disney's new two-dimensional animated film *The Princess and the Frog*—the first to feature an African American princess, named Tiana—can promote stronger as well as more diverse characters, while simultaneously marshaling Disney's trademark nostalgia in both the story line and the traditional hand-drawn medium. Disney has already made Tiana part of its existing Disney Princess franchise in anticipa-tion of the film's release in December 2009. While media coverage has focused on Disney's attempts to make the racial representations in the film as inoffensive as possible (even hiring Oprah Winfrey as a consultant on the film's politics),[80] it is difficult not to be cynical about what appears to be less a tribute to African American culture than a barely disguised attempt to round out the Disney Princess market base by targeting young black girls who may find Tiana dolls and products less alienating than the current Princess options (five white princesses and an Arab one).

It is unfortunate that so-called postmodern Disney has so far fallen back on an earnest affirmation of the iconic elements of Disney culture rather than bravely putting forth an actual critique of the classic Dis-ney formula. We end up with a next-generation advertisement for all things Disney and, if lucky, a token gesture toward feminism, rather than a sincere examination of the inadequacies of Disney culture (such as gearing one's whole life toward heterosexual union). *Enchanted*'s ultimate rejection of ironic self-parody suggests that Disney is not ready to relinquish its perennial appeal to childhood innocence. Yet, the Disney of the new millennium understands better than ever before how it is in the "identity" market. It recognizes how much power it has to provide consumers with identity models and seeks to do so when they are most malleable—in childhood and adolescence. This is a reality not lost on one of Disney's latest star creations, Vanessa Hudgens (tween idol Gabriella from *High School Musical*), who told reporters, "Disney is an incredible machine. They really have it down and figured it out. There's so much power with the [Disney] channel. Kids will watch anything that's on it. When these kids are put on these shows, the kids at home are living and breathing the channel, and they grow to love these people. It's crazy."[81]

Although it is unlikely that a corporation reaping such huge profits is going to change its game plan anytime soon, cultural producers other than Disney are producing thoughtful entertainment for young people. One example is the film *Penelope* (2006), a revision of classic fairy tale narratives about the eponymous young heiress who is born with a pig's snout instead of a nose because of an ancient curse laid on her family. The curse will be broken, so the story goes, if Penelope is loved by one of her own class. Consequently, her single-minded mother arranges for endless meetings with prospective blue-blooded suitors that always end with the young men fleeing at the sight of Penelope, who turns out to be an astonishingly well-grounded and intelligent young woman in spite of her mother's superficiality. This is demonstrated quite clearly when Penelope becomes an elementary school teacher, even after she gains a human nose. Contrary to her mother's traditionalist interpretation of the curse, Penelope does not need a man to love her—she simply needs to love herself. The moment she rejects her need for a husband and asserts, "I like myself the way I am," the curse is instantly broken. The film teaches young people to value self-respect over romantic love, while also presenting critical views of society's obsession with plastic surgery and the elitism that drives class snobbery. *Penelope* demonstrates the way in which fairy tales could be updated to create narratives that are empowering for youth. It also shows that Disney need not be constrained by the fairy tale genre and demands that parents, educators, and others question why Disney chooses to adhere so closely to the traditional formula. Deborah Ross reminds us that "the overriding goal is self-promotion—because Disney will absorb and use whatever works, or whatever sells the product."[82] What does a Disney production like *Enchanted* say about the way our culture is failing young people if there are so few narratives that promote self-respect among young women? Do we all think it is okay for corporations like Disney to foster young women's dependency on consumer products that promise to help them feel beautiful and generate desire in others? There currently appear to be so few alternatives to this disturbing trend of passive consumerism that a megacorporation like Disney can appear utterly confident in the existence of a large market for its products and the virtual absence of any public resistance toward its attempt to reduce children's identities to the role of consumer.

CULTURAL PEDAGOGY AND CHILDREN'S CULTURE

Given the corporate reach, cultural influence, and political power that Disney exercises over multiple levels of children's culture, Disney's animated films should be neither ignored nor simply censored by those who disagree with the conservative ideologies they produce and circulate. There are a number of issues to be addressed regarding the forging of a pedagogy and a politics responsive to Disney's shaping of children's culture. In what follows, we provide some suggestions regarding how parents, educators, and cultural workers might critically engage Disney's influence in shaping the "symbolic environment into which our children are born and in which we all live out our lives."[83]

First, parents, community groups, and other concerned individuals must be attentive to the diverse and often contradictory messages in Disney films in order to criticize them when necessary and, more importantly, to reclaim them for more productive ends. At the very least, we must be attentive to the processes whereby meanings are produced in these films and how they work to secure particular forms of authority and social relations. At stake pedagogically is the issue of paying "close attention to the ways in which [such films] invite (or indeed seek to prevent) particular meanings and pleasures."[84] In fact, Disney's films appear to assign, quite unapologetically, rigid roles to women and people of color. Similarly, such films generally produce a narrow view of family values coupled with a nostalgic and conservative view of history that should be challenged and transformed. Educators need to take seriously Disney's attempt to shape collective memory, particularly when such attempts are unabashedly defined by one of Disney's imagineers in the following terms: "What we create is a sort of 'Disney realism,' sort of utopian in nature, where we carefully program out all the negative, unwanted elements and program in the positive elements."[85] Disney's rendering of entertainment and spectacle, whether expressed in Frontierland, Main Street USA, or its online, video, television, and film productions, is not merely an edited, sanitary, and nostalgic view of history, one that is free of poverty, class differences, and urban decay. Disney's writing of public memory also constructs a monolithic notion of national identity that typically treats subordinate groups as either exotic or irrelevant to American history, simultaneously marketing cultural differences within "histories that corporations can live with."[86] Disney's version of U.S. history is not innocent; nor can it be dismissed as simply entertainment.

Disney's celluloid view of children's culture often works to strip the past, present, and future of diverse narratives and multiple possibilities. But it is precisely such a rendering that must be revealed as a historically specific and politically constructed "landscape of power." Issues regarding the representational politics of gender, race, class, caste, and other aspects of self and collective identity are defining elements of Disney's films for children and youth. Revealing and exploring the ideological nature of Disney's world opens up further opportunities for educators and others to use such texts in order to encourage meaningful critical engagement instead of simply passive absorption. Rustom Bharacuha argues that "the consumption of . . . images . . . can be subverted through a particular use in which we are compelled to think through images rather than respond to them with a hallucinatory delight."[87] One interpretation of the call to "think through images" is for educators and cultural workers to demonstrate pedagogically and politically that history and its construction of national identity must be contested and engaged, even when images parade as innocent film entertainment. The images that pervade Disney's production of children's culture, along with their claim to public memory, must be challenged and rewritten, "moved about in different ways," and read differently as part of the script of democratic empowerment.[88] It is within the drama of animated storytelling that children are often positioned pedagogically to learn which subject positions are open to them and which are closed off. Hence, the struggle over children's culture should be considered as part of a struggle over the related discourses of citizenship, national identity, and democracy itself.

Second, it is crucial that educators take seriously as an important site of learning and contestation the realm of popular culture increasingly appropriated by Disney to teach values and sell goods to children and young people. This means, at the very least, that those cultural texts that dominate children's culture, including Disney's animated films, should be incorporated into school curricula as objects of social knowledge and critical analysis. If the sinister grip that Disney exercises on children's imaginations is to be taken seriously, the cultural forms through which this happens must be taken seriously as worthy of study. This is a call both for making media literacy an essential part of what kids learn in schools[89] and for reconsidering the meaning, range, and possibilities of what counts as useful knowledge itself, while also offering a new theoretical register for addressing the ways in which popular media aimed at shaping children's culture are implicated in power/knowledge relationships. In simple terms, this means making popular culture an essential object of critical analysis in schools.

The pedagogical value of such an approach is that it alerts educators to taking the needs, desires, languages, and experience of children seriously. In part, this points to analyzing how entertainment can be addressed as a subject of intellectual engagement rather than as a series of sights and sounds that wash over us. Against those who insist that any attempt at a critical analysis violates the entertainment industry's sanctity as an element of popular culture, it must be made clear that there are other ways to engage popular forms than merely through the realm of pleasurable consumption. In this context it is crucial to address not just the pleasure created by the object but the pleasure created by learning and critical engagement. This suggests addressing the utopian possibilities in which children often find representations of their hopes and dreams but not relinquishing critical agency in the process. It also means recognizing the pedagogical importance of what kids bring with them to the classroom (or to any other site of learning) as crucial both to decentering power in the classroom and to expanding the possibility for teaching students multiple literacies, as part of a broader strategy of teaching them to read the world critically.

Third, it is crucial that educators and others pay attention to how diverse groups of kids use and understand these Disney films and visual media differently. We must talk to children and youth about these films and other aspects of popular culture so that we can better understand how young people identify with these cultural forms and what issues raised by them must be addressed. Such discussions would open up a language of pleasure and criticism that facilitates mutual learning and empowerment. If Disney's films are to be viewed as more than narratives of fantasy and escape, becoming sites of reclamation and imagination that affirm rather than deny the long-standing relationship between entertainment and pedagogy, it is important to consider how we might insert the political and the pedagogical back into the discourse of entertainment. A pedagogical approach to popular culture must ask how a politics of the popular works to mobilize desire, stimulate imagination, and produce forms of identification that can become objects of dialogue and critical investigation. This suggests that we develop new ways of critically understanding and reading electronically produced visual media. Teaching and learning the culture of the book can no longer be the staple of what it means to be literate.

Children learn from exposure to popular cultural forms, which provide a new cultural register to what it means to be literate. Parents, educators, and cultural workers must foster and attend to the cultural practices that shape students' knowledge and experience through their use of popular cultural forms. Youth should be taught to analyze critically the messages they consume as they navigate a vast range of electronic media in popular culture, but they must also be able to master the skills and technology to produce these forms, making their own films, videos, music, and websites. As Lee Artz suggests, it is not enough to hope that "individual subversive readings may prompt a social movement"; instead, "those who oppose Disney's autocratic production model and generic content should replace them with cooperative creations and narratives."[90] Thus, a cultural pedagogy also requires more resources for schools and other sites of learning, providing the opportunities for students and others to become, rather than merely consuming objects, the producing subjects of their own pedagogical creations. As cultural producers, young people will gain even more power over the conditions that influence them, while becoming attentive to the workings of power, knowledge, solidarity, and difference as part of a more comprehensive project for democratic empowerment.

Fourth, Disney's reach into the spheres of economics, consumption, and culture suggests that we analyze Disney within broad and complex relations of power (an analysis of this kind can be found in the following chapters). Eric Smoodin argues that the American public needs to "gain a new sense of [Walt] Disney's importance, because of the manner in which his work in film and television is connected to other projects in urban planning, ecological politics, product merchandising, United States domestic and global policy formation, technological innovation, and constructions of national character."[91] George Monbiot has rightly argued that we must understand what is old and new about Disney, but what brings these two moments together is Disney's wielding of "commercial, cultural, and political power in a way the world had never seen."[92] This suggests undertaking analyses of the Disney corporation that connect, rather than separate, the various economic and cultural formations in which the company engages. Clearly, such a dialectical practice not only provides a more theoretically accurate understanding of the reach and influence of Disney's power but also contributes to forms of analysis that challenge the notion that Disney is primarily about entertainment.

Disney exercises institutional and political power through its massive control over diverse sectors of what Mark Crispin Miller has called the "national entertainment state."[93] The availability, influence, and cultural power of Disney's films demand that they become part of a broader political discourse regarding who makes cultural policy. Questions of ownership, control, and the possibility of public participation in deciding how cultural resources are used, to what extent, and for what effect should become a central issue in addressing the world of Disney and other media conglomerates that shape cultural policy. In this context, Disney's influence in shaping culture cannot be reduced to critically interpreting the ideas and values promoted by the corporation. The production, distribution, and consumption of films and other products should be analyzed as part of a wider circuit of power. In other words, any viable analysis must understand and address how Disney, Inc., operates within the context of a larger cultural strategy and public-policy initiatives. Issues regarding how and what children learn could be addressed through broad public debates about how the distribution and control of cultural and economic resources could ensure that children are exposed to a variety of alternative narratives, images, and representations about themselves and the larger society. This form of analysis would combine research about Disney's reach and influence in the world and offer knowledge and strategies that address how cultural power and the shaping of children's culture could become matters of public policy on both a national and a transnational level.

The issue of what children read and see in public schools is quite clearly a matter of public policy, parental concern, and intervention. But when children's culture is shaped in the commercial sphere, the discourse of public intervention gets lost in abstract appeals to the imperatives of the market and free speech. Free speech is only as good as the democratic framework that makes possible the extension of its benefits to a wider range of individuals, groups, and public spheres. Treating Disney as part of a media sphere that must be democratized and held accountable for the ways in which it wields power, manufactures social identities, and subverts democratic agency must be part of the discourse of pedagogical analysis and public-policy intervention. This type of analysis and intervention is perfectly suited for cultural theorists and community activists willing to employ an interdisciplinary approach to such an undertaking, to address popular culture as an object of serious analysis, to make the pedagogical a defining principle of such work, to challenge the creeping commodification of everyday life, and to insert the political into the center of such projects.[94]

This suggests that cultural workers need to reexamine a politics of representation and a discourse of political economy, treating their varied interrelations as a form of cultural work that rejects the cultural/material divide. The result would be a new understanding of how such modalities inform each other within different contexts and across national boundaries. It is particularly important for cultural workers to understand how Disney films work as teaching machines, shaping individuals and social formations. The messages, emotional investments, and ideologies produced by Disney can be traced through the circuits of power that both legitimate and insert "the culture of the Magic Kingdom" into multiple and overlapping public spheres. Disney films must be analyzed not only for what they say but also for how they are apprehended by audiences within national and international contexts. That is, cultural workers need to study these films intertextually and from a transnational perspective. The Disney corporation itself is not ignorant of different cultural contexts. Indeed, its power, in part, rests with its ability to adapt to different contexts and to be embraced by different transnational formations and audiences. Disney engenders what Inderpal Grewal and Caren Kaplan have called "scattered hegemonies."[95] Although it is an icon of American culture around the world, the Walt Disney Company is not content to represent itself as a homogeneous corporate entity: every new place Disney ventures, it seeks to represent and commodify its new audience's culture back to both local and global consumer markets. It is precisely by exploring and addressing how

Disney's influence operates in particular spaces of power and specific localities—in different transnational locations—that we will be able to understand more fully the various agendas and politics at work as Disney is both reconstituted for, and interpreted by, different audiences.

Since the power and influence of Disney is so pervasive in American society and around the world, parents, educators, and others need to find ways to hold Disney accountable for what it produces. The defeat in 1995 of Disney's proposed three-thousand-acre theme park in Virginia suggests that Disney can be challenged, and the Disneyfication of American culture can be successfully opposed.[96] In this instance, a coalition of historians, community activists, educators, and other concerned groups mobilized against the land developers supporting the project, wrote articles against Disney's trivializing of history and its implications for the park, and aroused public opinion to generate an enormous amount of adverse criticism against the Disney project. What was initially viewed as merely a project to bring a Disney version of fun and entertainment to hallowed Civil War grounds in historic Virginia was translated by oppositional groups into a matter of cultural struggle and public policy. And Disney lost. There are other instances, too, when Disney's corporate ideology and practices have been challenged successfully by religious groups, individuals, and unions. In 2007, the Service Trades Council, which had been challenging Disney's outsourcing of overnight-shift custodial jobs at Walt Disney World, negotiated a successful resolution through the National Labor Relations Board. In this case, many workers who had been laid off got their jobs back, all 170 workers involved in the dispute received a cash settlement, and Disney agreed "not to unilaterally change employees' wages, hours, and working conditions or refuse to provide information requested by the union."[97]

The communities' and workers' resistance to Disney in Virginia and Orlando suggests that Disney cannot be allowed to shirk its public responsibility when it uses every means in its control to actively shape the field of politics and encroach on noncommercialized public space. And Disney must be held accountable not only for its direct impact on various cultural and political spheres but also for its claim on the public imagination. Rather than being viewed as an entertainment company innocently distributing pleasure to young people and adults, the Disney empire must be seen as an pedagogical and policy-making enterprise actively engaged in the cultural landscaping of national identity and the "schooling" of youthful minds. Walt Disney did not invent brand loyalty, but he took it to a new low in his commercialization and commodification of children's desires and needs. "Happiness," "fun," and "innocence" take on a not-so-hidden agenda in the Disney empire: they become synonymous with commercialization and high profit margins. This is not to suggest that there is something utterly sinister behind what Disney does. Rather, it points to the need to address in meaningful and rigorous ways the role of fantasy, desire, and innocence in securing particular ideological interests, legitimating specific social relations, and providing the content of public memory. Disney achieves its cultural power through consent, although it claims the authority to represent its version of reality as the truth. For this very reason, it is both possible and necessary for parents, educators, and others to challenge and disrupt the corporate power and the images, constructions, and values generated by Disney's teaching machine.

Chapter Four

Disney, Militarization, and the National-Security State after 9/11

I feel that if a thing can be proven un-American that it ought to be outlawed.

—Walt Disney[1]

Walt Disney's testimony before the House Un-American Activities Committee on October 24, 1947—in which he declared, "Everybody in my studio is one-hundred-percent American," while he also named a number of former employees who had organized a labor strike as "Communists"—signified the culmination of a long-standing relationship of collaboration between the Walt Disney Company and the American government.[2] Disney told the committee that he felt the best strategy for safeguarding "all of the good, free causes in this country, all of the liberalisms that really are American" would be to uncover the "un-American" labor activists who had infiltrated the motion picture industry and had propagated their Communist "ideologies," which in turn were directly responsible for activities such as the 1941 strike at the Disney studio in Burbank, California.[3] Meanwhile, other reasons cited for the strike, such as the company's "arbitrary and manipulative pay structure" and the illegal firing of union activists working with the Screen Cartoonists' Guild, were simply ignored.[4] According to Walt Disney in 1941, individuals such as the labor organizers who had "called my plant a sweatshop" needed to be "smoked out and shown up for what they are" in order to "keep the American labor unions clean"

and to preserve "good, solid Americans" from "the taint of communism."[5] Disney's justification of the state's use of repressive force in
order to secure American freedom may not sound quite so unfamiliar
today, following the events of September 11, 2001. Since 9/11, several
reports have emerged exposing a U.S. government that used illegal
wiretapping with impunity, lied about the reasons for invading Iraq in
2003, sanctioned the torture of alleged terrorists, and imprisoned so-
called enemy combatants—including children—denying them basic
legal rights such as the right to a fair trial.[6] Indeed, state repression and
patriotic correctness at their most extreme became the normal state of
affairs in a post-9/11 world characterized by domestic surveillance,
the erosion of civil liberties, and an ideological and military campaign
waged against the threat of "terrorism" that involved the construction
of a vast secret and illegal apparatus of violence.

Despite the Disney corporation's perennial claim that its products
are simply about entertainment, Disney/ABC's *The Path to 9/11* (2006)
and Disney/Pixar's *The Incredibles* (2004) both attest to the company's
endorsement of, if not active participation in, partisan political issues,
especially the "war on terror" and the emerging security culture in the
United States. Disney's history of making alliances with state power is
not surprising, given its corporate interest in reaching large audiences
and perpetuating dominant cultural forms, but not since its production
of several films for the U.S. military during World War II has Disney
participated in the dissemination of such overt political propaganda.
While the Walt Disney Company's patriotic fervor during World War
II has generated little critical response over the years, Disney's productions since 9/11 have been more controversial, yet few critics have gone
so far as to argue that the messages produced by *The Path to 9/11* and
The Incredibles do not support the status quo as much as they present a
reactionary politics, which not only justifies U.S. military power abroad
but also suggests deeply authoritarian ideas and practices are the best
way to secure the ongoing domination of American cultural identity at
home. Both films solicit their viewers' support and appear to occupy
solid (and therefore unquestionable) moral ground by taking a critical
stance that positions the lone protagonists outside repressive cultures
dominated by mindless bureaucracies. The films ultimately sacrifice
an understanding of the systemic causes of war and violence in favor
of blaming individuals who exhibit pathological behaviors that go far

beyond character flaws or mere cowardice. Of course, the demonization of the other and the representation of individuals who challenge institutional stagnancy as heroic are not new to those familiar with discourses of hyperindividualism, competitiveness, and jingoistic nationalism in the dominant media in the United States, but the justification of violence as the primary means to achieve these goals has not been asserted so boldly as before, except perhaps if one considers the history of Disney films.

At the onset of World War II, Walt Disney was not alone in his belief that film should play a dominant role in the teaching process or, as he claimed, in "molding opinion."[7] He was, however, at the forefront of a movement to recognize a "new aspect of the use of films in war": training industrial workers and soldiers.[8] Some historians try to account for Disney's participation in generating military propaganda by claiming that the studios were "taken over by the military as part of the war effort"[9] on December 8, 1941. But Richard Shale has meticulously documented Disney's much earlier attempts to court contracts with the aircraft industry, the U.S. Council of National Defense, and Canadian military supporters.[10] Indeed, despite a "popular (and frequently quoted) misconception" that the relationship between Disney Studios and the U.S. military was "unexpected or unsolicited," Shale observes an explicit shift in Disney's focus from "entertainment values to teaching values" that occurred before Disney acquired his first U.S. military contracts in December 1941.[11] For instance, in 1940 Disney approached the Lockheed Aircraft Corporation with the idea of generating a training film on flush riveting. And in the spring of 1941, with Canada already engaged in war, Disney convinced the commissioner of the National Film Board of Canada, John Grierson, that animated films were better positioned as teaching tools than documentary films because of their "capacity for simplifying the presentation of pedagogical problems."[12] Grierson then bought the Canadian rights to *Four Methods of Flush Riveting* and commissioned Disney to produce an instructional film that taught soldiers how to use an antitank rifle and four short films that encouraged Canadians to purchase war savings certificates.

Then, in the fall of 1941, Walt Disney toured South America at the bequest of the U.S. Office of Inter-American affairs, which was attempting to establish good relations and "hemispheric unity as explicated in Roosevelt's Good Neighbor policy."[13] With material collected on the trip, Disney proceeded to generate two feature films, *Saludos*

Amigos (1943) and *The Three Caballeros* (1945), both intended to celebrate Latin American culture while accentuating its similarities with North American culture (and downplaying or ignoring issues like national politics and poverty).[14] Born out of U.S. fear of a Nazi alliance with countries like Argentina, the films aimed to "enhance the Latin American image in the United States," while also "enhanc[ing] America's appreciation of Latin American Everymen."[15] Yet, in making *The Three Caballeros* palatable to white Middle America and American imperialism less threatening to southerners, Disney more often than not caricatures Latin American culture as a voluptuous, exotic female who is fleeing the attentions of a libidinous, but comically ineffectual Donald Duck.[16] There is little doubt that a relationship between Disney Studios and the U.S. government had been fully cemented by 1943, when 94 percent of the footage produced by Disney was under government contract.[17]

From 1941 to 1945, the Disney Studios produced dozens of short educational films, with their subjects ranging from aircraft and warship identification to dental hygiene to the household conservation of cooking oil for the making of military weapons. The studio also produced a number of anti-Nazi short films, including *Der Fuehrer's Face* (1943), *Education for Death: The Making of the Nazi* (1943), and *Reason and Emotion* (1943), two of which were nominated for Academy Awards. In these shorts, Hitler is depicted as waging a mind-control campaign over the German people based on the manipulation of emotions such as anger, love, fear, sympathy, pride, and hate, while also occasionally employing force, regimentation, depravation, and false rewards. Of course, the success of the films' efforts to expose Nazi propaganda overwhelmingly relies on the use of comic devices, caricatures, and stereotypes to make Hitler, Mussolini, and Hirohito seem irrational and absurd. Demonizing the enemy, according to Disney historian Leonard Maltin, "relieves aggression."[18] This claim, suggesting that the films function to disperse rather than focus emotional energy, clearly sidesteps the multiple ways in which the films, much like the propaganda they critique, attempt to shape their audience's emotional responses, such as when Donald Duck, clad in starred-and-striped pajamas, croons to the Statue of Liberty, "Oh, boy, am I glad to be a citizen of the United States of America!" Most significant about the techniques used by these Disney shorts is how they embody animation's capacity to draw clear, simple lines and present a selective representation of an otherwise complex reality. Through the use of comedy and comedic violence, in particular, Disney films are often released from the expectation that they might be attempting to do more than entertain. Viewers wooed by animation's unique capacity to create novel images through exaggeration, distortion, and aesthetic style are easily absorbed into an imaginary world that quite deliberately focuses their eyes on a constructed reality to the exclusion of other possibilities. The value of the anti-Nazi short films for today's audiences lies in their obvious attempt to win the hearts and minds of American viewers through clever visual and ideological manipulation, while ironically issuing repeated warnings to viewers not to allow emotion to short-circuit their critical faculties. A historical perspective on the subject matter sets in relief how Disney's critique of propaganda using the medium of animation inevitably ventures into the realm of propaganda itself.

During the war, a significant number of the studio's resources were devoted to making another feature-length propaganda film, *Victory through Air Power* (1943). The film, based in part on a book written by Major Alexander P. De Seversky, advocates the development of airplane and weapons technology as the means to win the war against the Axis powers. We are told the airplane will not only "revolutionize warfare" but is "the only weapon of war to develop such usefulness during peacetime." Dramatic music punctuates scenes that explore new models of airplanes with increased bombing potential. The United States as the "arsenal of democracy" is represented as a giant heart comprising factories that pump "war supplies" through "the arteries of our transport lines over distances that actually girdle the globe." This organic, humanizing image of "the great industrial heart of America" contrasts with the mechanical image of a spoked wheel used to represent the Nazi war industries, which are also vividly portrayed in dark reds and blacks suggestive of a hellish inferno. Japan is represented as a deadly, black octopus extending its "greedy tentacles" over its "stolen empire." We are told of the necessity for U.S. long-range bombers to strike at "the heart and vitals of the beast." With the lethal combination of the "superior" American "science of aviation" and "science of demolition," the "enemy lies hopelessly exposed to systematic destruction." At the same time, the film announces that "scientific bombing" will enable a "minimum investment in human lives," an oddly ambiguous use of language suggestive of two possible meanings in the context in which it appears: the assertion that aerial bombing of enemy territories requires a "minimum investment" of American soldiers and, what is both more sinister and perhaps in need of such coded language, the claim that bombing the enemy entails such "total destruction" that no human lives requiring "investment" will be left in its wake. Indeed, the film's climax consists of a montage of exploding bombs among Japanese cities and factories, which begin curiously unpopulated and end utterly annihilated. At the pinnacle of the climactic violence, the screen resolves into an image of a bald eagle descending upon and crushing the land-ridden octopus, which then dissolves into a dark cloud of smoke rising above Japan as "America the Beautiful" plays in the background.

Walt Disney believed that *Victory through Air Power* convinced President Franklin D. Roosevelt to support to long-range bombing.[19] For a contemporary viewer who has the benefit of hindsight, the unquestioned propaganda offered by *Victory through Air Power* leaves one with the eerie feeling that the perspective being shaped by the film would not only fail to question the use of technology such as the atomic bomb but even wholeheartedly celebrate it as the quickest and most effective way to win the war. Indeed, it is precisely the film's unflinching support of the development of bigger and better bombing technology, from small hand-dropped bombs to ten-ton delayed-action bombs and armor-piercing bomb rockets, that might seem most disturbing given the devastating effects of the bombing of Hiroshima and Nagasaki, as well as the postwar escalation of arms development during the Cold War and the ongoing expansion of the military-industrial complex in the United States.[20] But Walt Disney did not just support the development of larger weapons; he was a firm supporter of what might be called the atomic age and made the classic 1956 propaganda film *Our Friend the Atom*, which was also produced as a book and appeared as an atomic submarine ride in the Tomorrowland section of Disney's Magic Kingdom. In this instance, as Mark Langer points out, *Our Friend the Atom* was designed to "counter opposition to the military use of atomic weaponry."[21] The Magic Kingdom became an outpost for leading young people and adults to believe that an "Atomic reactor . . . is like a big furnace. An atomic chain reaction is likened to what happens when a stray ping-pong ball is thrown at a mass of mousetraps with ping-pong balls set on each one."[22] Disney played a formidable role in convincing every school child that atomic energy was central not merely to winning the Cold War but also to preparing them for a future that would be dominated by the United States and its use of new energy sources, which incidentally could be instrumental in elevating the United States to the position of the world's preeminent military power. Mouse power easily and readily made the shift to celebrating atomic power and militarism while enlarging Disney's role as a major purveyor of propaganda.

The Disney films discussed above alert us to the fact that Disney animators honed their skills and gained widespread popular appeal in the 1940s by first producing propaganda films for the U.S. government. This often neglected reality underlying Disney's origins as a cultural entertainment icon should make us all the more careful to heed Janet Wasko's warning that Disney encodes preferred readings of both its animated films and its own brand image to such an extent that "one of the most amazing aspects of the Disney phenomenon is the consistently uniform understanding of the essence of 'Disney.'"[23]

Attuned to Disney's willingness to assume an overt pedagogical role during World War II, several critics of a more recent Disney film, *Aladdin* (1992), noted that the timing of the film's production and release coincided with U.S. military efforts in the Persian Gulf war. According to Christiane Staninger, *Aladdin* is "a propaganda movie for Western imperialism" that "shows the supposed unworkability of Middle Eastern traditions and the need for American intervention."[24] Dianne Sachko Macleod takes this critique a step further, suggesting a link between Disney's "revival of British and French colonial stereotypes of Arab traders, fanatics, and beauties" and the "storehouse of racial and cultural images" used by the Pentagon to justify the war.[25] Macleod notes that regardless of the filmmakers' intentions, the film had the general effect of "privileging the American myths of freedom and innocence at a time of nationalist fervor."[26] Other connections between the film and the first Iraq war are not especially subtle: in addition to locating *Aladdin* in the fictional city of "Agrabah," it makes the villainous Grand Vizier Jafar look like a combination of Saddam Hussein and the Ayatollah Khomeini, while the two young heroes, Aladdin and Jasmine, not only look American—Disney animators made it publicly known that Aladdin was modeled after Tom Cruise[27]—but also, as Brenda Ayres suggests, display their heroism by "contesting (and changing) Arabian law and Islamic religious tradition."[28] While it is impossible to discern the actual motives of the Disney animators, it is equally impossible to ignore the cultural context in which the American public viewed *Aladdin*. At the time of the film's release, the dominant media were aggressively promoting similar images of liberation from barbaric traditions in order to justify the United States' "right to intervene in Middle Eastern politics."[29]

DISNEY'S CONSERVATIVE PATH

Despite the well-documented history of collaboration between the Walt Disney Company and U.S. military and state institutions, Disney has more recently claimed to have no interest in politics. How Disney's decision in May 2004 to block its Miramax division from distributing Michael Moore's *Fahrenheit 9/11* might qualify as a nonpolitical gesture is uncertain. At the time, a senior executive stated that "it's not in the interest of any major corporation to be dragged into a highly charged partisan political battle."[30] Not only were a number of Disney's top executives known to be campaign contributors to the George W. Bush administration,[31] but then CEO Michael Eisner was reported to have said that any criticism of the Bush administration might "endanger tax breaks Disney receives for its theme park, hotels and other ventures in Florida, where Mr. Bush's brother, Jeb, is governor."[32] Miramax arranged privately to buy Moore's film and distribute it independently, and in 2005, the founders of Miramax, Harvey and Bob Weinstein, did not renew their contracts with Disney.[33]

As suggested above, the company's alleged desire to remain outside politics contradicts the reality of Disney's historical pattern of intervening in political matters. It is hardly surprising, then, that in the wake of the unprecedented success of Moore's *Fahrenheit 9/11* documentary, Disney/ABC decided to produce its own account of the events leading up to the terrorist attacks on September 11, 2001. A $40 million miniseries titled *The Path to 9/11*, originally touted as a docudrama "based on the 9/11 Commission Report" and later as the "official true story," constituted a blatant political move on the part of Disney/ABC.[34] In addition, Scholastic, Inc., the educational distribution partner for Disney/ABC, sent one hundred thousand letters to high school teachers across the United States encouraging them to use *The Path to 9/11* in the classroom curriculum and directing them to online study guides.[35]

The miniseries was billed by its self-labeled conservative writer Cyrus Nowrasteh as an "objective telling of the events of 9/11"[36] but faced severe criticism for its partisan depiction of events and actors. *The Path to 9/11*, directed by evangelical Christian filmmaker David Cunningham,[37] depicted members of the Bill Clinton administration as totally incompetent, having repeatedly ignored opportunities to capture Osama bin Laden and overlooked warnings of an incipient attack before September 11, 2001. When prescreened to a select number of film reviewers before it aired on television, the miniseries was received with skepticism and outrage, not merely from Democrats and Clinton supporters. Robert Cressey, a top counterterrorism official to both the Clinton and George W. Bush administrations, argued that a scene depicting the Clinton administration's refusal to pursue bin Laden was "something straight out of Disney and fantasyland. It's factually wrong. And that's shameful."[38] Nearly one hundred thousand readers of the online journal *Think Progress* sent protest letters to Robert Iger, president and CEO of the Walt Disney Company, stating that the film inaccurately "places primary responsibility for the attacks of 9/11 on the Clinton administration while whitewashing the failures of the Bush administration."[39] According to Tom Shales, writing for the *Washington Post*, the miniseries qualified as an "assault on truth."[40] Shales added, "Blunderingly, ABC executives cast doubt on their own film's veracity when they made advance copies available to such political conservatives as Rush Limbaugh but not to Democrats who reportedly requested the same treatment. . . . Democrats have a right to be suspicious of any product of the conservative-minded Walt Disney Co."[41] A group of academic historians led by Arthur M. Schlesinger sent a letter to ABC calling for the network to "halt the show's broadcast and prevent misinforming Americans about their history."[42]

The film presents a number of clichéd stereotypes of "big government" and bureaucratic incompetence, depicting paper-pushing officials as woefully indecisive at crucial moments, primarily because they are too self-interested to put their necks on the line. Clinton, for example, is represented as not wanting to issue orders for military action against al-Qaeda because he's too worried about the effect such decisions might have on the polls, that is, when he is not caught up in dealing with the fallout from the Monica Lewinsky scandal. In one scene, General Ahmad Shah Massoud, leader of the Afghan Northern Alliance, which waits for U.S. approval to go after bin Laden, asks in a scornful tone, "Are there any *men* left in Washington?" Individuals working on the ground who buck procedure and orders from their superiors are, by contrast, willing to "take the heat." So, apparently, is George W. Bush, whose decisiveness in giving a strike-down order to the military after the 9/11 attacks really functions as the climax of the whole miniseries. One could imagine Bush political supporters cheering as this scene unfolded: finally, they could rest assured that there was a real man in Washington. Meanwhile, several FBI and U.S. customs agents recognize the nature of the "new kind of war" being waged against America, and their appeals to racial profiling and domestic spying appear justified in the film. For example, in a brief dialogue, one FBI agent states, "Americans have the right to be protected from domestic spying," and the central protagonist of the film, FBI counter-terrorism agent John O'Neil (portrayed by Harvey Keitel), replies, "Do they have the right to be killed by terrorists?" Heroic individuals such as O'Neil are willing to bypass "red tape" and stand in stark contrast to (1) politicians who are too worried about public opinion not to bow to the pressures of "political correctness," (2) uncooperative CIA officials who jealously guard intelligence when they are not mindlessly adhering to obsolete federal legislation that protects individuals' rights, and (3) various utterly casual security officials and workers who would rather appease suspicious-looking members of the public than be confronted with a situation that might embroil them in conflict. And that is not all. The film contrasts the coolness of John O'Neil's astute judgments with the irrationality of emotionally overwrought women, such as the ambassador to Yemen, Barbara Bodine (Patricia Heaton), and the fanatic zeal of the terrorists. In fact, many of the characters who represent terrorists such as Mohamed Atta (Martin Brody) and Ramzi Yousef (Nabil Elouahabi) share the same intense stare, bristly mustache, and swarthy skin exhibited by Hitler in Disney's World War II propaganda films. While it might be possible for a viewer to overlook insipid dialogue, fallacious logic, melodrama, and weak narrative structure, it is virtually impossible to ignore the film's use of racist and sexist stereotypes to lend legitimacy to all the standard bogeys of extreme right-wing ideology. And, most importantly, there remains the film's utterly deceptive self-presentation as a historically accurate depiction of events. Even lead actor Harvey Keitel told a CNN interviewer prior to the airing of the miniseries,

> I had questions about certain events—material I was given in *The Path to 9/11* that I did raise questions about. . . . Not all the facts were correct. . . . You cannot cross the line from a conflation of events to a distortion of the event. No. Where we have distorted something, we made a mistake, and that should be corrected. It can be corrected, by the people getting involved in the story that they are going to see.[43]

In response to the controversy surrounding *The Path to 9/11*, Scholastic, Inc., announced that its online study guide did not meet the company's "high standards for dealing with controversial issues" and would be replaced with new materials that would focus more on media literacy and critical thinking.[44] ABC also responded to protests by broadcasting disclaimers about the miniseries's "fictionalized" representation while airing a minimally reedited version on September 10 and 11, 2006. But ABC's rather inexplicable decision to air the broadcast without commercials—entailing a loss of $40 million[45]—fostered an illusion of the film's closer proximity to real life, if not also conveying the impression that it was a public service announcement. Most significantly, the broadcast that aired on the second night was framed by a strategic interruption—George W. Bush's Address to the Nation—prompting one journalist to note the "thematic synchronicity," as the president's speech called for ongoing support for the war on terror.[46] It is difficult to deny the *political synergy* suggested by the combination of the right-wing *The Path to 9/11* and Bush's speech—synergy being a profit-driven marketing strategy by no means unfamiliar to a megacorporation like Disney[47]—as Bush appealed to Americans to recognize the ongoing threat of terrorism and the necessity of preemptive action as the only way to safeguard "advancing freedom and democracy as the great alternatives to repression and radicalism."[48] When placed in the context of the film, Bush's success could be measured in terms of how the post-9/11 decisions made by his government succeeded where Clinton's administration apparently had failed. Furthermore, the timely juxtaposition allowed the film to gain a greater veneer of authenticity from the speech's presentation of topical and really existing political concerns, while the film in turn provided credible images and points of reference for listeners trying to engage the highly rhetorical, often self-referential use of language characteristic of Bush's speech. Additionally, the blurring of fact and fiction embodied by the film lent to the speech the mythic or symbolic power generated by extended narrative, and the grandeur of the presidential address added authority to the film.

As a context for Bush's speech, *The Path to 9/11* made an effort to point out some of the problems in law enforcement and governance that preceded the terrorist attacks of 9/11, but the nature of the critique—although presented as objective and all encompassing—never rises above criticizing particular individuals for their character failings. The film was cleverer, however, in the way it indicated the supposed gaps in the system and advocated taking a hard line, but offered no concrete alternatives. In doing so, the film left it to Bush to emerge as the ultimate hero, opening up a space for a timely description of the measures instituted since 9/11:

> We've created the Department of Homeland Security. We have torn down the wall that kept law enforcement and intelligence from sharing information. We've tightened security at our airports and seaports and borders, and we've created new programs to monitor enemy bank records and phone calls. Thanks to the hard work of our law enforcement and intelligence professionals, we have broken up terrorist cells in our midst and saved American lives.[49]

If *The Path to 9/11* presented a single narrative perspective (the "path" taken) as the infallible "truth," then Bush's speech, with a similar kind of religious confidence, also took for granted that only one predetermined course could secure the nation from the terrorist threat. At no point did the film or Bush's speech suggest that the situation was complex enough to necessitate the consideration of several possible paths; indeed, both narratives closed off the possibility of questioning the effectiveness of the security measures endorsed and instituted. Difficult questions—such as the extent to which freedom should be limited in order to be secured or the kinds of sacrifices entailed by "national security"—were simply ignored in favor of the message that Americans must do whatever it takes to defeat the "enemy." It is hard to believe that the gross trivializations of the complex issues surrounding terrorism and the war in Iraq in *The Path to 9/11* and Bush's address could almost escape public protest only five years after the horrifying events of September 11, 2001.

One notable exception to the general complaisance with which the public received *The Path to 9/11* involved a group of students at Ithaca College who protested the college's acceptance of a private donation from Robert Iger on the grounds that *The Path to 9/11,* touted as a docudrama, was actually an egregious display of media bias. Students argued that "accepting Disney money would send the wrong message about the importance of objectivity to the school's journalism and communications students."[50] Although a Disney spokesperson responded to the student protesters by calling them "people who can't distinguish between fact and fiction," Ithaca College president Peggy R. Williams lent credence to the students' concerns by reassuring them that Iger's donation "does not buy Disney any influence on campus. . . . Our curriculum decisions are our own."[51] Although certainly admitting no wrongdoing, Disney has uncharacteristically and tellingly opted not to sell *The Path to 9/11* on DVD—defying the expectations of both those who assumed the company would try to recover the costs of making the miniseries and vociferous right-wing groups who continue to support the film's representation of the events leading to 9/11.[52]

THE NATIONAL-SECURITY FAMILY: MEET THE INCREDIBLES

As films like *Aladdin* and *The Path to 9/11* suggest, the Walt Disney Company has an impressive ability to revise more or less familiar stories, updating the issues to make them resonate in people's lives at the current moment. It is how Disney offers audiences not simply escape but also a mode of relating to the real conditions of their existence that makes Disney films such a long-lived and potent force in U.S. and global popular culture. As Louis Marin suggests regarding the powerful cultural role of Disney theme parks, Disney represents both "what is estranged and what is familiar: comfort, welfare, consumption, scientific and technological progress, superpower, and morality." Importantly, Marin adds, "These are values obtained by violence and exploitation; [in Disney culture] they are projected under the auspices of law and order."[53] Marin's framework is especially useful for understanding a film such as *The Incredibles* as mediating the "imaginary relationship that the dominant groups of American society maintain with their real conditions of existence, with the real history of the United States, and with the space outside of its border."[54] In a post-9/11 world, Academy Award winner *The Incredibles* brings home the need not only to reclaim "superpower" identity as a quintessential American quality but also to recognize that American soil is not immune to the threat of violent attacks. In response to the forces threatening America—internally, the weakening of superhero resolve in the face of excessive bureaucracy, public cynicism, and unthinking adherence to the law; externally, enemies whose infantile resentment at being "not super" results in a genocidal campaign against everything "super," even to the extent of terrorizing an innocent public—the PG-rated film sanctions violence as a means to establish a new brand of "law and order." Although hearkening back to the nuclear family as the source of America's security and strength, the film diverges from past narratives in its emphasis on a natural order in which authority and power belong in the hands of the few strong leaders left in America, while the rest of us must duly recognize our inevitable "mediocrity." This overall message is especially disturbing in light of the events following 9/11, when the United States witnessed a growing authoritarianism throughout the larger culture.[55] Some consequences of the American response to the tragic terrorist attacks have been a general tolerance for the use of preemptive violence and coercion, control of the media, the rise of repressive state power, an expanding militarization, and a thriving surveillance and security industry that is now even welcomed in public schools. And these are only some of the *known* consequences: many of the effects of the Bush administration's policies are still coming to light. In 2009, President Barack Obama ordered the release of top-secret Bush administration memos that sanctioned the CIA's use of torture on terror suspects. A year previous, *New York Times* reporter David Barstow wrote an exposé of "independent" military analysts who appeared on television networks to inform the public with their expert and objective impressions of the war in Iraq (many were retired army generals and had direct ties to corporations that were courting government military contracts). It turned out the Pentagon was coaching the military analysts behind the scenes to put a favorable spin on the Bush administration's "wartime performance," with the apparent collusion of U.S. media networks, including ABC, which failed to check for, or simply ignored, evident conflicts of interest.[56] In addition to calling into question the journalistic integrity of the media, the scandal made it seem as if the Bush administration's public relations machine was taking its cues from corporations such as Disney by not only launching a marketing campaign carefully tailored to uphold its public image but also secretly controlling access to information and limiting public discourse, all in order to sell a sense of security to the American people.

An emphasis on controlling public speech and public spaces—not to mention autocratic rule, secrecy, and the appeal to security—is nothing new to Disney, whose theme parks, according to Steven Watts, "blur the line between fantasy and reality by immersing visitors in a totally controlled environment."[57] Disneyland is a useful space, apparently, to undertake surveillance, and Walt Disney offered the FBI "complete access" to Disneyland facilities in the 1950s for "use in connection with official matters and for recreational purposes."[58] Indeed, the development of a cordial relationship between Walt Disney and FBI director J. Edgar Hoover is now better understood not only in relation to Walt Disney's fervent anticommunism but also in light of revelations that he may have served as "a secret informer for the Los Angeles office of the Federal Bureau of Investigation."[59] Certainly, as Watts indicates, it is known that Disney was appointed a special FBI agent in part because of his desire to root out so-called communist agitators from the film industry.[60] More recently, Eric Smoodin notes that the Disney corporation remains "interested in constructing surveillance as entertainment," as suggested by the marketing of products such as a Mickey Mouse doll with glow-in-the-dark eyes that illuminate sleeping children for the benefit of parental scrutiny.[61]

The Incredibles, with its complex appeal to several levels of audience, received overwhelming praise from film critics, who admired not only its retromodern aesthetic and detailed animation but also its "stinging wit."[62] However, most reviewers who observed an "edge of intellectual indignation"[63] focused on the first thirty minutes of the film in which the main character, Mr. Incredible (voiced by Craig T. Nelson), is forced to conceal his superhero identity as a consequence of public disaffection and a string of lawsuits (he is sued after rescuing a suicidal man named Sansweet who claimed Mr. Incredible had "ruined [his] death"). With "average citizens" now proclaiming they want "average heroes," Mr. Incredible; his superhero wife, Elastigirl/Helen (Holly Hunter); and their children become the middle-of-the-road Parr family, trying to maintain a normal suburban lifestyle by suppressing their superpowers in what one reviewer suggests is a "suspicious society that's decidedly below-Parr."[64] As suggested by a *Boston Globe* film review, Bob Parr's cubicle office job as a claims adjuster at Insuricare is designed to evoke identification with the "middle-age blues felt by audience members."[65] But many reviewers, in choosing to highlight the film's critique of suburban conformity and corporate greed, misread or overlook the film's central message, which does not elicit identification on the part of a mere newspaper journalist or academician: in fact, normal people who wrongly identify with superheroes and devalue their worth are society's worst threat. The film's villain, Buddy aka Syndrome (Jason Lee), begins as Mr. Incredible's "number one fan" but then transgresses the boundary between admiration and emulation. Conflict arises when Buddy asserts that his rocket boot technology enables him "to be super" without being born with superpowers. When rejected by Mr. Incredible, who prefers to "work alone," Buddy turns the pathological injury into villainy with an ideological goal: to provide the technology "so that everyone can be superheroes. . . . And when everyone's super, no one will be." The connections between Buddy and the dominant media's portrayal of international terrorists are multiple: his fixation on demolishing a superpower, his development of high-tech weaponry, his narcissistic rage, his ideological purpose, and, what resonates most clearly, his plan to gain power over a fearful public by launching a plane at Manhattan. At one point, Buddy even tells Mr. Incredible, "Now you respect me, because I'm a threat. . . . It turns out there's a lot of people, whole countries, who want respect. And they will pay through the nose to get it." Given the film's resounding judgment of Buddy/Syndrome—he is shredded by a jet turbine while attempting to kidnap the Parr baby—it is difficult to understand how the film's message could be interpreted, as one reviewer suggests, as empowering viewers to recognize the "secret identities we all keep tucked away in our hearts."[66] Even if one were to extend an allegorical reading of *The Incredibles* to argue that all Americans are super, it would not be possible to elide the film's clear validation of a social hierarchy along primordial lines.

Throughout the film, the plight of the super family is closely linked to their superiority. The Incredibles' son Dash (Spencer Fox), frustrated by not being able to demonstrate his speed in school sports competitions, acts out in his fourth-grade class by playing pranks on his teacher. Dash wins his father's admiration, but the thought of a graduation ceremony for fourth-graders leads Mr. Incredible to burst out, "It's psychotic! They keep creating new ways to celebrate mediocrity, but if someone is genuinely exceptional . . . " Later in the film, Elastigirl reassures daughter Violet (Sarah Vowell), "Your identity is your most valuable possession. . . . Doubt is a luxury we can't afford anymore. You have more power than you realize. Don't think. Don't worry. If the time comes, you'll know what to do. It's in your blood." As A. O. Scott astutely recognizes in a *New York Times* review, the movie argues, "Some people have powers that others do not, and to deny them the right to exercise those powers, or the privileges that accompany them, is misguided, cruel and socially destructive."[67] Being "super" in such a framework does not mean being smart or being virtuous; it simply means possessing innate power. The highly advanced modern society produces mediocrity because its ethics (a belief in social justice and equality) counter the effects of natural selection by nullifying Darwinian fitness as the condition for survival.

If the film indeed offers up "the philosophy of Ayn Rand"—who opposed collectivism, altruism, and the welfare state in favor of egoistic individualism—then it turns to violence as the means to achieve supremacy.[68] At no point during *The Incredibles'* "eardrum-bashing, metal-crunching action sludge" and its self-referential mockery of "monologuing" does the film suggest that reasoning, discussion, or any other form of peaceful resolution might be pursued instead of violence. More in keeping, however, with Disney conventions than Rand's philosophy is the film's conflation of the pursuit of individualism with the protection of the nuclear family. One reviewer cleverly summarizes the film's main theme as "the family that slays together stays together."[69] In this way, the white, nuclear, middle-class family becomes the ethical referent for a bombproof collectivity: only a muscular protection of one's own will ensure stability, identity, and agency, not to mention consumerism, heterosexuality, clearly defined gender roles, parenthood, and class chivalry. The result is that the film brings "individuals and their families to the centers of national life, offering the audience an image of itself and of the nation as a knowable community, a wider public world beyond the routines of a narrow existence."[70] But the American nation drawn by the film is imaged as one that neither shies away from use of force nor requires any justification for its display of blatant chauvinism when confronted by others.

The Incredibles further contrasts the banality of suburban life with the glamour and excitement of "hero work." The elaborate security compounds of Syndrome's island and the home of fashion designer Edna Mode (Brad Bird) are suped up with the latest high-tech gadgetry, the exhilarating navigation of which bears a close resemblance to video game playing, particularly in the medium of computer-generated animation. And even if the filmmakers' intended to parody gated homes à la Hollywood Hills in their representation of Edna Mode's mansion, the cumulative message makes security and surveillance systems seem not only unthreatening but also quite normal—at least as familiar as, say, the presence of gates and cameras at Walt Disney World. In fact, Syndrome's island has a developed monorail system, which implies a double reference both to the James Bond movie *Dr. No* (1962) and to Disney World itself. Referentiality seems to come full circle as *The Incredibles*' island imitates Bond films that likely drew on the model of Disney theme parks in portraying the villain's lair. For instance, Bond's antagonist in *The Man with the Golden Gun* (1974) "inhabits a politically autonomous island that features an amusement park funhouse,"[71] an allusion that betrays cultural anxiety about a rigidly controlled theme park environment governed by an autocrat who deliberately toys with defenseless people's perceptions and plays upon their fears. The Bond films were tapping into a darker side of the Disney-designed spaces, also noted by M. Keith Booker, who writes, "The fictional utopias portrayed in the [Disney] parks have a definite dystopian side, as anyone who has ever been bothered by the efficiency with which the parks are able to control and manipulate the vast populations who visit them has noticed."[72] Yet, the lush tropical island in *The Incredibles* works less to expose the dark side of a totally regulated world than to associate it with exotic thrills and gamelike suspense as the superheroes infiltrate Syndrome's compound—a brilliant advertisement for a family adventure at Walt Disney World, if there ever was one. More disturbing is the recognition that as dominant culture in the United States accepts the expansion of a security-military-surveillance-intelligence complex, negotiating such altered environments can be reduced to slapstick comedy (when, for instance, Elastigirl finds herself stretched between two security doors and must fight against a number of armed guards). Not rendered entirely harmless, the island environment also represents the ideal locale for the Incredible children to rise to the challenge of a real danger—their mother tells them that unlike "the bad guys" on "Saturday morning cartoons . . . these guys will kill you"—and to engage the enemy in a display of family loyalty and heroic exceptionalism.

Because "calls to action litter the film," critics such as David Hastings Dunn have suggested that *The Incredibles* is "an allegorical tale justifying U.S. foreign policy under George W. Bush."[73] Indeed, the only imaginable way the "slightly fascist" *Incredibles* could be labeled a "family-friendly film,"[74] as one critic claims, is if one assumes the "super" refrain throughout the film is an oblique reference to American superiority and supremacy, such that viewers are included as part of one big national family, a family that has recently demonstrated its mettle on the world stage by waging wars against Afghanistan and Iraq. Indeed, Mr. Incredible repeatedly argues for an ethic of intervention and pushes aside anyone who poses an obstacle to action. Those individuals who wish to prevent superheroes from acting are fundamentally weak: people who claim their right to noninterference, politicians who cravenly seek public approval, lawyers who succumb to financial pressures, teachers who suppress any challenges to their authority, and employers who expect blind obedience to corporate policy. Interventionism is legitimated when Bob/Mr. Incredible helps an elderly woman with her insurance claim, only to face his irate boss, who indicates that Bob's loyalties must be redirected to one specific purpose: "Help *our* people! Starting with our stockholders." While the diminutive Mr. Huph (Wallace Shawn) launches into a speech about the necessity for the "little cogs" in the company machine to "mesh together," Mr. Incredible is prevented from saving a man in the street who is being mugged. The film deserves credit for extending a clichéd critique of office work as crushing of individual creativity to a representation of greed and corruption plaguing private corporations charged with providing public services. Unfortunately, the only solution to the social ills of exploitation and dehumanization proffered by the film is to put one's faith in the individuals who have the power to subjugate a clear and unambiguous enemy, in other words, a militaristic version of the old adage "Father knows best." Before we join the throngs of enthusiastic reviewers who laud the film for its exposure of corporate abuses of power, it should be understood that the film is as much invested in showing how postindustrial capitalism—and liberal democracy even more so—elevates the weak manipulators above the authentic strongmen. Instead of presenting a viable solution to the ravages of neoliberal economics on social democracy, *The Incredibles* offers only one reactionary alternative devised in the realm of fantasy: superheroes will save us as long as we recognize our natural inferiority and give them our unqualified vote of confidence. The huge, hard-bodied Mr. Incredible is ready to rescue America from the city slicker, ladies' man softness of the postwar era. (Admittedly, this superhero for a "postfeminist" generation has an exceedingly competent female sidekick/wife, but one who tellingly possesses the complementary superhero power of extreme malleability).

When considered alongside the blockbuster success of *The Incredibles* and its overarching message in 2004, it probably should not surprise us that George W. Bush was reelected the same year—in part because his public relations team managed to convince voters that, in an insecure world rife with terrorist threats, they should depend on his uncompromising judgments of good and evil, his impervious cowboy-like manner, and his "strong, stable personality." What makes the Incredibles appear to be superheroes is the same quality that apparently made George W. Bush seem presidential: the ability to act free from the paralyzing effects of thoughtful consideration. This orientation toward decisive action in the film becomes an end in itself since, as Jeremy Heilman points out, "There are no scenes in which characters learn to use their power responsibly (except for those that extol conformity), and no moments in which loss of life is felt."[75]

According to George Soros, the events of 9/11 renewed a "distorted view" of American supremacy that "postulates that because we are stronger than others, we must know better and we must have right on our side."[76] If American patriotism reached a fever pitch in the aftermath of 9/11, then *The Incredibles* clearly tapped into a desire to assert U.S. preeminence on the world stage. Indeed, all the superheroes are American, and the only non-American with any power is a villainous French mime named Bomb Voyage. The overall message of the film, as Hastings Dunn points out, is a perennial neoconservative theme: "America's failure to spread its values can lead to 'blowback' from former clients and protégés."[77] The only response offered by the film to a society supposedly weakened by a misguided egalitarianism and the post–Cold War softening of American resolve is to minimize institutional and legal controls while letting unrestrained power achieve its deserved place of domination. For "supers" to dictate the common good once again, *The Incredibles* concludes, "it's up to the politicians." It is difficult to imagine a more resounding dismissal of democratic processes than this final assertion, suggesting less the need for political accountability and public participation than the need for emboldened leaders whose decisive action should be divorced from the values and constraints imposed by the mediocre masses.

DISNEY AND THE RHETORIC OF INNOCENCE

The bizarre way in which *The Incredibles* marries two dangerous social ideals—a Darwinist notion of survival of the fittest and a retrograde identity politics based on biological superiority—can verge on acceptability when it is packaged as a Disney animated film that carries the overarching association with childhood innocence. Audiences are meant to appreciate the fact that if in a fit of rage Mr. Incredible destroys a car, or another human being for that matter, then it is simply a natural expression of his innate "super" identity and not something that requires moral assessment. Or, worse yet, it is something that can only be considered as intrinsically good. By appealing to the view that "might is right," the film fails to open up the possibility that values and ethics are constituted by various social mechanisms and material relations of power. Instead, the tautological rationale suggests that being "right" is simply entailed by being "super," such that the imperative to conquer the enemy who threatens one's way of life remains not only above question but also without any negative consequences (after all, the enemy is not "super" like us). The presumption of innate American benevolence is implied by a reading of *The Incredibles* as a national allegory. At stake in this concept of America as a superpower is the belief that its leaders and the entire populace are incorruptible and therefore exemplify absolute goodness.[78]

As we have seen in previous chapters, this notion of a benign, incorruptible nature is nothing new to Disney, whose cultural productions rely on innocence as a rhetorical tool to legitimate dominant relations of power. *The Incredibles* slightly modifies the concept of childhood innocence by linking it to a citizenry in need of a blameless and absolute

paternalistic authority to safeguard its interests. The appeal to innocence often enables animated Disney films to fly below a critical radar.
The Incredibles probably does so, despite its authoritarian overtones,
because of the historical and cultural context in which it was received.
After the tragic events of 9/11, Americans sought an opportunity to envision themselves as proactive agents of history rather than its passive
victims and as part of a community with strong leadership that could
instill hope for security and redemption in a world that seemed hostile
to such desires.

However, when politics is cloaked in the guise of innocence, more
is at stake than a simple affirmation of desire. At stake is the way in
which Disney films garner the cultural power to influence how people
think not simply through their particular mode of representation but also
through shaping the knowledge and subjectivities of their viewers in
order to valorize some identities while disabling others. Film watching
involves more than entertainment; it is an experience that reproduces
the basic conditions of learning. To understand Disney films, we need
to understand how Disney culture influences public understandings of
history, national coherence, and popular values in ways that often conceal injustice, dissent, and the possibility of democratic renewal. While
the retro style and clever allusiveness of *The Incredibles* appeal to what
is aesthetically pleasing about America's past, there is no acknowledg-
ment of an underlying totalitarian ethos driving, for instance, U.S. military and imperial expansion during the Cold War. Although weakling
institutions and individuals hinder all things "super," Mr. Incredible, as
an exemplary cultural icon, enables the reconstruction of American history purged of its seamy side, not least of all through an appeal to nostalgia, stylized consumption, and a reinvigorated patriotism. Moreover,
The Incredibles' comic representation of 1950s suburban mediocrity
does little to challenge the prevailing discourses of patriarchy, class,
and sexism. In fact, the film pays tribute to the consumerism, patriarchy, and family values associated with 1950s sitcoms by suggesting that
the failing of such a family orientation lies not in its oppressive control
but in how settling into a mundane reality and accepting the onset of
complacency sap its inherent magisterial vitality. Taking what it considers best from that era, the film revitalizes conservative ideology for a
new generation of video-gaming kids, sexing up the suburban doldrums
with designer superhero garb and high-tech stunts that substitute spectacle for critical engagement.

The Incredibles and *The Path to 9/11* are films produced at a particular historical moment that share the theme of defending U.S. hegemony and values against the insidious forces of a weak-willed political correctness at home and envious terrorists determined to destroy the American way of life abroad. One interesting outcome of the comparison can be seen in the way the different film genres elicited much different responses from the public despite their thematic similarities. *The Path to 9/11*'s claim to portray historical events objectively in the form of a documentary-style ABC miniseries drew some public resistance, whereas the animated Disney film whose very representation defies objectivity drew virtually none. But the messages of *The Incredibles* are no less persuasive for being more fantastic.

Clearly, *The Incredibles'* inscription of biological supremacy represents not only an assertion of dominant family values but an ideological justification for gender- and race-based conceptions of U.S. global imperialism and national identity. *The Path to 9/11* is less clever in concealing its affirmation of racist and sexist attitudes and its legitimation of violence, but *The Incredibles* is far more dangerous in that it has been viewed in a generally unfiltered manner by millions of children and adults worldwide. Recognizing the conservative influence of Disney films—a conservatism that manifests with unprecedented boldness in *The Incredibles*—should not entail avoiding them, suppressing them, or complacently accepting their cultural ascendancy. It should involve making explicit how and what we learn from the very political messages being taught by Disney films, rather than accepting them at face value or dismissing their existence altogether.

Consuming culture even as a form of entertainment is fundamentally a pedagogical experience, and the more educators, parents, students, and other cultural workers become active in their attempts to decode the complex representations being offered by Disney, the more rich and rewarding our experiences with popular culture will become. For this reason, a nuanced criticism of Disney films would not assume that they inherently disempower the audience but would instead view such cultural encounters as opportunities that can empower children and adults by creating the conditions that give people control over the production and types of knowledge and values arising from their experiences as cultural consumers. Being resisted here is the attitude that turns Disney's native utopianism into an excuse to adopt a stance that willfully overlooks the risks incurred by allowing a multinational corporation to escape any critical scrutiny as it reproduces dominant forms of identity, authorizes particular forms of history, and validates "hierarchies of value as universally valid, ecumenical, and effectively consensual."[79] Nothing could be more dystopian in its consequences than the abdication of our responsibility to be critical and thoughtful of the ways the U.S. media represents America to itself and others. Disney should not be allowed to dictate, limit, and monopolize the only current and future possibilities imaginable for an increasingly global culture that must be able to imagine a better life—a life built upon the precepts of compassion and justice rather than American-centered images of power, nostalgia, insularity, and world domination.

Chapter Five

Globalizing the Disney Empire

Why be a governor or a senator when you can be king of Disneyland?

—Walt Disney

"Disneyland Comes to Baghdad." This headline appeared in a 2008
article in the London *Times*, which revealed that a company responsible for "imagineering" parts of Disneyland had been hired by a
private development firm to design the "Baghdad Zoo and Entertainment Experience."[1] The new theme park in Iraq is slated to be built on
the existing site of the al-Zawra park and zoo, a public space adjacent
to the Green Zone, which will be transformed into a privately owned
compound featuring glitzy displays, rides, a skateboard park, a concert
theater, a museum, hotels, and upscale housing. The announcement of a
Disney-style park in Baghdad was subsequently covered by progressive
news outlets in the United States as an example of how Pentagon-led
reconstruction efforts do not simply attend to the needs of the country's
devastated citizenry. Critics rightly observed that the park is a barely
disguised promotion of American cultural values in the name of entertainment; the new complex is intended to help legitimize the U.S. occupation of Iraq by working to "depoliticize Iraqi youth and curb anti-
American sentiment."[2] Instead of focusing on repairing infrastructure
such as hospitals and schools or providing Baghdad's inhabitants with
better access to food and clean water, the developers will give Iraqi kids

157

"opportunities to enjoy their childhood" by donating "200,000 Califor-
nia-style skateboards to Iraqi children" and encouraging them to forget
their real-life woes, if not their own cultural heritage and identities, by
paying to play in the multi-million-dollar entertainment complex.³ The
$500 million project was promoted as potentially beneficial to Iraqis
in a number of ways: it could provide employment for some of the
half-million skilled workers left jobless after the U.S. invasion; it could
contribute to healing ethnic conflict (Shias and Sunnis could enjoy the
park together); or it could simply keep kids occupied so that they would
not become recruits for an escalating resistance against the occupation.
Although critics pointed out that hype surrounding the park just glosses
over the U.S. government's involvement in selling off state-owned
Iraqi resources, spaces, and factories to American private enterprise, the
head of the development firm certainly made no effort to conceal his
motives, stating, "I wouldn't be doing this if I wasn't making money. I
also have this wonderful sense that we're doing the right thing—we're
going to employ thousands of Iraqis. But mostly everything here is for
profit."⁴

Although "Disneyland Baghdad" is not actually a Disney venture,
the park's conceptualization as a harbinger of American imperialism
is valuable for the ways it can be likened to, and distinguished from,
Disney's corporate empire. The story speaks to the belief on the part of
U.S. authorities in Iraq that spreading American cultural symbols—here
a fantasyland stamped with a "Made in America" logo—is tantamount
to spreading American economic values, such as free enterprise, consumerism, and leisure, which in turn provide the foundations for the
displacement of hostility and eventual acceptance of the U.S. presence
in Iraq (if not full assimilation to secular American political values).
This narrative also makes clear what Zygmunt Bauman has called negative globalization, in which democratization becomes synonymous with
market forces.⁵ When democracy is equated with the marketplace, a
dangerous form of depoliticization occurs in which history and memory
are erased and cultural identity becomes either inconsequential as a
political determinant or simple fodder for commercialization. It has
become increasingly evident that the rising tide of free markets has less
to do with ensuring democracy than with spreading a reign of terror
around the globe, affecting the most vulnerable populations in the cruel-
est of ways. The global politics of commodification and its underlying

logic of waste and disposability do irreparable harm, especially to children, and the resulting material, psychological, and spiritual injury must be understood not merely as a political and economic issue but also as a pedagogical concern.

Critics have long targeted the Walt Disney Company for advancing a public pedagogy equally invested in both the shaping of childhood identity and the "Americanization" of other cultures. For example, Ariel Dorfman and Armand Mattelart's seminal study of Disney comics produced for Latin American readers in the 1960s suggested that Disney deployed imperialist strategies by filling the comic books with pro-capitalist content. It is not unlikely, given the history of Disney's collaboration with the U.S. government (discussed in chapter 4), that Disney may very well have been conscripted into the Cold War battle for hegemony throughout the Americas, particularly as it pertained to Chile, which at the time was witnessing a series of socialist reforms.[6] While Walt Disney has been described as "a true-blue patriot who saw himself as a proselytizer for the values of the American heartland,"[7] other, more significant advantages arose from the company's tight alliance with the American government. In one glaring example, Disney was perceived to be such a good corporate citizen that in 1965 the state of Florida essentially handed over to the private corporation all the rights and powers of an independent municipality to govern a land base twice the size of Manhattan. What has become Walt Disney World as we know it today functions much like a "state-within-a-state."[8]

There is little doubt that the Walt Disney Company was founded upon and forged in the crucible of free market capitalism, which coincided with the emergence of supporting ideologies such as American triumphalism, possessive individualism, and a growing faith in privatization over public management. And there is no doubt at all that Disney, like every other multinational corporation, has a major interest in seeking out new markets and securing lifetime consumers in already established markets. Making profits for shareholders, creating a market base that continues to buy, and shaping culture toward consumption, then, are its main corporate goals. This means promoting the twin ideas that Disney has attractive products to offer potential buyers and that consumption is a fundamental good, certainly on a personal level but also quite possibly on a societal level too. It is hardly surprising, then, that Disney, as a global media conglomerate, would capitalize on the mutual reinforcement made possible by blending major elements of its economic policies with its cultural products. The cycle of reinforcement allows those people exposed to the cultural products that ritualize and extol consumption to be shaped into lifelong consumers by identifying with products that affirm their everyday choices, practices, and goals as laudatory ones. But there is more. Disney's investment in negative globalization is also evident in its ongoing global efforts to replace public space with privately owned and administered spaces. The shrinking of those public spaces where norms are debated, values confronted, ideas negotiated, citizenship skills honed, and ideas lifted into the political and public realm makes it more difficult for individuals and social groups to fight the values and power of global corporations like Disney. Disney's global reach is tantamount to the opposite of democratization. It is an attempt to shrink the spaces in which democracy can emerge and moral responsibility can be practiced, substituting consumers for citizens and entertainment for the capacities of civic engagement.

The reality of globalization and Disney's status as a multinational media conglomerate seeking out new markets in non-Western countries together change the rules of the game as far as cultural imperialism is concerned. While there was a time, as Mark Phillips notes, when Disney simply offered global consumers repackaged versions of standardized products that had been designed and marketed in the United States,[9] the company now goes much further to customize its products. As Disney distributes its wares all over the globe and gains prominence through its theme parks in France, Japan, and China, it appears very willing to adapt its content to local contexts or even to become a distributor for indigenous content. For instance, in 2007 it coproduced with a state-run Chinese film company a Mandarin-language feature film, which appeared in English as *The Secret of the Magic Gourd*.[10] It also hired a Japanese animation house to adapt an American Disney Channel series based on the *Lilo and Stitch* film characters for Japanese television.[11] And it sponsored a dance competition in India in 2006 that involved hundreds of school-age kids developing their own choreography for the Hindi version of *High School Musical*.[12] Increasingly, Disney is recognizing that its brand name need not be synonymous with American values—or even Western values—but can function like a shell invested with various "localized content."[13] So *The Secret of the Magic Gourd* tells the story of an introverted boy who ends up rejecting the magic gourd's offer to make his dreams come true in favor of working hard with others to achieve a collective goal. This film seems to embody a level of respect for cultural differences that was not evident in Disney's own version of a Chinese legend, *Mulan* (1998), which Annalee Ward has aptly described as presenting "a conflicted version of Chinese culture, one that attempts to acknowledge the collectivist mind-set but in reality sets in within a Western idea of individualism."[14]

The key for Disney is to capitalize on positive perceptions of affluent U.S. culture — the American "'dreamworlds' of consumption, property, and power"[15] — while also making its products seem as universal as possible. On the one hand, for many nations around the world, U.S. brands are desirable because they are "symbols of wealth and modernity and freedom."[16] With more of their citizens able to participate in the global marketplace as consumers, countries like Japan and China measure their growing affluence based on their ability to attract foreign investment and foreign goods in the marketplace. On the other hand, too much specifically American culture spreading overseas becomes threatening to other nations' sense of autonomy and identity. So, for example, Disney's development of a theme park near Paris famously prompted one French critic to denounce Euro Disney as a "cultural Chernobyl" that was going to poison European traditions.[17] For Disney, as a purveyor of cultural goods, these very different modes of reception mean walking a fine line in how it markets its products overseas both as exotic foreign wares (that is, essentially American) and as the culturally sensitive efflorescence of a budding global village. According to Janet Wasko, "Brands based on media products, such as Disney, present far more overt and often more complex values and forms of signification."[18] The complexity of Disney cultural products is probably why they are so popular on a global scale and, at the same time, provoke so much resistance. The multivalent meanings and contradictions ascribed to Disney enable vastly different audiences and individuals to shape, recontextualize, and appropriate what Disney signifies in accordance with their own politics and desires. For Disney, the global megacorporation, the kind of meanings brought to bear on its offerings must be carefully considered in tandem with its marketing strategies, but the end goal is the same: whatever enhances its brand recognition and sells its products is good for business. While Disney is well aware of the need to treat different parts of the global order differently, aligning its own interests with the particularity of historical traditions, places, and cultures, this market-based attentiveness to context excludes any nonmarket rationality that promotes either values such as generosity and human solidarity or modes of cultural pedagogy that nurture politically empowering capacities central to individual and collective agency.

Disney appears more than willing to adapt its message in order to gain new markets, and the strategy works. For example, the Global Disney Audiences Project found that Disney's international reception across different cultures remains remarkably consistent and extraordinarily successful. The project, which conducted surveys of over 1,250 young adults in eighteen countries, discovered that Disney was ubiquitous across the globe: for instance, 98 percent of respondents had seen a Disney film.[19] A question asking respondents to describe Disney conjured up the following terms: fun, happiness, fantasy, imagination, and family.[20] As Janet Wasko and Eileen Meehan note, these associations—which suggest that people worldwide essentially either accept Disney's brand image at face value or have been so thoroughly submerged in Disney's "symbolic universe as [children]" that they rarely question its message—are so powerful that even those respondents who expressed dislike for Disney seldom offered alternatives for what Disney "means"; in fact, the utter lack of oppositional readings led the researchers to conclude that audiences were nothing if not "constrained" in the way they related to the Disney brand and its texts.[21] While this demonstrated a significant degree of homogeneity in terms of Disney's generic symbolism and the way its products are consumed, there was far less consensus on whether Disney should be viewed as uniquely American, Western, or universal in nature. Of course, this type of question would require the respondents to apply their own definition to each of the relevant terms, which have certainly become murky concepts (what is "American"? what is "Western"?) under the contemporary pressures of globalization. Unsurprisingly, then, there appeared to be a wide variation in perceptions of Disney's national or international status as a corporation as well as the national bias, or lack thereof, of its product content. Perhaps more interesting is the fact that the researchers discovered that both fans and critics of Disney managed to "compartmentalize" their awareness of Disney's business practices, such as excessive advertising, while not recognizing in Disney the merging of corporate culture, entertainment, and education. Disney, the corporate powerhouse at the center of the national entertainment state, remained conceptually distinct from Disney the benign purveyor of family-oriented entertainment.[22] In other words, most people happily participate in consuming Disney products despite occasionally vocalizing a marked ambivalence toward the corporation. Overall, the study suggested, according to Wasko, that "despite cultural and language differences and certain individualized product offerings, Disney had been amazingly successful in consistently communicating specific values" on a global scale.[23]

Disney's vigorous efforts to generate a coherent brand image and encapsulate its many products and services within the seductive symbolism of childhood innocence and wholesome family fun actually make Disney a particularly useful case for understanding corporate strategies in an increasingly globalized environment. At the same time as Disney represents nostalgia and tradition, it has become a global leader in transforming digital technologies into media platforms and developing a consumer-centered discourse that deflects criticism away from, while it softens, what can only be called boldly commercial self-promotion. In understanding Disney, it becomes possible to trace a shift away from the homogenizing and rationalizing orientation of All-American Fordist industrial models toward a post-Fordist global economy of immaterial production, affective labor, and emotion management. Disney is significant because, through decades of expansion, diversification, and integration since 1923, it has maintained control over and propagated a recognizable corporate identity that envelops all its products and activities, unlike other multinational corporations and media conglomerates that seem increasingly to fragment into niche markets as they cross national boundaries.

Alan Bryman maps out Disney's global strategies, using the corporation as a metaphor for shifting cultural and economic landscapes. The process Bryman calls "Disneyization" involves applying theme park design (itself based on cinematic narratives and the spectacular)[24] to everyday consumer habits and spaces such that variety and "a sense of the dramatic" work together to increase "the likelihood that the consumer will engage in other types of consumption."[25] Bryman focuses on four main principles that characterize Disneyization: theming, hybrid consumption, merchandising, and performative labor. Put together, these elements focus on "modes of delivery of goods and services," staging that delivery in a way that creates "an ambience of choice."[26] The application of these principles results in spaces and experiences that multiply the opportunities for consumption, seek to heighten the "inclination to consume," and offer the illusion of a "world of variety and choice in which the consumers reign supreme."[27] Bryman makes an important distinction between Disneyization and Disneyfication, in that the latter typically describes the reconfiguration of a cultural narrative, object, or space in accordance with Disney's own core values (such as childlike innocence and pleasure), while the former reflects larger, systematic changes to the underlying structures of cultural production and consumption within a commodified setting, of which Disney theme parks are one example. Extending Bryman's analysis further, it would seem that navigating a Disneyized space offers individuals the opportunity to customize their experiences within limits that are scripted by the designer but hidden from view, producing an effect not unlike surfing a heavily hyperlinked website. The Walt Disney Company announced in 2009 that it would be redesigning its chain of 340 Disney Stores to mirror a theme park design, thereby embodying the very principles Bryman has identified as Disneyization. The refurbishment, whose "goal is to make children clamor to visit the stores and stay longer," will cost approximately $1 million per store. Based on the prototype called Imagination Park, the renovated stores will be entirely networked with interactive technology to create a multisensory recreational experience that encourages consumer participation and emphasizes community through collective activities.[28] In this way, consumers can generate a narrative for their own consumption that makes them producers of meaning and grants them the capacity to customize their identities through the stories that are created around the objects and processes of consumption. Such power is not necessarily false, and it is undoubtedly seductive in a world of narrowing opportunities for agency and expression—perhaps even more so for children and youth for whom such opportunities are few and for whom the spectacular has not yet lost the appeal of novelty— but it cannot ultimately empower people beyond the overarching confines of being individual consumers.

There are several impacts of this new model that views social relations as primarily mediated and managed by consumption (with consumption turned into both the consuming of cultural products and a productive act in itself). And these impacts appear throughout society, in both local and global contexts, as we witness the "growing interpenetration of the economic and the cultural."[29] For instance, spaces that were once constructed through "forms of public culture," as noted by Sharon Zukin, now become privatized, controlled, and framed by corporate culture.[30] These spaces, from suburban shopping malls to tourist spots to city centers, encourage leisure while also "priming the young for consumerism."[31] Corporations like Disney try to provide "enhanced" experiences for an overworked, overeducated middle class that wants to maximize its leisure time. Disney accordingly not only presents "one of the best-known symbols of capitalist consumerism"[32] but also claims to offer consumers a stable, known quantity in its brand-name products. In this sense, Disney's corporate strategies are brilliant. Global corporate control involves the "production of subjectivity that is not fixed in identity but hybrid and modulating,"[33] only to sell consumers the illusion of fixity. In other words, the consistency presented by Disney culture acts as a temporary salve to growing feelings of uncertainty and insecurity produced by economic dislocations and social instability, while multinational corporations such as Disney are one of the globalizing forces largely responsible for the instabilities and upheavals facing the nation state. The sovereignty of national governments is increasingly challenged by the power of multinational corporations and the logic of the marketplace they embody; unemployment rises as jobs are filled by cheaper labor in regions such as Southeast Asia; governments are downsized and their services are privatized; social services and social security are gutted; corporations receive incentives in the form of huge tax breaks or bailouts with taxpayers' money; legislation is passed that further deregulates the market; and democratically elected governments fail in their responsibilities to foster a just and equal society. Given these conditions, it is no wonder that individuals find comfort in the stable meanings they can ascribe to Disney and turn to consumption for even the semblance of personal agency. But the consumption of cultural products by its very nature also elicits consumer demands for quality and depth, which require that Disney adapt to local conditions and cultures as it expands to markets outside the United States. For instance, scholars have argued persuasively that while Tokyo Disneyland is a physical replica of Walt Disney World, its corporate culture and offerings have been thoroughly "Japanized."[34] According to Jeremy Weber, capitalism adapts to local conditions in ways that secure its profit-making power: "The market does not simply obliterate all earlier traditions. It is opportunistic. It will enhance and concentrate on those features of a society which turn a profit or change them in such a way that they will make money."[35] Consequently, everything potentially becomes a commodity, including, and perhaps most especially, identity. Global capitalism manages and controls diversity by commodifying and selling different identity positions, while also encouraging self-commodification (particularly of youth) through various marketing trends and technological means, such as online virtual worlds.[36]

At the same time, access to the consumer panacea is limited to those who can afford to pay for it. Those people who do not represent profit for corporations become losers in a global game in which the corporations themselves act as the referees. Multinational corporations move "beyond and above the traditional boundaries of nation-states,"[37] exerting exploitative control over the poor and unemployed in developing countries who work in their factories for poverty wages in unsafe conditions, while disenfranchising anyone else who cannot freely exercise a "right to consume." The consequence is a redefinition of citizenship on the global scale in the oxymoronic form of a personal autonomy that is utterly dependent on the exclusionary capacity to consume. Bryman makes this point very clearly: "From the position of Disneyization, it is not just that the poor are flawed consumers that is striking, but that they are *limited citizens*. Their ability to enter the temples of Disneyization is limited not just by their capacity to purchase its offerings but also because they are heavily guarded and under surveillance."[38] Unfortunately, the only real winners in this global game are the corporations and the handful of technocrats who form the corporate elite. The concept of social justice becomes utterly bankrupt under the oligarchic rule of a single world market by corporate giants who feed upon a starving citizenry. Under these conditions, civil society and every other public sphere that serves as an "open terrain of political exchange and participation" are stealthily and systematically dismantled. This trend is advanced the furthest by those culture industries that produce and regulate public opinion and discourse. Disney is leading the worldwide transformation of civic culture into a "spectacle [that] destroys any collective form of sociality—individualizing social actors in their separate automobiles and in front of their separate video screens—and at the same time imposes a new mass sociality, a new uniformity of action and thought."[39] Multinational corporations such as Disney have become "the aristocratic articulations" of a global monopoly of power and coercion that is imposed from above and that achieves control through circuits that do not reveal themselves because they operate on the "terrain of the production and regulation of subjectivity" itself[40]—that is, in the realm of cultural production and consumption.

Walt Disney was making a joke when he declared himself "king" of Disneyland, but his statement makes visible the fundamentally antidemocratic nature of corporate power. A king is vested with the power to rule independently of his subjects. But a smart king also recognizes that happy subjects are a boon to his ongoing power and to the royal coffers. Disney was right to recognize that real power did not lie in the hands of elected public officials. He was prescient of the fact that someday the authority of "senators" and "governors" would wane and that a new sovereign power would emerge. But Disney was wrong when he suggested that a human being would be at the center of this new social order. It is the global market led by multinational corporations that is now sovereign and autonomous. With the demise of democracy, citizens are no longer political agents actively involved in the collective governance of the nation. There was a time when elected officials promised to uphold the public interests of their constituents, but today's corporate state exists for one end only: to generate profits for shareholders. As Sheldon Wolin points out, genuine democratic ideals have been supplanted by a notion of "'shareholder democracy' that gives a 'sense of participation' without demands or responsibilities."[41] All of this means that Disney culture—even its most "corporatized" elements—might seem nonpartisan on the surface, but the market logic and the material reality underlying its global authority and economic force are not. They have very real political consequences, despite the company's appearance of disinterest in affairs of state and civil society. The ultimate corporate goal is to achieve a profit-driven monopoly that wrests power away from individuals and public bodies. Although the political outcome is authoritarianism, politicians and public officials in developed countries around the world increasingly implement policies in the name of "neoliberalism" or free-market fundamentalism that basically subscribe to an ideological belief in unchecked corporate power.[42]

As Disney expands globally, the contradictions between its brand image and its corporate policies emerge more clearly and open up new opportunities for resistance to its power. As Jeremy Seabrook points out, "Despite the rigid neoliberal economic orthodoxy now established globally, a great variety of cultural forms remain."[43] This has become particularly evident in China, a country embedded with socialist principles, where Disney is aggressively attempting to expand its market and where it also depends on up to nine thousand factories to make the consumer products that are distributed worldwide.[44] If Disney on U.S. soil has managed to keep from public view the exploitative practices through which it pays pennies to an impoverished Chinese garment worker to make a T-shirt that sells for US$20, it will have a much harder time marketing Hong Kong Disneyland or the projected Shanghai Disneyland to Chinese consumers whose critical acuity has been trained to identify capitalist exploitation and who are much closer to witnessing the real conditions under which producers of Disney goods actually work, however well concealed. The fact that Disney has come under greater scrutiny for its labor, environmental, and cultural policies and practices is evident in the company's first-time publication in March 2008 of a "Corporate Responsibility Report" that argues Disney is making strides toward becoming a better "corporate citizen."[45] It is also true that individuals are forging alternative identities in relation to the global commercial media, while antiglobalization movements are making visible the ways in which global markets display values antithetical to democracy.[46] The Campaign for a Commercial-Free Childhood in the United States started an educational movement to teach parents, educators, and others the social and personal costs of tolerating the commercialization of children's culture.[47] In 2009, China Labor Watch (CLW) mobilized in the wake of news of the tragic death of an underage worker in a Disney factory and launched a letter-writing campaign calling on Disney to work with the factory to monitor and remediate the use of child labor and unsafe working conditions, instead of simply moving its business to another factory in its expansive supply chain.[48] Examples like these might compel us to ask again an incisive question first posed by Janet Wasko and Eileen Meehan: "Could the contradictions of capitalism ultimately unravel on a matter as simple as Disney's exploitation of children?"[49]

Getting beyond Disney means viewing children as an important social investment and recognizing how commercial values have numbed the public's ability to sense the danger such values present to children.

It also means viewing democracy as a process that involves every member of society striving toward a collective existence that is more equal and more just, rather than reducing it to simply a label defined by its difference from more overtly authoritarian forms of government. And democracy certainly does not reside in a fantasy world of consumption in which pixie dust and mass entertainment merely cover up an utterly impoverished experience devoid of social meaning and purposeful significance. A number of important issues must be addressed as part of the larger struggle of mounting opposition to megacorporations such as Disney. First, democracy and democratization must be separated from a market-driven society. Democracy is not capitalism, and Disney is not the apogee of democratization. Corporate power is the enemy of democracy and must be acknowledged as such. Corporations are not elected; yet, increasingly they have the cultural and material power to shape the lives of millions of people around the world. The power of such corporations must be limited and regulated, and this task demands a new understanding of governance, resistance, and politics—what Peter Marcuse calls a "restructuring of global institutions and regulations . . . [either] eliminating global institutions entirely or replacing them with a completely different system of relations, both economic and political, within nation-states and among them."[50] Second, it is crucial to recognize that fighting the social exploitation produced by corporations such as Disney is important but not enough. We need to understand how such corporations produce particular identities, desires, needs, and modes of consent. In other words, we must be attentive to their meaning-making pedagogies as they work and circulate through diverse technologies and sites. Public pedagogy provides the supportive culture for Disney to inculcate its values, turn children into consumers, and hide its ruthless expansion of corporate power behind its stylized claim to innocence. The spread of global markets and consumer values would be impossible without the power and reach of Disney's cultural apparatuses and multiple teaching machines. Third, it must be clear that technological development and negative globalization are not the same thing. The globalization of power by corporations such as Disney is not synonymous with the development of new media technologies. In fact, these technological developments should be harnessed for progressive purposes and used in ways that undermine the economic and pedagogical power of Disney and other megacorporations. As the June 2009 political uprisings in Iran illustrated, new electronic technologies and the popular social-networking sites they have produced have transformed the global landscape of media production and reception as well as the ability of oppressive state power to define the boundaries of what constitutes the very nature of political engagement. The key issue here is to push democratization and all of the conditions that support it as part of a broader struggle against the forces of negative globalization. The use of digital media, particularly the Internet, can mount a serious challenge to both repressive state practices and the power of corporations to commodify everything in their path.

We should expect more from our lives than submission to existing structures of power, and we should demand more for the sake of the next generation of young people who have to live in the world we have created. The following sections provide three different contexts for understanding and challenging the Disney empire as a particular embodiment of globalizing capital. They begin at the top with Disney's corporate leadership and end with an account of grassroots protests against Disney's principles and practices. The discussion of Disney's corporate culture and its role in fostering a global corporate elite is followed by a look at the ways in which Disney theme parks in global contexts become limited sites of appropriation that suggest nevertheless how consumption provides some room for contesting dominant cultural meanings. Finally, this chapter considers modes of resistance initiated by various activist organizations that not only foreground the new media and its centrality to democracy but also open up new and hopeful possibilities for revitalizing democratic participation in a globalized world.

GLOBALIZING CAPITAL AND THE TRANSFORMATION OF DISNEY'S CORPORATE CULTURE

> It doesn't matter whether it comes in by cable, telephone lines, computer, or satellite. Everyone's going to have to deal with Disney.
>
> —former Disney chairman and CEO, Michael Eisner

With the 2007 release of *Pirates of the Caribbean: At World's End*, Disney knew it was promoting the most expensive film ever made (estimated at $300 million), but it may not have known that the screenwriters had created a fable of our time. The film was the third installment in a series of blockbusters that provided the backstory for a Disney theme park attraction, and this one displayed a decisively more political edge. The film opens with Lord Cutler Beckett, head of the East India Company, declaring a "state of emergency" that not only suspends the legal rights of the colonists but allows for the immediate execution, without benefit of habeas corpus, legal counsel, or trial, of all those deemed to be pirates or their associates—including, apparently, the mere child who is the camera's focus. The bizarrely anachronistic nature of the film's opening seems to link eighteenth-century British imperialism to George W. Bush's "war on terror" and the arbitrary way in which U.S. laws were applied and manipulated and international law was disregarded under his leadership. Unfortunately, this reading is not sustained through the rest of the film. Yet, the initial subversive message is clear enough: the pirates facing the gallows are symbols of those deemed "terrorists," including children, whose rights have been suspended and who have been persecuted and even tortured by a vengeful, imperialist U.S. government in the aftermath of September 11, 2001.[51] In the film, Beckett defends his genocidal vendetta against the pirates, as well as his dishonor and betrayal, with the refrain "It's just good business," revealing the imbrication of politics and economics in the era of global capitalism. In fact, the pirate ship, as a free-floating entity not tied to any national territory, becomes a perfect symbol for the transport and flow of multinational corporate capital in a postindustrial world, signaling the obsolescence of the car as the central signifier of a past American industrial era.

Although we can read the film's opening in this radical way, the remainder of the plot unfolds as conventional Disney fare, conveying slightly modified versions of pro-American nostalgia and the celebration of entrepreneurial capitalism. Throughout the film, the head of the British East India Company is represented less as a corrupted defender of the empire against renegade pirates than as a type of 1980s corporate raider. According to Beckett in the second *Pirates* film, small-scale entrepreneurs of the likes of Jack Sparrow are "a dying breed. The world is shrinking; the blank edges of the map filled in." Beckett's pathological desire to assume control of all the world's resources is underscored by his use of thug mercenaries and his wanton destruction of nature (he orders his minions to destroy a sea monster, the last of its kind). Because Beckett is a figure of the "Old World" and the only character who speaks with a formal British accent, all the negative associations of monopoly capitalism become projected onto this stereotypical antagonist of American "freedom," now embodied by the clever, comical, honorable, even multicultural pirates. This representation of the "British as the 'old masters' and British influence as an unjust yoke to be thrown off is deeply ingrained in American cultural history."[52] Despite the topical allusions of the film's opening, rapacious imperialism ultimately becomes projected onto the distant past, far from the boardrooms of today's multinational corporations. The pirates are represented in an equally unambiguous light. With the exception of Sao Feng, pirate lord of the South China Sea—the only character other than Beckett to use the phrase "good business," thereby linking him to the evil empire[53]—all the pirates appear as heroic freedom fighters who represent the "everyman" exploited by greedy imperialists, exhibit an entrepreneurial spirit, respect each other's autonomous territories, and have a legislative council that upholds the "pirate code." One pirate even uses diplomacy before resorting to trickery to release the sea (another symbol of nature) from the bounds imposed by humans, stating, "Better were the days when mastery of seas came not from bargains struck . . . but from the sweat of a man's brow and the strength of his back alone." If the film can avoid implicating corporate Disney while it shows the corruption of legitimate authority in its zeal to monopolize power and property, it also shows the virtue of small-scale capitalist enterprise. That a Disney film boldly attacks the principles underlying a profit-driven monopoly—granted one that is suitably distanced through its projection back into eighteenth-century Britain—is yet another sign of the effectiveness of Disney's branding strategy. Disney perennially appeals to the rags-to-riches tale of Old Walt arriving in California with nothing but his suitcase and building from the ground up a small animation studio, conquering as David did Goliath all his giant Hollywood competitors. In fact, such a narrative about Disney as a smallish, family-oriented business was used very effectively to oust Michael Eisner, Disney CEO and chairman from 1984 to 2005, who was demonized as a money-grubbing, rapacious bean counter whose policies had destroyed the "soul" of the Walt Disney Company.

When Eisner took the helm of Disney in 1984, the company was clearly floundering. It had narrowly escaped a takeover by corporate raiders. Initially, Eisner was deemed an apt heir to Walt's crown. He put in place an aggressive expansion plan that within a decade turned the animation studio with two theme parks and a market capitalization of $1.8 billion into a $57 billion massive media conglomerate and real estate developer with extensive holdings in the United States and around the world.[54] Eisner's management policies, his attentiveness to making Disney profitable, and his brash arrogance were viewed as strengths—at least in the 1980s, which witnessed the emergence of celebrity CEOs like Donald Trump and an ethos of cutthroat corporatism, captured in films like Oliver Stone's *Wall Street* (1987). In this sense, Eisner and his "raw corporatism" were products of his time.[55] Under his reign, several new animated films became huge box office hits, which, together with the new trend in home video releases, made Disney a household name. But a series of well-publicized problems surfaced between Eisner, other top Disney executives (in one instance generating a lawsuit that cost the company $280 million), and members of the board, all of which James B. Stewart documents meticulously in *Disney War*.[56] Dissent within the ranks led to a well-organized public campaign against Eisner, led by none other than Roy E. Disney, Walt Disney's nephew, and another ex–board member, Stanley Gold. They launched a website called SaveDisney.com and posted blogs that encouraged shareholders to reject Eisner's leadership. Eisner had developed a reputation as a tyrant with a penchant for micromanagement, bottom-line downsizing of Disney's creative divisions, stacking the board with pliable supporters, and increasing his own yearly remuneration. In the last instance, Eisner had collected $575 million in executive pay in 1997 (a $750,000 salary, a $9.9 million bonus, and $565 million worth of stock options).[57] He then published a memoir titled *Work in Progress* in 1998, while Disney stock was plummeting. By 1999, Disney's profits had fallen by more than one-third and continued to do so through to 2002.[58] Eisner faced increasing criticism, being variously figured as the "Louse in the Mouse House"; Snow White's eighth dwarf, Greedy; and Lord Farquaad in the rival DreamWorks's animated production, *Shrek* (2001).[59] In true Disney fashion, a story was published on SaveDisney. com that turned Eisner into an "evil ogre" who had usurped generous King Walt's kingdom and engaged in "looting, pillaging, outsourcing, and the constructing of 'great, gaudy, dreadful structures with tacky, garish facades.'"[60] According to one former Disney employee, Old

Walt was a real innovator, while Eisner was simply a pretend "emperor who has no clothes."[61] At the company's annual meeting in May 2004, 43 percent of the shareholders voted against Eisner's reelection to the board. He was subsequently stripped of his title as chairman but remained CEO until September 2005. Disney shareholders had staged a mutiny that was deemed a historic victory, "unprecedented . . . in the annals of American business."[62]

Thousands of people with a stake in Disney had spoken when the company's board, as well as government and other regulatory bodies, failed to exert their influence by forcing Eisner to follow the proper procedures of corporate governance. A series of scandals would soon unfold surrounding Disney under Eisner's leadership. First, the publication of Stewart's *Disney Wars* exposed further instances of mismanagement, which the board failed to address. When Eisner did not immediately step down as CEO and then suggested he would run for chairman of the board when his term as CEO had ended, Roy Disney and Stanley Gold launched a lawsuit against the Disney board, asserting that it had lied to shareholders when it promised to conduct a global search for a CEO to replace Eisner instead of just installing Eisner's own handpicked successor, Robert Iger. The court did not dismiss the suit, and the resulting pressure was finally great enough to force Eisner out. Eisner responded quickly by having the board appoint Iger as CEO (a year before Eisner's expected retirement), and Iger then diplomatically settled the suit by hiring Roy Disney as a consultant and conferring on him the title of director emeritus.[63] In 2004, a second revelation was made when the Securities and Exchange Commission charged Disney with failing to disclose to shareholders certain relationships between the company and the board of directors during the period from 1999 to 2001, such as the fact that Disney employed three children of members of the board. According to the commission, lack of disclosure impeded "shareholders' ability to evaluate the objectivity and independence of directors."[64] In fact, the picture that emerged from various legal and corporate accounts of Disney under Eisner's management shows not only a culture of cronyism, backroom dealing, and kickbacks for compliance but the "abject failure of the Disney board" as the checks and balances mechanism within corporate governance.[65] Finally, in June 2006, the Delaware Supreme Court passed its ruling on a ten-year class action suit led by shareholders that had charged Disney's board of directors with wasting company assets and failing in its fiduciary duty (specifically by complying with Eisner's decision to act without its authorization in the hiring and firing of his long-time friend Michael Ovitz as company president—the result for Ovitz was "one of the most excessive employment contracts in the history of corporate America," which ended up costing the company over $130 million).[66] Although the court ruled that the directors of the Walt Disney Company had not breached their fiduciary duties, the court's recorded opinion was that the case had "clarified how ornamental, passive directors contribute to sycophantic tendencies among directors and how imperial CEOs can exploit this condition for their own benefit, especially in the executive compensation and severance areas." Sadly, the court's decision merely affirmed "the long-held rule that directors enjoy wide insulation for liability for most decisions, regardless of defects in the process by which those decisions are made,"[67] suggesting in larger terms a profound failure of U.S. corporate law to ensure effective corporate governance when a company's directors act in bad faith. But the court did state unequivocally that Disney's boardroom culture had been "unwholesome," a damaging description to say the least for a company that gains its earnings from the family-entertainment business.[68]

Indeed, Disney's own public relations image with its appeal to Middle America's moral standards provided the language for shareholders to launch their campaign against Eisner and fight for corporate accountability. Because of the company's unique position as a purveyor of wholesome family entertainment, the company's own public relations imagery became the basis for shareholders to demand that it live up to its promises. While the shareholders as owners of the company certainly had a stake in making their investments profitable, the basis on which the anti-Eisner campaign flourished was the sudden realization that Disney in reality was nothing like the fantasy world of truth, virtue, and happiness on which it relied to market its products. It is impossible to determine whether the shareholders actually believed in the "magic" of Disney, but they used Disney's own corporate rhetoric as the basis for demanding corporate accountability. In so doing, they brought to the foreground of public perception the contradiction at the heart of the Disney's dual identity as a profit-seeking megacorporation and the moral center of American popular culture. The corporate reforms achieved were significant but limited by the very nature of the campaign. After all, the protest against Eisner centered on a personality cult around the company's originating figure, Walt Disney himself. Eisner's actions provoked the sentiment that he was "the latest in a series of pretenders to the throne that Walt had occupied."[69] According to Mark Phillips, global public perception of Disney in the 1990s was that its creative essence and moral goodness remained intertwined with the paternalistic figure of "Uncle Walt," while "business practices [were] not associated with Walt but instead [were] ascribed to Michael Eisner and the [then] current Disney corporate team."[70] This means that the shareholders' revolt judged its success solely by its ability to get rid of Eisner, whose removal in turn would fully restore the company's integrity. Eisner became in this sense the scapegoat for a conservative movement seeking to purge the company of unscrupulous corporate values in an effort to return to the mythical values that originated with, and were first embodied by, Walt Disney. Of course, it makes sense from the investors' point of view that they did not take their critique of the corporate side of Disney any farther than seeking to oust Eisner, as they hardly wanted to undermine the company's credibility. At the same time, they did not want to return to the small-scale and ailing operation Disney had been before Eisner became CEO. And Eisner was seen as not only greedy but cheap. In 2002, Eisner announced a cost-cutting strategy that would focus on making film sequels and knock-off television programs instead of investing in new projects.[71] In this way, the shareholders certainly had better long-term foresight than Eisner, whose demeaning treatment of the company's creative contributors and alienation of Pixar and Steve Jobs would have probably left Disney with only second-rate programming. In terms of the investors' interest in the future success of Disney, it was much better to represent themselves as loyal Disney fans who had been betrayed by a rogue individual (much like *Pirates of the Caribbean*'s Lord Cutler Beckett), an individual who had not only bit off more than he could chew in trying single-handedly to manage a growing multinational media conglomerate but was also gnawing away at the hand that fed him.

Considered from a larger perspective, the fall of Michael Eisner represents much more than a symptom of the growing pains of Disney's transformation into a multimedia megacorporation. It reveals worldwide cultural, political, and economic changes that have occurred as an effect of negative globalization and the widespread acceptance of neoliberal ideology. Fundamental to the construction of the neoliberal subject is the acceptance of this official set of orthodoxies: the public sphere, if not the very notion of the social, is a pathology; consumerism is the most important obligation of citizenship; freedom is an utterly privatized affair that legitimates the primacy of property rights over public priorities; the social state is bad; all public difficulties are individually determined; and all social problems, now individualized, can be redressed by private solutions. The undermining of social solidarities and collective structures, along with the collapsing of public issues into private concerns, is one of the most damning elements of neoliberal rationality. Zygmunt Bauman elucidates this issue in the following comment:

> In our "society of individuals" all the messes into which one can get are assumed to be self-made and all the hot water into which one can fall is proclaimed to have been boiled by the hapless failures [of those] who have fallen into it. For the good and the bad that fill one's life a person has only himself or herself to thank or to blame. And the way the "whole life-story" is told raises this assumption to the rank of an axiom.[72]

Defined largely by "the exaggerated and quite irrational belief in the ability of markets to solve all problems,"[73] the public domain is emptied of the democratic ideals, discourses, and identities needed to address important considerations such as universal health care, ecologically responsible mass transit, affordable housing with ethical lending practices, subsidized care for the young and elderly, and government efforts to reduce carbon emissions and invest in new forms of energy. As safety nets and social services are hollowed out and communities crumble and give way to individualized, one-man archipelagos, it is increasingly difficult to develop social movements that can act in concert to effect policies to meet the basic needs of citizens and to maintain the social investments needed to provide life-sustaining services.

The Disney shareholders organized a collective protest against Eisner that essentially drew attention to his corporate mismanagement. But the protest was limited because it was based on the hyperindividualized corporate mentality for which it was criticizing Eisner himself. In their protest against Eisner, the Disney shareholders missed the fact that replacing the CEO—admittedly one whose bold leadership style and emphasis on merchandising and branding had "exposed the profit-driven underbelly of Disney's 'magic'"—was not going to change the reality that Disney was no longer "untainted by the sordidness of brand capitalism."[74] Disney was a corporate leviathan whose power and relative autonomy exceeded the grasp of any single individual and would function in the same structural ways regardless of what kind of rhetoric or personal style the person in charge used. The events surrounding Disney in 2004 can teach us about the limitations of resistance within a corporate framework, while Eisner's blatant disregard for the already minimal regulations imposed on corporate management carries with it another very important lesson. Eisner's actions, whether driven by personal hubris or not, reveal the brutal nature of corporate power and the latitude it enjoys within an increasingly unregulated global setting. Eisner made quite clear the truth underlying corporate propaganda: as Chris Hedges writes, "Corporatism is about crushing the capacities for moral choice."[75] If *Pirates of the Caribbean: At World's End* was a coded critique of megalomaniacal CEOs and an affirmation of a loose collaboration of privateers as the ideal business model, then the fact still remains that corporations do not function at all like Disney's pirates but instead like real historical pirates: they seek to operate outside the law, they avoid oversight by moving outside territorial jurisdictions, their only moral imperative is profit, they pillage and extract resources wherever they find them, and they readily resort to coercion to achieve their ends.

A "free market" should never be equated with justice or democracy. Corporations are not democratic entities: they are hierarchical, they rule according to economic principles that benefit shareholders, and they only care about public dissent when it might deter consumers. Eisner made grotesque sums of money from 1995 to 2000, to be sure, but he was not alone. The average CEO compensation in 2001 was $38 million.[76] In 2005, "average CEO pay was 369 times that of the average worker, compared with 131 times in 1993 and 36 times in 1976."[77] The result, as Peter Dreier observes, is massive disparities in wealth across society: "At the pinnacle of America's economic pyramid, the nation's 400 billionaires own 1.25 trillion dollars in total net worth—the same amount as the 56 million American families at the bottom half of wealth distribution."[78] As many Americans face the pressures of higher mortgage rates, soaring college tuition, galloping health-care costs, and bleak possibilities for retirement savings, their quality of life plummets, while corporate welfare and executive compensation go through the roof. Corporate capitalism over the past thirty years has created an exclusive club of global billionaires whose collective income, explains Zygmunt Bauman, "equals the combined incomes of [the planet's] 2.3 billion poorest people (45 percent of the world's population)."[79] In the United States, the gross inequalities produced by a government that sells out to corporate lobbyists and embraces neoliberal principles in its policy formation can be seen in the growing concentration of wealth among the richest groups, which has given rise to a gap between the rich and the poor unlike anything replicated since the 1920s.[80] Of course, there is more at stake here than the emergence of a new class of rich tycoons, a decadent materialism, and an instrumentalized worldview in which the future can only be measured by immediate financial gains. There is also the growing threat to the planet as democracy is largely redefined in the interests of corporate values and profits. It is clear that corporate wealth translates into political and economic power for the rich and impoverishment for everyone else. Government policies are made into laws that benefit the rich through tax subsidies and legal protections, while undercutting, underfunding, and eliminating social protections aimed to help the poor, aged, and sick, including children. And yet, even as the public sentiment turns against these excesses at a time of financial turmoil following the economic crisis of 2008 and a few of these CEOs get vilified in the press, little is said about the fundamentally antidemocratic tendencies and corrupt practices underlying corporate politics. It is not enough simply to challenge "this bonus payment or that bailout [when] the pernicious superstructure of the corporate state itself" remains unchallenged.[81]

Indeed, Disney under Robert Iger's leadership is not actually charting a new course so much as amplifying its efforts to commercialize its products, utilize new technologies, and "leverage its brand" in international markets, reaping profits to such a degree that Michael Eisner begins to look small-time. For example, the company's corporate speak refers to the "Disney Difference. . . . Our portfolio of Disney businesses combine to create a highly effective marketing engine that helps increase revenue while affording numerous efficiencies."[82] The Pirates of the Caribbean franchise, for instance, not only promotes the theme parks, films, reams of merchandise, video games, and a virtual world but probably also helps to sell tickets for Disney's two cruise ships, which make stops at Disney's private Caribbean island, Castaway Cay. And, of course, Disney, like many other twenty-first-century corporations, now realizes that consumers and their ever-expanding social networks have become the most effective marketing device. When the ships land at a port and satisfied guests disembark to tour the city, they become walking advertisements for Disney in a number of locations that Disney might not otherwise receive high visibility. But whereas brash showman Eisner exuded confidence in Disney to the point of rupturing the pixie-dust illusion, "cool-headed" Iger goes for the soft sell, staying out of the limelight and using a consumer-centered discourse typical of the next generation of affirmational advertising.[83] This more flexible, "collaborative" approach relies heavily on market research and understands the benefit of flattering the egos of savvy consumers, particularly in the marketing of popular culture, which no one needs but will want because each consumer can use the symbolic investments in Disney products to construct him- or herself as a unique "brand."[84] Iger expressed this new consumer-oriented discourse perfectly when he stated, "Consumers have a lot more authority these days and they know that by using technology they can gain access to content and they want to use the power they have. . . . We can't stand in the way and we can't allow tradition to stand in the way of where the consumer can go or wants to go."[85] In other words, Disney is not going to compensate for what people lack or unilaterally "make dreams come true"; instead, it will help enterprising consumers be who they want to be by providing socially recognizable modes through which they can maximize their own creativity. What makes this "flexible" approach so effective in a marketplace flooded with cynicism is that it appeals to consumers' sense of entitlement and egoistic self-indulgence, while it makes the consumer appear all-powerful. Disney, conversely, appears to abstain from dictating the meaning of its products to consumers, who can now figuratively and literally generate their own content. This is evident in the fact that Disney under Eisner may have jealously guarded intellectual property rights and pursued even the most minor infringement, but the company now tolerates YouTube postings called "mashups" that add new soundtrack music to snippets from Disney films.[86] The new "hip" Disney seems almost to be applauding the creative ingenuity of Internet pirates as incentive for its imagineers to find a way to provide innovative content more quickly and cheaply. Disney's expansion into virtual space, much like the physical space of Walt Disney World, becomes a "kind of spatial analogy of monopoly capitalism that incessantly produces rhetoric about free enterprise."[87] Iger's approach also acknowledges a global shift away from grounding products and corporate identities in nationalist discourses. When others speak of shrinking their carbon footprint, Disney proclaims that it "continues to make great strides toward broadening its global footprint."[88] Of course, this benign, humanizing image reveals how cleverly Disney's new corporate philosophy appropriates language from progressive social movements in order to conceal the tremendous efforts exerted and dollars spent by the corporation in order to influence consumers, both in the media and in the boardroom. Through this distorted lens, globalizing corporations do not exploit and deplete resources, stomping on and crushing everything in their path, but merely go on an adventurous trek across the planet. What becomes evident when examining Disney's corporate culture is the way in which cultural content, such as the films it makes and the corporate language it uses, legitimates its economic practices, though in an oblique rather than a directly propagandistic way. Disney is breaking down cultural and economic barriers; yet, as its privateers seek out new markets from which to profit, it is quickly discovering that even the most extensive corporate planning cannot fully anticipate what will emerge when an iconic American dreamworld like Disneyland is transplanted into new contexts.

IT'S A SMALL WORLD: DISNEY THEME PARKS GO GLOBAL

> From a cultural perspective, we don't believe that the world is flat. Disney executives on the ground are creative, not just distribution executives.
>
> —Disney President and CEO Robert Iger[89]

In the wake of the onset of economic recession in the United States in 2008, when attendance at Disney's American theme parks was on the decline, Disney decided to focus more aggressively on developing its overseas markets. But the above statement by Robert Iger about Disney's perception of global culture being "not flat" is curiously ambiguous. It seems to communicate a recognition of cultural diversity that cannot simply be run over roughshod, such that Disney must be "creative" about selling its content outside the United States. At the same time, the historical allusion positions the company as having fully modernized its approach to global culture—much like the Renaissance explorers who embraced the new technologies of navigation and sailed out on journeys around the world, despite the superstitious warnings that they might fall off the edge of a "flat" planet. Of course, this metaphorical connection to a cosmopolitan past most notable for its "discovery" of the New World carries the taint of economic imperialism: Disney may be more sensitive to other cultures, but the bottom line is that it is more profitable to send a creative team into the field instead of trying to envision products that might sell in India, Russia, and China while sitting at an office desk in California. Iger's statement, while admitting that diversity poses a challenge that requires adaptation by Disney (a novel recognition for the habitually conservative corporation) carries the implication that such diversity is a resource that can be immensely lucrative when well researched, managed, and relentlessly commodified.

As far back as 1982, Disney's EPCOT Center's World Showcase attempted to tame "the specter of cultural and economic globalization" by offering guests an innocuous simulation of cultural exchange that merely encouraged further insularity rather than tolerance of cultural difference.[90] According to Elayne Rapping, the It's a Small World attraction embodies Disney's version of a globalized world: "Cultures are gobbled up, reproduced as Disney images, and put up for sale to those who cannot afford to visit the real locales or be trusted to look squarely in the face of the real people who live there. No one yells or spray paints 'Yankee go home' at Epcot." Disney the corporation would not be quite so protected from hostile encounters in its overseas ventures, particularly in Europe. The company evidently had much to learn about the reality of cultural appropriation and exchange when it embarked on developing its theme parks in France, Tokyo, and Hong Kong. The missteps taken by Disney in the past twenty-five years in its eagerness to stretch its influence across a global market are informative. Disney's investments in theme parks outside the United States have not actually been huge financial successes for the company for reasons as different as cultural clashes with the local population, limited ownership by Disney, and disputes over infrastructure development. It might seem counterintuitive that the cultural issues would be the greatest in the case of the western European theme park, which opened outside Paris in 1992. But if Michael Eisner became the poster boy in the 1990s for CEOs blinded by arrogance and greed, turning Disney into a much maligned symbol of corporate mismanagement, then the reputation of Euro Disney (now named Disneyland Paris) fared little better as it became the touchstone for criticisms of American arrogance, on the one hand, and cultural imperialism, on the other. Disney learned one of its hardest lessons about the need to adapt to local conditions from its experiences with Euro Disney, which was $2 billion in debt as of 2005.[91]

In the bigger picture, Euro Disney actually represents the culmination of a series of costly land-development debacles that had embroiled the Walt Disney Company since the mid-1980s. One typical example displays Disney's arrogance in its dealings with the city of Seattle. Disney planners were hired to redesign its civic center. Stacy Warren documents how Disney trivialized public input and then proposed that the city put up a fence and charge an admission fee for entrance to the public space. This Disney plan was rejected, but for those involved it symbolized "the true private and exclusionary nature of Disney's so-called public-planning venture."[92] The negotiations with Seattle appeared typical of the company's approach to urban planning as "an efficient and ruthless enterprise" that colonized public spaces by taking them "out of local hands" and imposing "pan-national Disney cultural economies on local ones."[93] A similar fear of Disney's inevitable degradation of local culture was expressed by French intellectuals who denounced the Euro Disney development as a barely disguised vehicle of vulgar American imperialism that would "bombard France with uprooted creations that are to culture what fast food is to gastronomy."[94] It probably did not help matters when Michael Eisner tried to appease the park's critics by saying that Disney culture was "European folklore with a Kansas twist."[95] While the negative implications of Eisner's statement were clearly lost on him, Europeans seemed well aware that "crafty revisions of the literature, history, and religion of particular cultures [are] not only one of the realities of colonial expansion but a Disney trademark."[96] Touting Americanized versions of European traditions went side by side with Disney's public relations efforts to praise French cuisine, but to little avail. Critics from the outset lamented the aesthetic principles on which Disney theme parks are built: one particularly vituperative French journalist referred to Euro Disney as "a horror made of cardboard, plastic, and appalling colors, a construction of hardened chewing gum and idiotic folklore taken straight out of comic books written for obese Americans."[97] And while the most trenchant criticisms drew attention to the issue of cultural imperialism as well as aesthetics (with hardly disguised elitist and anti-American overtones), most of the public views missed entirely the fact that selling America only entered the minds of investors so long as America was saleable in foreign markets. As Andrew Lainsbury asserts, "Imperialism can no longer be viewed as a uniquely 'American' strategy: it has become a global *corporate* phenomenon."[98] The days when Disney viewed itself as a noble emissary of American patriotic fervor are now long gone: global Disney is about promoting market values and can only be said to promote American values where the latter happen to overlap with the former.

Early on, several controversies involving the management of Euro Disney plagued Disney and seemed to legitimate the French media's accusations of cultural insensitivity. Indeed, it appeared as if the company "did not bother to research the habits of French people" but simply assumed "that foreigners should have to adjust to its standards."[99] Disney had initially hired American executives to manage the park, twenty-three of whom would eventually be replaced by European nationals. When the park opened, alcohol was banned in keeping with the American "family-friendly" parks, but this ran contrary to the French custom of having wine with meals. Disney relented on the issue of serving alcohol after incurring a $34 million loss in the first six months of operation.[100] Disney also imposed its standard strict dress code for employees that banned facial hair and prescribed "limited use" of personal makeup, which provoked the protestations of French labor unions as well as hundreds of resignations on the part of Euro Disney's workforce, who argued that Disney's code was a violation of personal liberty and even "human dignity."[101] Local perceptions that Disney was focused only on American business interests were not helped by the theme park's original name, Euro Disney, which for citizens of the European Union naturally evoked connotations related to money. Eisner explained, "As Americans, we had believed that the word 'Euro' in front of Disney was glamorous and exciting. For Europeans, it turned out to be a term they associated with business, currency, and commerce."[102] The park's name was officially changed to Disneyland

Paris in October 1994. Although Disney made repeated adjustments to
the American park model, such as attempting to shorten queue lines in
deference to European cultural norms, its actions did not seem to go
far enough to dispel French suspicions that what had been grafted onto
the small community of Marne-la-Vallée on the outskirts of Paris was
simply another version of Walt Disney World in Florida, "the fullest
representation of commodified space in North America."[103] After all, as
far back as 1973, the French intellectual Louis Marin had equated entering Disneyland with falling into "an empty abyss," while the park itself
he described as a degenerate utopia that provided imaginary support for
an American ruling class.[104] Marin's likening of the visitor's experience
of Disneyland to being shipwrecked on a deserted island would ring all
the more true for the "shipwreck" that Disney's European theme park
venture would become.

Disney's theme park initiatives in other global contexts, particularly in Japan and China, have encountered issues of a different kind.
Problems derived from economic considerations, such as profitability,
and infrastructure development have greatly outweighed local hostility
toward Disney's mystification of American culture. In fact, Disney's
grand complexes in Japan and China are still widely perceived as the
visual embodiment of human society's triumphant progress toward modernity and all the benefits entailed by industrialization, including better
urban infrastructure, more advanced technology, and higher standards
of living. Accordingly, Disneyland seems to retain much of its utopian
symbolism in recently developed and developing parts of the world that
associate its simulated structures with the leisure and luxury enjoyed
by middle-class Americans. In this context, as suggested by Mitsuhiro
Yoshimoto, "the opening of Tokyo Disneyland in 1983 gave a generation of Japanese a sense of completion or achievement."[105] Researchers,
such as Jonathan Weber, who have explored the cultural reception of
Disney theme parks in Tokyo and Hong Kong tend to agree that the
company treads carefully between, on the one hand, presenting America
as the exotic "other" for consumption by more or less curious park
goers—a kind of "Occidentalism" that counterposes the West's long
history of Orientalism—and, on the other, carefully tailoring the park's
content and services to local tastes.[106] Tokyo Disneyland's substitution
of the consummate American nationalist symbol, Main Street USA,
with its World Bazaar is an oft-cited example of how the Japanese are

not enthralled by everything American but are actually quite selective about what they find appealing. Disney's cartoon portrayals of cute, furry animals, for instance, seem to mesh quite well with Japan's own animated tradition and aesthetic taste for all things cute (*kawaii* is the term for a whole Japanese cultural movement centered on cuteness).[107] Indeed, Tokyo's simulated urban environments not only preceded the development of Tokyo Disneyland but could also be said to exceed in their scale, intensity, and elaborateness anything built by Disney. Far from colonizing Japan, Tokyo Disneyland represents the Japanese appropriation of an element of foreign culture that appears to blend almost seamlessly with Japan's own. Evaluating the extent of Disney's cultural influence and economic power on the global stage, then, means paying close attention to local reception and its specific contexts, particularly the ways in which actual cultural exchange contradicts or limits theories about unrestrained U.S. imperial domination.

Scholars have shown a number of ways in which Japan has carefully negotiated its encounters with Western culture, even as its history reflects a long tradition of syncretism with cultural forms, beliefs, and practices from other regions in Asia. As Mary Yoko Brennan points out about Tokyo Disneyland, "The process of assimilation of the West, the recontextualization of Western simulacra, demonstrates not that the Japanese are being dominated by Western ideologies but that they differentiate their identity from the West in a way that reinforces their sense of their own cultural uniqueness and superiority, or what we might call Japanese hegemony."[108] One example of Japan's participation in the global culture industry is its toy manufacturing, which rapidly developed after World War I and contributed to the general development of manufacturing industries in Japan. As Gary Cross and Gregory Smits have documented, the story of Japan's toy industry essentially parallels that of the United States' toy industry, with the first plastic toys appearing on the market in the 1950s.[109] When the United States began outsourcing production and exporting children's popular media and toys to Europe, Japan was exporting its products to Southeast Asian countries like South Korea.[110] The Japanese government promoted toy manufacturing in the 1960s as a way to revive the postwar economy, giving initial stimulation to the practice of year-round gift giving and a multigenerational fascination with toys that still permeates Japanese culture.[111] Finally, Japanese companies were able to dominate the global market in the area of children's computerized toys beginning in the 1980s, when firms like Nintendo pioneered the world's most popular video game consoles.[112] Mitsuhiro Yoshimoto adds to this narrative the fact that Japanese electronics giants began their incursion into Hollywood studios in the 1980s.[113] This means that Japan was active in generating its own commercialized children's culture and focusing on transnational capitalist growth, which was linked to the economic policies put in place during the boom years of the 1980s. Japan may have drawn some of its merchandising and mass marketing strategies from corporations like Disney, but it was clearly never dominated by American toy manufacturing, unlike some countries in Europe and Latin America.

Extrapolating from the particular case of the toy industry, it becomes apparent, as Yoshimoto argues with respect to Japan's relationship to Disney, that Japan's acceptance, even "obsession," with Western culture does not coincide with its economic subordination.[114] Japan's highly commercialized culture and embrace of technology accept the possibility of manufactured identity and absorb other cultures into its own as objects of consumption in order to create a whole world within Japan itself. In doing so, Japan does not lose a sense of its unique cultural identity; rather, in a quintessentially postmodern way, Japan perpetually re-creates its native difference through constant encounters with foreign "others."[115] Paradoxically, Japan's openness to the "dehistoricization and decontextualization that is at work in the Japanese discursive space" makes Disneyland a perfect materialization of "contemporary Japanese nationalism."[116] As Shunya Yoshimi suggests, Tokyo as a postmodern city could be described as more "Disney" than Disneyland, with several of its spaces having been thematically planned like one giant Disneyized space before the theme park even arrived in Tokyo.[117] The commodification and simulation of spaces and identities, then, suggests a fundamental compatibility between some dominant elements of Japanese culture and Disney, as does their mutual acceptance of privatization as a cultural and economic principle. Indeed, one of the most important elements distinguishing Tokyo Disneyland from other Disney theme parks is the fact that it is entirely owned by a Japanese corporation. Its perennial high rates of attendance make Tokyo Disneyland one of the most successful theme parks in the world. Not only is the park not a joint venture between private interests and the local government, unlike Disneyland Paris but Hong Kong Disneyland, and the Walt Disney Company only receives royalties on admissions (10 percent) and sales of food and souvenirs (5 percent).[118] As Aviad Raz points out, the autonomy of the management at Tokyo Disneyland enables a much higher degree of localized practices of consumption, despite the marketing of the park as a "100 percent copy of the American original."[119] For all of these reasons, Tokyo Disneyland remains a unique challenge to the kinds of grievances and fears surrounding American cultural imperialism that French critics would express regarding Euro Disney.

The reciprocity between contemporary Japan and other cultures, described by Raz as "the dynamic and bilateral nature of the flow of popular culture between first-world cores such as Tokyo and Los Angeles,"[120] stands in stark contrast to traditional Western models of identity based on an absolute opposition between the self and the other that often translates into a relationship of domination and subordination. There is something potentially redemptive in such a cosmopolitan model, which might enable cultures around the world to coexist based on a mutual respect and appreciation for difference. As Jonathan Weber points out, at the very least it does not look like the arrival of a "shallow global monoculture" is imminent.[121] The drawback of this model, embodied by Tokyo Disneyland, is that it remains limited by an emphasis on highly commercialized modes and relations that are accessible only to those who can afford them. While it is clear that each society mediates global market culture differently and that neoliberal globalization cannot be reduced to yet another version of Western dominance, those who are too affirmative about "Japanization" overlook the fact that the critical appropriation of corporate offerings remains a luxury of affluent countries, in which consumption rules the day. It ignores the way in which neoliberal globalization divides the world: the consumers on one side, the disposable, dehumanized remnants on the other. Indigenous cultural forms in developing countries are less likely to stand on equal footing with Disney's marketing juggernaut than those in developed countries. Most significantly, celebrating cultural participation in these brave new worlds of consumption means strengthening the economic and cultural power of private corporations and weakening democratic citizenship, the end point of which must resemble something more like Aldous Huxley's dystopia than the world according to Walt Disney. Having said this, postmodern Japan's relationship with Disneyland at least enables a better understanding of how global capitalism is slowly hybridizing a world culture through the commodification of identity and the spread of commercial values. The good news is that, as Disney becomes more global, the contradictions—such as those between American nationalism and transnational capitalism—surface in more visible ways, opening up opportunities for the development of new modes of resistance.

Disney currently heads a group of multinationals that are hastening the "worldwide triumph of American-style capitalism,"[122] but in becoming global, Disney has loosened its ideological ties to a patriotic nationalist agenda. In the development of its newest theme parks in Hong Kong (opened 2005) and Shanghai (projected for 2014),[123] Disney appears eager to build partnerships with local governments. In the case of Hong Kong Disneyland, the government of Hong Kong invested $2.9 billion in taxpayer dollars (80 percent of the initial costs) and owns a 57 percent stake in the park.[124] This joint arrangement helps reduce the financial risk for Disney, while it gives the government an important stake in the success of the venture. The effects of this private-public partnership for citizens of Hong Kong remain to be seen. Although the success of the park has been affected by overcrowding and disputes among stakeholders that have slowed park expansion,[125] Disney at least opted for a more culturally sensitive approach to the park's design, having hired a Chinese feng shui master to ensure "a flow of positive energy"—it probably does not hurt, too, to conjure some of the luck and financial prosperity that the Chinese believe will come from paying proper attention to certain design details, such as avoiding the number 4 (which in Chinese is pronounced like the word for death).[126] Disney views Hong Kong as an important gateway to mainland China, which historically has been a closed market to purveyors of American culture. Disney already has forty-two hundred "corners" in Chinese stores, designed to lure members of a growing middle class into the snares of Disney's merchandising network.[127] Additionally, in preparation for the development of Shanghai Disneyland and specifically deemed by Disney to be part of a "brand-building process," the company entered into a partnership with China's Communist Youth League (CYL): "With some 70 million members, the CYL offers the park a major entrée into China's youth market. Disney is working with the organization to present activities that include storytelling, drawing, and interactive games.

Those sessions are often centered around Disney characters."[128] Donald Duck may once have comforted American children by dreaming in stars and stripes, but Mickey Mouse now marches with Chinese youth on the other side of the globe.

Neoliberal global capitalism is less concerned with nationalism than with creating corporate empires. Indeed, even more threatening than the specter of all aspects of culture becoming fodder for Disney's profit margins is the ongoing, wholesale redirection of global systems, economies, politics, and cultures toward the growth of neoliberal forms of capitalism. Not only does Disney's worldview support neoliberal expansion, but it represents individuals, societies, and global culture as seemingly free of conflict, politics, and contradictions, while also offering a rationale for abstracting corporate culture from the realms of power, politics, and ideology. Against this Disney dreamworld, one has to ask what price the public pays by simply focusing on the pleasure and fun that culture industries such as Disney provide while ignoring the growing influence they have in shaping so many other facets of national and global life. Privatized utopias of neoliberal consumerist society offer the public only a market-based language that produces narrow modes of subjectivity, defining what people should know and how they should act within the constricted interests and values of what Zygmunt Bauman has called "an order of egoism."[129] Perhaps in the development of theme parks, Disney can rest assured that consumers will not vocalize resistance to the expansive range of "consumer choice" symbolized by the Disneyfied spaces. But there is growing dissent among those global communities whose relationship to Disney culture as either the exploited or the excluded adds urgency and legitimacy to their protests against corporate power.

GLOBAL RESISTANCE TO DISNEY: LABOR MOVEMENTS AND CORPORATE ACCOUNTABILITY

The economic conduct of corporations is in dire need of reform. Because of its size and scope of activities, Disney is as good an example as any. With one hand, the company was accepting praise for its high-profile sponsorship of Celebration's model of urbanity. With another, it was busy recruiting foreign nationals willing to labor for a minimum wage that buys much less than it did thirty

years ago. All the while, it was turning a blind eye to the uncounted
Asian factory workers toiling over its T-shirts and toys for starvation wages. This is not publicly minded policy, nor is it intended to
be. It is the intolerable face of capitalism with no footing in humane
conduct, rewarding the affluent and punishing the poor.

—Andrew Ross, *The Celebration Chronicles*[130]

As global capital spreads around the world, the ideas and practices fuel-
ing neoliberal consumerism shelter people from a global perspective on
issues such as poverty, environmental destruction, and the exploitation
of labor in the developing world. Neoliberalism's lens is one narrowed
to individualized concerns only, much in the same way that Disney's
construction of utopian spaces and narratives ignores the lived reality
of so many people around the world. As Rapping remarks, "It is no accident that Disney's central ambassador is a neutered, hairless civilized
rodent—by nature the filthy scourge of every slum in the developed
world."[131] A stuffed Mickey Mouse toy symbolizes to a middle-class
American all the joys of childhood. But to a Chinese migrant worker
laboring in a sweatshop in Guangdong Province, Mickey Mouse means
thirteen-hour workdays (around two hundred hours of overtime per
month) with no overtime premiums, absurdly high quotas on piece-
rate production, below legal minimum wages, rental fees to live in
rat-infested dormitories, pay withheld for forty-five days at a time,
prolonged exposure to unknown chemicals in synthetic stuffing, no
Social Security benefits, and no job protection when voicing complaints
about horrendous working conditions.[132] This is a reality for hundreds
of thousands of people who are behind the manufacturing of Disney's
consumer products and who are struggling to survive. For decades,
Disney has hidden this reality behind a fantasy that is only sustainable
among affluent and privileged consumers in the developed world, not
the hard-working producers who suffer by virtue of their global location within a cutthroat commercial market that extracts as much profit
as possible. Disney has been remarkably successful at convincing consumers that its products are safe, clean, and good for children, even as
the company recognizes that many of its factories use child labor. What
happens when resistance to Disney's corporate power is waged outside
the framework of financial investment (shareholders) and consumerism
(theme park goers)? Due to the efforts of a number of activist organizations, the reality of Disney's production operations in the developing

world is coming to light. A significant protest movement focuses on demanding corporate accountability for Disney's use of sweated labor around the globe. There are also indigenous-rights movements outside the United States whose heightened consciousness of a history of forced assimilation and cultural appropriation—not to mention Disney's specific contributions to American colonial indoctrination of Latin American workers with the educational short films on health it produced in the 1940s[133]—has led to protests against Disney's distortions of culture. After considering a few instances of global resistance to Disney's corporate practices waged on the level of cultural politics, the rest of this section will focus on labor organizations that work to expose the gross exploitation of international factory workers, whose working conditions and pay fall egregiously short of the minimum requirements to ensure human dignity and a living wage. Cultural and economic producers are the lifeblood of capitalism, but Disney seems more than willing to count on an endless supply of minds and bodies, leaving more than a few corpses in its wake as it lumbers its way across the globe.

Uniting global resistance movements in their efforts against corporate power is the use of multimedia and information networks, such as the Internet, to educate a global public and generate bad publicity for corporations like Disney, which depends heavily on its pristine public image to market its products. In this way, individuals and groups utilize the same tools as Disney in order to subvert the company's cultural authority. One example is the website LosDisneys.com, a brilliant parody that envisions what might happen if Disney was given free reign to take over the United States. The focus of the site is an open-source video game, first made available online in 1997, while the site also offers a message board to post critical discussions about "the ever-expanding Disney Empire."[134] In truly postmodern fashion, the site uses entertainment and satirical exaggeration as a way to expose the full ramifications of the corporate logic underlying Disney's utopianism:

> The year is 2015. Steeped in national debt, the United States reluctantly allows the Walt Disney Company to purchase the entire peninsula of Florida in the largest geographical acquisition since the Louisiana Purchase. Under its new president, formerly ousted CEO Michael Eisner, the newly sovereign state is renamed Los Disneys. Your job is to attempt to seek and destroy the cryonically frozen head of Walt Disney. However, doing so inadvertently triggers Eisner's doomsday device, sending a

series of thermo-nuclear warheads hidden deep beneath the surrounding waters of the peninsula to devastate every major city in the world—unless you can stop it.[135]

The video game cleverly turns the symbolic violence inflicted on democratic public spheres by private corporations such as Disney into a reality that players can experience interactively. The incorporation of vibrant imagery, fantastic conspiracy theories, and apocalyptic overtones allows the site to maximize the impact of its subversive pedagogy, using Disney's cultural tools against itself. At the same time, the site spoofs Disney's earnestness, providing a Web-based community with the impression that critiquing Disney can be as much fun as consuming Disney. Los Disneys's representation of Disney's genocidal drive to appropriate the land and citizenry and subject both to authoritarian control is mere fiction. But others have protested Disney's very real appropriation of history and culture. The Mexica Movement, an indigenous-rights educational organization, launched an international boycott of Disney because ABC radio stations featured right-wing talk show hosts who were using hate speech and inciting racist violence against Mexicans and Central Americans.[136] The organization also expressed outrage at Disney's plans to make a film based on the life of Mexican indigenous leader Emiliano Zapata and to cast Antonio Banderas, a Spanish actor, in the role of Zapata. The group likened the hiring of Banderas to having Brad Pitt play Malcolm X and picketed for a year in 2002 outside the Los Angeles theater staging a production of *The Lion King*.[137] Disney eventually cancelled the film. In yet another example of Disney's brazen disregard for indigenous peoples, *Pirates of the Caribbean: Dead Man's Chest* portrays eighteenth-century Carib peoples as "a gang of voracious cannibals," reissuing a blatant colonial stereotype that modern anthropological accounts have contradicted.[138] It was shot on location in Dominica, the home of one of the last remaining communities of Carib people, descendants of the indigenous group first stigmatized by Christopher Columbus, most of whom were killed by disease and war in the seventeenth century.[139] Despite strong objections voiced on the part of Carib leaders, the film's script remained unchanged. Even more than disrespect for political protests and the careful work of social scientists, the film demonstrates that Disney is willing not only to engage in a desecration of historical truth but also to cannibalize the culture of already marginalized communities. It seems the world's most disenfranchised peoples become fodder only too often for Disney's global expansion, whether the sacrifice entails the exploitation of their cultural identity or their physical labor.

Disney utilizes workers around the world in order to make the thousands of Disney consumer products that flood store shelves each year. Disney not only hires some factories directly but also licenses vendors who subcontract the manufacturing of Disney toys, clothing, and other products. One of the pioneering efforts to hold Disney accountable for its corporate practices was a video produced by the National Labor Committee (NLC) titled *Mickey Mouse Goes to Haiti* (1996). The documentary paints a grim picture of how corporations like Disney use Haitian workers to produce their consumer products. In particular, the film points to the gross discrepancy between what Haitian garment workers are paid compared to the profits reaped by Disney when it sells the products to consumers back in North America. On a given day, a worker might make dozens of clothing items, each selling for $12 in the United States, but only be paid $2.40 in wages. In other words, the worker receives only 0.05 percent of the market value of the product. The relatively high cost of food in Haiti means that workers do not make enough money to pay for food, schooling for their children, and shelter for themselves and their families, and so they end up in a downward spiral of debt accumulation. Meanwhile, workers who organize to protest starvation wages or even speak honestly about their working conditions, such as being harassed to work more quickly or receiving only dirty water to drink, are promptly fired. Without the intervention of the international community and the corporations who use the factories, the film suggests, Haitian workers will suffer increasing exploitation as neither the factory bosses nor the government step up to protect their rights. In fact, the factory owners are the only citizens recognized by the government, and they successfully lobby to avoid increases in the minimum wage. The film points out that a living wage would mean an increase from 28 cents to 58 cents per hour, a difference that would barely make a dent in Disney's profit machine but would mean relief from indentured servitude for a Haitian worker. *Mickey Mouse Goes to Haiti* provoked an important response from other human rights organizations, students, and trade unionists back in the United States. Thousands of people wrote damning letters to then CEO Michael Eisner with comments like "I don't see how you can walk down the street without having to hide your face because of guilt. It's sad that you can't spare 50 more cents to the people who made you a billionaire."[140] Disney initially dodged responding directly to the campaigners and the film's allegations, but the company did establish its Code of Conduct for Manufacturers in 1996, following the principles outlined by various labor-standards organizations and the International Labour Organization (ILO). The code requires that manufacturers abstain from employing children under age fourteen and from using involuntary labor, coercion, harassment, and discrimination, while respecting employee rights to associate without interference, work in a safe and healthy environment, and receive proper wages in compliance with the wage and hour laws in the country of operation.[141] Unfortunately, on a subsequent visit to Haiti, the NLC found that none of the workers had ever heard of the company's new code of conduct.[142]

Then, in 1998 the North American Congress on Latin America reported union busting at Haitian factories that were producing Disney goods. Workers were also deliberately being fired before their three-month probation was up so that the factory would not have to pay severance or benefits. It noted cases in which factory management coached workers to lie to monitoring teams, while workers who had spoken honestly were suspended from work without explanation.[143] Acknowledging none of these documented incidents, Disney reports on its corporate website that it ceased commissioning its products from factories in Haiti in 1999 "due to political instability."[144] On its website, Disney also paints an image of a supply chain that seems much less like a linear chain and more like an unwieldy monster with tentacles spreading out into various regions of the globe. In 2008 alone, Disney had twenty-three thousand active factories making products, along with eight thousand licensees and vendors who contract their own Disney merchandise.[145] With so many layers of licensing and contracting, how can Disney adequately monitor all the production facilities let alone track where its products are even being made? In fact, Disney-employed monitors, along with external monitoring firms, were only able to assess 15 percent of the factories the company had contracted in 2008.[146] Of these assessments, over half the factories in every region outside North America had health and safety violations, while factories across Asia and the Middle East all had high rates of violations that involved coercing overtime hours, failing to comply with monitoring, and paying less than the minimum wage.[147] What really matters to the company is not improving the working conditions of laborers but managing public perception. According to one labor organization, Disney's code of conduct and auditing system are largely designed to "assuage fears that cheap goods actually bear a human cost" rather than to actually foster substantive improvements.[148] Disney's motivation is not even disguised in its 2008 annual report, which suggests that its "corporate responsibility" initiative "reinforces the attractiveness of its brands and products and strengthens bonds with consumers and neighbors in communities the world over."[149] Apparently, Disney cares about the perception that it is making an effort, not the reality of having made substantive improvements. Moral responsibility is reduced to paying lip service to its attempts to be a better "corporate citizen." Meanwhile, consumers are relieved of the need to be conscientious about their own choices when they can rest assured that Disney's corporate conscience is operating on their behalf. This may sound cynical. Even more cynical, however, is the recognition that Disney is a corporation particularly vulnerable to criticisms of its labor practices, leaving the question open as to what kinds of checks might be effective against other multinational organizations who do not share Disney's vested interest in maintaining its public image as a provider of children's culture and family entertainment?

It is nevertheless significant that the work of labor activist organizations has made inroads with Disney, pointing to where the company's monitoring processes have failed and exhorting Disney to make improvements. Students and Scholars against Corporate Misbehavior (SACOM) is an activist group based in Hong Kong, which, since 2005, has monitored Disney's corporate practices with the goal of ensuring that Disney works to "improve the working conditions in its supplier factories in China."[150] The organization released several reports documenting labor violations uncovered by students in mainland China who worked in the factories and experienced the conditions firsthand. The activists are united in their desire "for a more open, democratic, fair, sustainable China" and their aim to "awaken the conscience" of major multinational corporations is the first step toward this goal. The organization's strategies focus on "name-and-shame" campaigns that "use the media to amplify the scandal" in order to pressure corporations, while making the public aware of the consequences of their consumption patterns.[151] Emerging from SACOM's reports is a strong sense of the ineffectiveness of the measures put in place by Disney to safeguard workers. Monitoring teams often lack the time to verify the paperwork supplied by factories, so the violations remain undetected. Although the Chinese government passed legislation in 2008 requiring written contracts of employment, workers in many factories are made to sign "one-sided 'contracts' in which wage, work hours, and benefits are simply left blank. Managers then collect the contracts and complete them as they see fit."[152] Factories that are informed about upcoming audits provide workers with scripted answers to the auditors' questions. The workers are warned to reveal nothing but what is provided by the script.[153] Meanwhile, most workers remain unaware of the Disney Code of Conduct and other international labor standards.[154] Clearly, the code is ineffective if workers are not informed that it exists and cannot demand compliance from their employers. SACOM asserts,

> Disney should disclose its full list of outsourced Chinese manufacturers for public scrutiny and ensure that its suppliers comply with local labor laws. It should also give every Chinese worker at every Disney supplier a copy of Disney's Code of Conduct translated into Chinese. Furthermore, it should promote workplace democracy by respecting workers' right to create mechanisms of worker representation at all Disney suppliers.[155]

Disney's response to SACOM has produced decidedly mixed results. Although Disney in general seems willing to address problems at its factories—collaborating, for example, with McDonald's and other stakeholder groups to implement in-factory improvements at ten suppliers in southern China[156]—it also seems heavily dependent on the information and resources supplied by grassroots organizations. In response to a SACOM report about a toy factory, Disney claims that it has installed a confidential worker helpline with the assistance of a "civil society organization" and is working with the International Council of Toy Industries's ethical manufacturing program to evaluate the factory's compliance with labor standards.[157] But why does Disney, a giant corporation that makes billions of dollars in profits every year, need to rely on underfunded, overworked organizations to monitor factories, communicate with workers, and provide on-site educational training? While Disney touts its collaboration with nongovernmental organizations, it is clearly reaping the benefits. Disney's Corporate Responsibility Report also blames local management for a lack of compliance but meanwhile awards contracts to the lowest bidders who can fill the order as quickly as possible. As SACOM points out, factory management has resorted to "concealing labor abuses in order to survive in the 'race to the bottom' of the global economy"—and it is the global corporations pitting factories around the world against each other that provide the impetus for cheaper labor and increasing violations rather than reforms.[158]

More significantly, Disney's reaction to publicity surrounding labor-code violations in its factories seems more often than not to be withdrawal of its business from the factory, abandoning the workers rather than supporting remediation. Despite the proactive rhetoric Disney uses to describe the measures it has taken, cutting its losses and running does not approximate "corporate responsibility." In July 2009, another activist group, China Labor Watch, revealed the tragic death from an industrial accident of an underage worker at a paper factory—a Disney supplier—in southern China. Liu Pan began working at the factory when he was only fifteen years old, although Chinese law stipulates eighteen as the minimum age for work in hazardous occupations. The seventeen-year-old's body was so completely mutilated as he was clearing jammed machinery that he was unrecognizable to his parents who journeyed from their home in Sichuan Province to the Guangdong factory to retrieve his body. CLW noted that the particular factory had passed Disney's labor-certification test repeatedly over the past two years and questioned how "Disney's audit failed to notice the use of child labor and untrained workers operating dangerous machinery."[159] Disney initially agreed with CLW's request to oversee reforms in collaboration with workers and factory management, which is also known for practices such as forced overtime and not providing workers with written contracts.[160] When the story broke in the *New York Times* and Disney appeared to hastily withdraw its business from the factory, CLW petitioned Disney to address the problems at the factory "rather than abandoning the factory in search of another cheap supplier to exploit."[161] CLW had learned from past cases that Disney repeatedly abandoned factories where it had identified labor-code violations. Fortunately, continued pressure from CLW resulted in Disney's implementing a series of reforms,[162] which offers some hope for a better future for Disney workers around the world.

These various protest movements provide both political and pedagogical models of how megacorporations can be exposed for the exploitation they promote and the human suffering they inflict in the name of profit making as well as how a wide array of tactics and strategies can be used to fight for both immediate reforms and long-term structural transformation. Those whose voices are removed from the narratives of official power have found new ways to counter such narratives, challenge them, and offer counternarratives in their place. The Internet, mobile technologies, and other new media, in particular, embody a distinct mode of representation and signal the potential for a more capacious politics that can correct what Nick Couldry calls the "current injustices of representation."[163] These media provide new public sites of visibility for an unprecedented look into the workings of labor exploitation, state-sponsored violence, and civil unrest. They can be used to challenge state and corporate power through their ability to facilitate public exchange and social relations while constituting a new sphere of politics that cannot be controlled by traditional forces of repression. Global publics of opposition are emerging through electronic circuits of power that offer up wider spheres of communication, dialogue, and resistance—and new ways to conceptualize the possibility and value of political engagement in creating alternative public spheres that enable people, especially youth, to claim their own voices and challenge dominant forces of oppression.

Global resistance must prioritize the safeguarding of youth—their health, education, and rights—if the world has any chance of achieving sustainability. Young people—as a concrete embodiment and symbolic reflection of the abstract forces that govern the social sphere—are one of the most significant modalities through which to understand and launch an effective resistance to neoliberalism. The concept of youth has the potential to provide a universal value and ethical position that can unite people across the political spectrum and globally, but only if the particular contexts surrounding youth—such as their exploitation and commodification at the hand of corporations like Disney—are combined with the larger contexts of politics, economics, and culture as corporatism expands across the globe. The future task will then be to mobilize diverse publics and political struggles with the goal of building global organizations and long-term social movements that have the capacity to challenge antidemocratic forces and institutions through a variety of channels and actions.

CONCLUSION

Democratic politics once recognized its dependency on the people it governed and to whom it remained accountable. But no one today votes for which corporations have the right to dominate the media and filter the information made available to the public; no electoral process determines how private companies grant or deny people access to adequate health care and other social services. The reign of the market in a neoliberal economy is not restricted to a limited term of appointment, despite the market's unprecedented sovereignty over the lives of citizens in democratic countries and despite the fact that sovereignty in such circumstances becomes essentially defined as the "power and capacity to dictate who may live and who may die."[164] We are currently witnessing the unleashing of a powerfully regressive symbolic and corporeal violence against all those individuals and groups who have been "othered" because their very presence undermines the engines of wealth and inequality that drive the neoliberal fantasy of perpetual consumption, power, and profitability. Global flows of capital feed a planetary corporate empire that now works in tandem with a rampant culture of corruption and secrecy both in multinational corporate structures and at the highest levels of government. As finance capital reigns supreme over global society, democratization, along with the public spheres needed to sustain it, becomes an unsettled and increasingly fragile project.

While the state still has the power of the law to reduce individuals to impoverishment and to strip them of civic rights, due process, and civil liberties, neoliberalism increasingly wields its own form of sovereignty through the invisible hand of the market, which now has the power to produce new configurations of control, regulate social health, and alter human life in unforeseen and profound ways. Underlying the transfer of sovereignty to corporations is a widely endorsed assumption that regardless of the suffering, misery, and problems faced by human beings, individuals are not only responsible for their own fate but must rely ultimately on themselves for survival. Meanwhile, long-standing histories of racist and class-based exclusion—driven by colonial fantasies that regard the racial "other" as less than human or dismiss the unemployed worker as a disposable by-product of the capitalist order— continue to inform the withdrawal of moral and ethical concern regarding from these populations.[165] As a mode of rationality, neoliberalism enables and legitimates the practices of managerialism, deregulation, efficiency, cost-benefit analysis, and privatization, all of which function in the interest of "extending and disseminating market values to all institutions and social action."[166] As neoliberalism extends the logic of the market economy into all aspects of daily life, the boundaries of the cultural, economic, and political become porous and leak into each other, shaping not only social relations, institutions, and policies but also desires, values, and identities in the interest of constructing "the citizen-subject of a neoliberal order."[167] Under neoliberal rationality and its seductive mode of public pedagogy, not only are the state and the public sector reduced to the phantoms of market choices, but the citizen-subjects of such an order navigate the relationship between themselves and others through the calculating logics of competition, individual risk, self-interest, and a winner-take-all ethic reminiscent of the script played out daily on "reality television." In resisting globalizing capital, we must oppose its concerted assault on the very existence of politics and democracy, as well as the educational conditions that make such as assault possible. Central to such a challenge is the necessity of addressing how neoliberalism as a pedagogical practice and a public pedagogy operating in diverse sites has succeeded in reproducing in the social order a kind of thoughtlessness—a social amnesia of sorts—that makes it possible for people to look away as an increasing number of individuals and groups are made disposable, relegated to new zones of exclusion marked by the presupposition that life is cheap, if not irrelevant, next to the needs of the marketplace.

In the past thirty years, we have witnessed neoliberal ideology construct "the market as the very paradigm of freedom, [such that] democracy emerges as a synonym for capitalism, which has reemerged as the telos of history."[168] If unregulated capitalism should not be equated with democracy because free markets lead private corporations to seek out power, monopolies, and profit through the exploitation of humans and the natural world, then nor can democracy be reduced to the way government is organized around an electoral system. Democracy must mean more. It must refer to a process of always becoming more democratic, never accepting things as they are but always struggling toward a more just and equal world. One of the great challenges facing global democracy is the need to recognize and further the elements of human agency that are both products of and challenges to the market's ultimate disregard for human life. It is precisely in the struggle over a democratic ethos that we must mobilize global movements and modes of resistance that reject and transform the narratives, values, and seductions of a neoliberal ethos. Needed today are growing modes of global resistance, escalating calls for more rights legislation, and an expanding influence of international law.[169]

A genuinely global public sphere also demands a certain kind of citizen informed by particular forms of education, a citizen whose education provides the essential conditions for democratic public spheres to flourish. This new public has to be cosmopolitan, transnational in its scope, global in its sense of responsibility, and educational in its mobilizing functions. As Nick Couldry has argued, part of the struggle for a vibrant democracy requires figuring out where emergent democratic publics can be created, how public connections can be sustained beyond the private sphere, and how neoliberal discourse and a multinational corporate oligarchy can be countered with an enlarged notion of the social and a "shared space of public action" where norms of collective agency can be developed and democratic politics sustained.[170] Engaged and substantive citizenship requires a commitment to debate, dialogue, and matters of justice and power and a willingness to listen to the claims of others. But we cannot achieve the strengthening of the social bonds of democracy simply through the exchange of ideas, as important as this may be. Also needed is the promise and reality of new spaces in which to cultivate the capacities for critical modes of individual and social agency, as well as the crucial opportunities to form alliances in the collective struggle for a new politics that expands the scope of vision, the operations of democracy, and the range of democratic institutions.

As outlined above, the struggle for corporate accountability can take place at the level of ownership, consumption, and production, but it is seemingly most transformative at the level of production, where there is a clear sense of a global oppositional framework in development. Disney demonstrates its willingness to struggle over global popular culture by adjusting its corporate language and philosophy to the shifting assumptions and practices that characterize the changing roles and conceptions of work, consumption, the family, and identity in postindustrial societies. Effective resistance on the part of activist groups requires the same adaptability. It means understanding analytically how political economy and culture operate together to support a global corporate empire but can be redirected to build global democratic partnerships. It means not simply playing the game according to the rules set by Disney but changing the very terms on which corporate power is engaged. Any viable mode of collective resistance to neoliberal logic must refuse a vocabulary of impoverished oppositions, one "that strives to reduce expansive vocabularies of politics, social debate, and intimacy to a straightjacket of absolute oppositions: nature and abomination, truth and concealment, good and evil."[171] Against such oversimplifications, there is a growing need for modes of critique that not only take seriously how power and consent shape the terrain of everyday life but also embrace a politics of possibility that engenders a global resistance, one that moves beyond the borders of the local to rewrite the global politics in which we think and live. Jean Comaroff reminds us the struggle is just beginning:

> As conventional politics falters in the face of ever more elusive collaborations of wealth, power, and the law, social activism has sought to exploit the incoherence of the neoliberal order against it, finding productive footholds within the *aporias* of the market system. While it has hardly forced a capitulation on the part of governments and corporations, it has won some significant concessions.[172]

All of the labor, student, and activist movements discussed above are motivated by a sense of political and ethical urgency, while at the same time they develop anew modes of pedogogy in which the political becomes a space of possibility both within and outside the boundaries of the nation-state. If belonging to a global community is not to be understood as a private affair but as a vibrant experience in which people learn how to participate in and shape public life, it must begin with a kind of education that provides the decisive traits of courage, critical thinking, civic engagement, responsibility, and respect, all of which connect the fate of each individual to the fate of others, the planet, and global democracy.

Conclusion

Turning the World into a Disney Store

The Southern Baptist Convention in June 1997 generated a lot of media attention when it called for a boycott of the Walt Disney Company for promoting "immoral ideologies such as homosexuality." The Southern Baptists were angry because Disney sponsors an unofficial "Gay Day" at its theme parks, extended health benefits to the domestic partners of gay employees in 1996, and published the book *Growing Up Gay* with its subsidiary Hyperion Books in 1995. According to Herb Hilliger, a convention spokesman, the last straw came in April 1997 when the lead character of the sitcom *Ellen* had the audacity to come out as a lesbian on the Disney-owned ABC.[1] Against the Southern Baptists' homophobic rhetoric, the land of the Magic Kingdom actually looked progressive—even though Disney was one of the last studios to extend health benefits to same-sex partners.[2] The boycott ended in 2005—the same year Disney released *The Chronicles of Narnia: The Lion, the Witch, and the Wardrobe*, a film based on C. S. Lewis's Christian allegory—when Southern Baptists were apparently reassured that Disney under Robert Iger would serve "families of America by providing only those products that affirm traditional family values."[3]

But the Southern Baptists had got it right in assuming that something was amiss in Disney's portrayal as an icon of pristine innocence, childhood fun, and healthy family entertainment. Unfortunately, they got it wrong when they condemned Disney for refusing to endorse homophobic practices in it labor operations and appealed to the company's traditional brand image: the image of conservative, white American

205

family values—values in which the heterosexual patriarchal family unit becomes normalized, wrapped in the patriotic and nostalgic aura of a bygone era of small-town Midwestern Protestant ideals. The digital revolution in technology has not changed the fact that Disney still promotes elements of this timeworn image, but it is becoming increasingly evident that such a pretense to innocence camouflages a powerful cultural force and corporate monolith. For this same reason, Disney should not be heaped with unstinting praise when it supports gay-friendly policies. As Sean Griffin points out, Disney has recognized a lucrative market for its products, particularly among "white, middle- or upper-middle-class gay men, the subgroup within the homosexual population with the most disposable income." It is important to remember that progressive corporate policies reveal more about Disney's business savvy than its alleged "gay agenda." In Disney's case, such policies not only reinforce the company's corporate identity as a model of social and civic responsibility, but they simultaneously turn the gay community's "subversive strategy into a potential for more profit." The credit for promoting social justice, as Griffin argues, should go to those individuals who have managed to use "corporate space as an opportunity to make connections and bond together in a shared expression of their existence in the face of a still vibrant hatred and oppression."[4]

Far from being a model of moral leadership and social responsibility, the Walt Disney Company increasingly co-opts subversive elements within public culture, monopolizes the media, limits the free flow of information, distorts historical memory, undermines substantive public debate, and constructs children's identities primarily within the ideology of consumerism. In doing so, it poses a serious threat to democracy by corporatizing public spheres and limiting the avenues of public expression and choice.[5] Disney does not, of course, have the power to unilaterally engage in armed warfare, dismantle the welfare state, or eliminate basic social programs for children. In fact, Disney's influence is subtler and more pervasive. It shapes public consciousness through its enormous economic holdings and cultural power. Michael Ovitz, a former Disney executive, says that Disney is not a company but a nation-state, exercising vast influence over global constituencies.[6] Influencing multiple facets of cultural life, Disney ranks within the top two hundred companies in the Fortune Global 500 and controls ABC and ESPN, numerous television and radio stations, Internet sites, motion picture studios, multimedia companies, and major publishing houses.

In 2008, Disney pulled in a record $37.8 billion in revenues from all of its divisions.[7] What the 2008 financial meltdown in the United States would seem to demonstrate is that Disney and other megacorporations are in fact more powerful than nation-states, as they remain immune from the kind of accountability measures that limit government power. A decade of growth in the 1990s enabled Disney to provide prototypes for developing American culture and civility, including a model town, a school system, and the Disney Institute, where it offers business owners tips on how to apply "Disney magic" to their organizations and provides accredited continuing-education programs for doctors, nurses, human resources managers, health-care administrators, and accountants. Disney has increased its holdings even more in the new millennium, buying up successful franchises to target preschoolers, such as Baby Einstein and Club Penguin, and appealing to older youth with online movies and television shows, interactive websites, and video games. Not content to peddle conservative ideologies merely to English-speaking countries, Disney continues to diversify its products on the Internet and in global markets, such as Hong Kong, where it opened a theme park in 2005. The sheer size of the Disney corporation in 2009 makes the traditional image of the artistically creative yet entrepreneurial small-town American company seem truly a thing of the past. Today's Disney rarely refrains from adapting its brand image in order to achieve the widest possible consumer base. And the multinational megaconglomerate will face difficulty restricting the associations made with its brand as it grafts itself onto other countries around the globe. This was recently made evident by a *Slate* article recounting a reporter's impressions of a billboard in Beijing:

> I was stopped in my tracks by a billboard that made the controversial 1990s Calvin Klein underwear ads look artistic by comparison. Staring down at throngs of shoppers . . . was a white girl who looked all of 12, reclining in a matching bra-and-panties set adorned with Disney's signature mouse-ear design. In a particularly creepy detail, the pigtailed child was playing with a pair of Minnie Mouse hand puppets.[8]

As pointed out by the reporter, Daniel Brook, an ad that so overtly sexualizes children, particularly one bearing the Disney logo, would never be tolerated in the United States. Disney's public relations department had just expressed outrage at a May 2008 issue of *Vanity Fair* magazine for printing photos of Miley Cyrus wearing nothing but a satin sheet. When Brook spoke with Disney management about the lingerie ad featuring a prepubescent model, he was told that in "other parts of the world this is not unusual at all" but was still assured the billboard would be promptly removed. Brook did not, however, remark explicitly upon what the Chinese billboard strongly implied about perceptions of Westerners in other countries: namely, that children are often and repeatedly exploited as commodities, if not sex objects, in the American media—and Disney is really no exception.

From its inception, Disney has understood the crucial connection between profits and selling culture to mass audiences. But Disney has mastered an understanding of how people learn through media consumption and how this grants a corporation overwhelming power to shape people, politics, and the larger culture. As one of the most powerful media conglomerates in the world, Disney promotes all the messages that serve corporate power—hierarchy, consumer agency, free markets, cultural homogeneity, and political conformity—waging battle against those individuals and groups who believe that democratic public life requires democratic cultural institutions, including the mass media. Extravagant, feature-length animated films, theme parks, and the Disneyfication of West Forty-second Street in New York City certainly may have entertainment and educational value, but such activities cannot be used as a defense for Disney's stranglehold on the message and image business, its stifling of dissent, its abusive labor practices in the United States and overseas, or its relentless corporatizing of civic discourse—all of which undermine cultural and political life in a vibrant democratic society.

Many critical interpretations of Disney miss that resistant readings of Disney culture or a subtle alteration of the cultural content produced by Disney toward a more progressive worldview cannot change the basis of the company's threat to civic life, which comes from its role as a transnational communications industry capable of exercising corporate power and ideological influence over vast segments of the globe. In the Magic Kingdom, choice is about consumption, justice is rarely deemed the outcome of social struggles, and history is framed nostalgically in the benevolent, patriarchal image of Walt Disney himself. In the animated world of Disney's classic films, monarchy replaces democracy as the preferred form of government, people of color are too often cast as either barbarous or stupid, and young Barbie doll–like princesses such as Ariel, Pocahontas, and *Enchanted*'s Giselle reaffirm the worst kind of gender divisions and stereotypes. Combining economic control with pedagogical influence, Disney has become a major player in global culture, and the first casualties of its dominance in popular culture are, of course, those who are most defenseless—children. More insidiously, Disney uses its much-touted commitment to wholesome entertainment to market an endless array of toys, clothes, and gadgets to children. Beneath Disney's self-proclaimed role as an icon of American culture lies a powerful educational apparatus that provides ideologically loaded fantasies. Walt Disney imagineers have little to do with "dreaming" a better world or even commenting on the world that today's kids actually inhabit. Compare the raw exposure of social issues and personal struggle on the Canadian television show *Degrassi: The Next Generation* with the Disney version of young people's lives in *High School Musical*. Fantasy for Disney has no basis in reality, no sense of real conflicts, struggles, joys, and social relations. Fantasy is a marketing device, a form of hype rooted in the logic of self-interest and consumerism. Disney's claim to innocence takes a big hit when, in its rapacious desire to expand its profit margins, it violates its own claims to modesty. For instance, as Brooks Barnes points out, the most expensive piece of clothing sold by the Walt Disney Company in 2002 was a "$75 sweatshirt embossed with the mug shot of Mickey Mouse."[9] Today, the Disney name with a host of new designer labels sells "$3,900 designer wedding gowns . . . $6,000 chandeliers patterned after the Art Deco décor in Mr. Disney's former office," and a sequined Mickey Mouse T-shirt for $1,400.[10]

Disney's view of children as consumers has little to do with innocence and a great deal to do with corporate greed and the realization that behind the vocabulary of family fun and wholesome entertainment is the opportunity to teach children that critical thinking and civic action in society should be far less important to them than assuming the role of passive consumers. This does not bode well for young children. The American Psychological Association (APA) reported in 2004 that "children under the age of eight lack the cognitive development to understand the persuasive intent of television advertising and are uniquely susceptible to advertising's influence." For this reason, the APA Task Force on Children and Advertising recommended a ban on advertising that targets children under the age of eight.[11] It is hard to imagine a corporation like Disney, which now owns the Baby Einstein and Club Penguin franchises, voluntarily refraining from advertising to children under eight years old.

Eager to reach children and teens, who "influence parental purchases totaling over . . . $670 billion a year," Disney relies on consultants such as marketing researcher James McNeal to reach very young consumers.[12] McNeal can barely contain his enthusiasm about targeting children as a fertile market and argues in *Kids as Customers* that the "world is poised on the threshold of a new era in marketing and that . . . fairly standardized multinational marketing strategies to children around the globe are viable."[13] In recent years, these strategies seem to be especially focused on children from ages eight to twelve, also labeled "tweens," who "spend $30 billion of their own money each year and influence another $150 billion of their parents' spending."[14] McNeal and his client, the Walt Disney Company, view kids as a lucrative market and their identities are limited as to what they consume. With so many dollars at stake, serving the public good becomes an afterthought in the battle to manipulate and commercialize children's desires and imaginations.

In its search for new markets and greater profits, Disney presents its theme parks and entertainment as objects of consumption rather than as spheres of participation. Each new product represents an advertising spectacle designed to create new markets, commodify children, and provide vehicles for merchandizing an endless array of toys, gadgets, clothes, home accessories, and other products. Films and television shows serve as launching pads for a vast array of video games and toys. Disney franchises, such as Cars and Pirates of the Caribbean, are used as a pretext to convert Walmart, JCPenney, Toys 'R' Us, McDonalds, and numerous other retailers into Disney merchandising outlets. But the real commercial blitz is centered on Disney's own marketing and distribution network, which includes the Disney Store, the Disney Channel, *Disney Magazine*, Disney.com, Disneyland, and Walt Disney World.[15]

Given the media attention on advertising directed at children, the growing prevalence of eating disorders and obesity among kids, and the exploitation and sexualization of youth in the fashion industry, there is surprisingly little public outcry over the baleful influence Disney exercises on young people. The emerging marketing trend toward promoting self-branding through consumption (as the preeminent manifestation of personal and social agency) seems even more disturbing as Disney expands the age of its traditional audience into infancy, on the one hand, and adolescence, on the other. But the general public, even conservative Christian denominations such as the Southern Baptists, appear indifferent to Disney's role in directing children's desires and needs through the lure of an endless chain of commodities. What does it mean when a corporation like Disney convinces children that the only viable public space left in which to experience themselves as autonomous beings is the toy section of Walmart or the Apple iTunes Store?

Growing up corporate has become a way of life for American youth, and companies like Disney constitute a new global force in shaping youth around the world as consuming subjects. Corporate mergers, such as Disney's buyout of ABC and Pixar Studios, consolidate corporate control of assets and markets, extending the influence of media conglomerates over public opinion. An accelerated commercialism has become apparent in all aspects of life, including the "commercialization of public schools, the renaming of public streets for commercial sponsors, Janis Joplin's Mercedes pitch, restroom advertising, and [even the marketing] of an official commercial bottled water for a papal visit."[16] Accountable only to the bottom line of profitability, companies such as Disney carpet bomb their audiences with commercials and magazine ads.[17] Michael Jacobson and Laurie Ann Mazur estimate that each day, "260 million Americans are exposed to at least 18 billion display ads in magazines and daily newspapers [as well as] 2.6 million radio commercials, 300,00 television commercials and 500,000 billboards"—and these statistics do not include daily encounters with telemarketers and the now ubiquitous advertising on the Internet.[18]

Although it is largely recognized that market culture exercises a powerful role educationally in mobilizing desires and shaping identities, it is still a shock that an increasing number of pollsters report that young people, when asked to provide a definition for democracy, refer to "the freedom to buy and consume whatever they wish, without government restriction."[19] Growing up corporate suggests that as commercial culture replaces public culture, the language of the market becomes a substitute for the language of democracy; at the same time, the primacy of commercial culture has an eroding effect on civil society as the function of public pedagogy shifts from creating a "democracy of citizens [to creating] a democracy of consumers."[20] Confusing democracy with the market does more than hollow out those public spheres whose roots are moral rather than merely commercial; it also fails to heed an important insight expressed by Federico Mayor, former director general of UNESCO, who argued rightly, "You cannot expect anything from uneducated citizens except unstable democracy."[21]

Disney's role as the arbiter of children's culture may seem abstract when expressed in these terms, but Disney has long been perfecting a very practical approach to marketing its products. Although computer technology has opened up many more ways to access potential consumers—as is evident in Disney's use of its website to provide live streaming of the Disney Channel film *Camp Rock* to 863,000 viewers in addition to the 24.5 million watching the television broadcast[22]—Disney's approach to marketing was perhaps cemented by the promotional blitz it arranged for the animated film *Hercules*. As far back as 1997, the mix of educational strategy and greed was fully evident.[23] Disney was providing a special showing of the film on June 21, 1997, a few weeks before its general release. But to get a ticket for the special showing, people had to go to an authorized Disney Store to buy a box for $7 that contained a ticket, a collector's pin of one of the characters in the film, a brochure, and a tape of a song in the show performed by Michael Bolton. Disney was in full force, in this instance making sure that every kid knew that along with the film came stuffed animals, figurines, backpacks, lunch boxes, tapes, videos, and a host of other gadgets soon to be distributed by Mattel, Timex, Golden Books, and other manufacturers of children's products. Once again, children became the reserve army of consumers for the culture industry. More egregiously, Disney, like other corporate giants in children's culture such as Mattel and Hasbro, routinely exploits workers in industrializing countries such as China, Mexico, and Indonesia.

Disney's efforts to turn the film hero Hercules into an advertisement for spin-off merchandise were shameless. The story used to be that Hercules proved himself through a series of brave deeds, but Disney turned him into a public relations hero with a marketable trade name for products such as Air Hercules sneakers, toy figurines, and action-hero dolls, all of which could be bought in an emporium modeled shamelessly in the film after a Disney Store. Disney executive Tom Schumacher claimed that the film was about building character and exploring what it means to be a celebrity, while Michael Eisner claimed that it was about "sophisticated style, and a hip sense of humor."[24] Clearly, "character" for Disney executives has less to do with developing a sense of integrity and civic courage than with getting a laugh and building name recognition in order to sell an endless stream of consumer goods. Character in the land of the Walt Disney imagineers is more about winning a popularity contest than anything else. The case of *Hercules* makes it much more difficult to believe that the Disney dream factory is a guardian of childhood innocence when it so blatantly appears to be a predatory corporation that uses children's imaginations as simply another resource for amassing earnings.[25]

Historical memory has shown clearly the dangers of unbridled corporate power in the United States and around the globe—a reality made more acute by the worldwide economic crisis of 2008 and 2009. Slavery, segregation, the exploitation of child labor, the sanctioning of cruel working conditions in coal mines and sweatshops, and the destruction of the environment have all been fueled by the law of maximizing profits and minimizing costs, especially when there has been no countervailing power from civil society to hold such powers in check. This is not to suggest that corporations are the enemy of democracy but to highlight the importance of a strong democratic civil society that sets limits on the power and authority of corporate culture. John Dewey was right: democracy requires work.[26]

Alex Molnar is also right in warning educators, parents, and others that the market does not provide "guidance on matters of justice and fairness that are at the heart of a democratic civil society."[27] Corporate culture, when left to its own devices, respects few boundaries and even fewer basic social needs, such as a safe food supply, universal access to quality health care, and safe forms of transportation. Moreover, as multinational corporations become more powerful by amassing assets and increasing their control over the circulation of information in the media, there remains little countervailing discourse about the role they play in undermining the principles of justice and freedom and in limiting the range of views at the center of our civic institutions.[28] This is particularly true for the public schools whose function, in part, is to teach about the importance of critical dialogue, debate, and decision making in a participatory democracy.[29]

What strategies are open to educators, parents, and others who want to challenge the corporate barons who are shaping children's culture in the United States and around the world? First, it must become clear that Disney and other multimedia conglomerates are not merely about peddling entertainment: they are also about politics, economics, and education. The power and influence of globe-trotting corporations such as Disney must be acknowledged for the threat they pose to children's culture and public life in general. Disney does not give a high priority to social values, except to manipulate and exploit them. With every product Disney makes, whether for adults or children, there is the accompanying commercial blitzkrieg that aims to reinforce excessive consumerism, selfishness, and individualism. This commercial onslaught undermines and displaces the values necessary to define ourselves as active and critical citizens, rather than as consumers.

Moreover, driven by the imperatives of profit, Disney and other megacorporations reward ideas, messages, and values that are supportive of the status quo and corporate power while marginalizing dissident views. A vibrant democratic culture is not served well by shrinking the range of critical public spheres, discourses, and relations necessary for the full, active participation of its citizens in shaping political culture. Disney, Time Warner, and other corporate giants constitute a media system, or national entertainment state, that has "negative implications for the exercise of political democracy: it encourages a weak political culture that makes depoliticization, apathy and selfishness rational choices for the citizenry, and it permits the business and commercial interests that actually rule U.S. society to have inordinate influence over media content."[30]

Second, battles must be waged on numerous fronts to make clear the political, economic, and cultural influence that media industries such as Disney exercise in democratic society. This suggests at the least the hard pedagogical and political work of getting the word out that "fewer than ten transnational media conglomerates dominate much of our media; [and] fewer than two dozen account for the overwhelming majority of our newspapers, magazines, films, television, radio and books."[31] Academics, teachers, parents, and others must engage in public debate in numerous venues and spheres over the implications of media concentration for commercializing public discourse, limiting the range of dissent, restricting access to channels of communication, and shaping national and global views, desires, and beliefs.

While the challenge to such media concentration has typically involved the traditional liberal call for regulation, progressives must interrogate the limits of such regulation and press for more radical structural changes. Educators, parents, community groups, and others must call into question existing structures of corporate power in order to make the democratization of media culture central to any reform movement. In part, this suggests taking ownership away from the media giants and spreading it among many sites in order to make the communications industry more diffuse and accountable. Monopolies are a political and cultural toxin in the economic as well as the cultural sphere, as demonstrated by the stock market crash of 2008. The influence of corporate giants can be broken through broad-based movements using a variety of strategies, including Internet blogging and videos, public media, organized campaigns, teach-ins, and boycotts, all of which can raise public consciousness, promote regulation, and encourage antitrust legislation aimed at breaking up media monopolies and promoting noncommercial, nonprofit public spheres.[32]

Progressives also need to press for a combination of state-supported, nonprofit, noncommercial television, radio, journalism, websites, and other cultural formations resistant to the pernicious influence of advertisers and corporate interests. At the same time, progressives must be vigilant in not yoking public broadcasting to state control.[33] Clearly, any commitment on the part of the government to cultural democracy must be tied to subsidies that allow independent media to flourish outside the commercial sphere.

Defending media democracy is no less important than demanding that schools teach media literacy, which will help students by providing them with more choices regarding what they watch, hear, buy, and consume. Media literacy as a political strategy means teaching methods of interpretation and providing tools useful for social transformation. As a form of political education, media literacy teaches students not only how to interpret critically the knowledge, values, and power produced and circulated through diverse technologies and public spaces but also to link such understanding to broader public discourses that invoke the interrelated nature of theory, community, personal identity, and social change. Makani Themba captures this sentiment in claiming that "media literacy must be more than helping children and families take a discerning look at media. We need to work together to forge new partnerships—new covenants—that address corporate irresponsibility and government neglect. We must not only talk with kids and admonish them to stay on track, we must also hold those businesses accountable who prey on our young people."[34]

These educational issues are important but become meaningless if isolated from issues of institutional and economic power and how it is used, organized, controlled, and distributed. For example, as important as it is to teach students to learn how to read ads in order to understand the values and worldviews they are selling, it is not enough. Such literacy should not be limited to matters of textual interpretation or stop with the recognition that media culture is about business rather than entertainment. Parents, educators, and others need to take an ethical stance against the manufactured myths, lifestyles, and values created by media giants like Disney in order to sell identities and increase profits.

Children are growing up in a world shaped by a visual culture under the control of a handful of megacorporations that influence much of what young people learn. We need a new language to address these forms of power and their interlocking systems, which dominate the production of knowledge on a national and global level. Against the power of a global culture industry driven by commercialism and commodification, it is crucial that we reclaim the language of critical citizenship, democracy, and social values. Financial and institutional support is necessary to develop those public cultures and spaces in which open deliberation, critical thought, and public education are not undermined by the imperatives of big business and advertising but are shaped by those social and critical values necessary for building democratic communities, identities, and social relations. This suggests curbing the power of big media and weakening the influence of advertising in shaping cultural life. Media giants such as Disney must be challenged. Disney has created an empire capable of exercising unchecked corporate power within "the injustices of an unregulated global economy."[35]

It is as important now as it was in the 1990s to challenge Disney's self-proclaimed role as a purveyor of "pure entertainment" and to take seriously Disney's educational messages aimed at teaching children selective roles, values, and cultural ideals.[36] Progressive educators and other cultural workers need to pay attention to how the pedagogical practices produced and circulated by Disney and other mass media conglomerates organize and control a circuit of power that extends from producing cultural texts to shaping the contexts that will profoundly influence children and others.

As dominant products of popular culture, Disney's films, television programs, newscasts, and other forms of entertainment should become objects of critical analysis, understanding, and intervention both inside and outside schools. It is almost a commonplace that most of what students learn today comes from electronically generated media spheres. Consequently, young people need to acquire the knowledge and skills to become literate in multiple languages and technologies so as to be able to read critically the various cultural texts to which they are exposed. This is not to suggest that we should junk a traditional literary canon for Disney studies but to suggest that we rethink how we raise and teach kids, understanding that most learning takes place in cultural spheres outside the classroom.

All people, but especially young people whose identities are forming in relation to popular culture, need to become multiply literate regarding diverse spheres of learning. The issue of what is valuable knowledge and what connects to kids' lived experiences raises interesting questions that point in different directions: What does the current generation of young people need to learn to live in a substantive democracy, to read critically in various spheres of culture, to engage those critical traditions of the past that continue to shape how we think about the present and the future, and to critically analyze multiple texts for the ideologies and identities they provide and the maps they draw that guide us toward a world that will be either more multicultural, diverse, and democratic or its very opposite?

Youth and others involved in resistance movements need to learn how to produce their own websites, videos, newspapers, radio and television programs, music, and whatever other technology is necessary to link knowledge and power with pleasure and the demands of public life. But for such skills to become useful, they must be connected to the larger project of radical democracy and technological justice, that is, to the struggle for local communities to have universal access to the Internet, public broadcasting, and the institutional spaces for theater, newspaper, and magazine productions. Put simply, young people need access to subsidized, noncommodified public spheres that allow their artistic, intellectual, and critical talents to flourish.

Involving youth in the task of making the pedagogical more political is a first step toward providing them with the skills to govern and not simply to be governed. Educators, parents, and others will find a useful resource in the Media Education Foundation (www.mediaed.org), founded by educator and filmmaker Sut Jhally, which produces and distributes documentary films as teaching tools that address critical issues in the mass media. In 2001, the Foundation released *Mickey Mouse Monopoly: Disney, Childhood and Corporate Power*, a concise examination of Disney culture that makes excellent use of footage from Disney films to illustrate larger issues involving the representation of gender and race. The Campaign for a Commercial-Free Childhood (www .commercialexploitation.org) is a national coalition of concerned citizens engaged in research, advocacy, and education regarding the harmful effects of marketing on children. The MoveOn organization (www .moveon.org) promotes political and civic action aimed at "bringing real people back into the democratic process by making sure legislators hear their voices." In addition to using media resources, such as television and print advertisements, to stir up public debate, MoveOn directly engages in campaigns for media reform. These are only a few examples of progressive organizations that attempt to revitalize democratic public spheres. Other organizations have emerged that focus specifically on youth with the goal of enabling young people both to politicize their own education and to participate in educating the larger society. Adam Fletcher has pioneered the Freechild Project (www.freechild.org), which connects kids with important informational resources (such as how to make a video) so that they can launch their own campaigns for social change. Making the political more pedagogical means that activists and others must attend to how people connect intellectually and affectively to the language, values, and political issues that shape their lives. This is no small matter because consciousness is the basic condition for agency to develop and for political action to become realizable.

Corporate power is pervasive and will not yield its control over resources willingly. Effective resistance to corporate culture requires developing pedagogical and political strategies that both educate and transform, that build alliances while recognizing different perspectives, and that foreground the struggle over democracy as the central issue. Any attempt to challenge media giants such as Disney demands linking cultural politics with policy battles. Changing consciousness must become part of a practical politics designed to change legislation, regulate the communications industry, reorganize and distribute resources, and redefine the relationship between pedagogy and social justice with the understanding that critical thought is the foundation for social and personal agency. Building alliances is especially important, and progressives need a new language for bringing together cultural workers that ordinarily have not worked well together. This suggests finding ways to organize educators and activists at all levels of schooling in order to gain control over those pedagogical forces that shape our culture. And this means addressing the pedagogical influence of those cultural industries that have supplanted the school as society's most important educational force.

There is also the crucial imperative to reinvigorate unionized labor, whose funds and power can help fight for social justice, particularly through gaining access to the media as a site for public pedagogy.[37] Unions must be convinced that the struggle over wages, better working conditions, and health benefits becomes more meaningful and effective when linked to the broader discourse of democracy and populations who are often marginalized.

Finally, we need to organize those cultural workers who inhabit the cultural spheres that produce, circulate, and distribute knowledge but who seemed removed from matters of education, politics, and culture. Artists, lawyers, social workers, and others not directly connected to formal education should nevertheless view themselves as public intellectuals engaged in a pedagogy that offers them an opportunity to join with others across the globe to expand noncommodified public spheres.

These suggestions are premised on an expansive view of the pedagogical and the political, one that chooses not to determine or restrict in advance the strategies for how political activism will work most effectively to foster genuine democracy. The only certainty is that hope must form the basis for collective resistance. As market culture permeates the social order, it threatens to cancel out the tension between market values and those values representative of civil society that cannot be measured in strictly commercial terms but that are crucial to democracy, values such as justice, freedom, equality, health, respect, and the rights of all people as equal and free human beings. Without such values, young people are relegated to the role of profit-generating machines, and the growing disregard for public life is left unchecked. What kind of world will be present when today's youth assume the mantle of citizenship? While the task of resistance to Disney's corporate and cultural monopoly is daunting, we cannot leave the future of democracy hanging precariously in the balance. Disney got its eye blackened when active citizens successfully resisted its 1995 attempt to create a theme park at a historical Virginia landmark. This victory, while modest, suggests that dominant power is never total, resistance is possible, and creating a public voice is fundamental to any struggle for social justice.

We should not underestimate the political power and cultural force of corporations such as Disney in undermining democratic public life and turning every aspect of daily life into either a commercial or an appendage of the market. It is crucial that we make visible the threat such corporations pose to democracy everywhere. Contesting the ideological underpinnings of Disney's version of common sense is the first step in critically engaging the ways in which corporate culture has refashioned the relationships between education and entertainment, on the one hand, and institutional power and culture, on the other, subordinating their democratic potential to profits and consumer entertainment. The ongoing Disneyfication of society in the United States and around the world must be halted and reversed. Challenging Disney's authority and power effectively will require a collective effort that is informed by broader political and pedagogical movements. Working together, we can create public spheres that educate for critical consciousness, close the gap in wealth and resources between the rich and the poor, and gain control over the mechanisms that will turn a truly democratic media into a plausible reality rather than just a far-off dream.

Notes

PREFACE

1. See Donald F. Roberts, Ulla G. Foehr, and Victoria Rideout, *Generation M: Media in the Lives of 8–18 Year-olds*, Henry J. Kaiser Family Foundation, March 2005, www.kff.org/entmedia/upload/Generation-M-Media-in-the-Lives-of-8-18-Year-olds-Report.pdf (accessed August 22, 2009), and Victoria Rideout and Elizabeth Hamel, *The Media Family: Electronic Media in the Lives of Infants, Toddlers, Preschoolers and Their Parents*, Henry J. Kaiser Family Foundation, May 2006, www.kff.org/entmedia/upload/7500.pdf (accessed August 22, 2009).

2. Juliet B. Schor, *Born to Buy: The Commercialized Child and the New Consumer Culture* (New York: Scribner, 2005), 25; Roberts, Foehr, and Rideout, *Generation M*, 6, 9.

INTRODUCTION

1. Stuart Hall, "The Centrality of Culture: Notes on the Cultural Revolutions of Our Time," in *Media and Cultural Regulation*, ed. Kenneth Thompson (Thousand Oaks, CA: Sage, 1997), 232.

2. Disney press release, "Disney Creates One-Stop Online Resource for Parents," Walt Disney Interactive Media Group Newsroom, March 13, 2007, http://corporate.disney.go.com/wdig/press_releases/2007/2007_0313_family-com.html (accessed May 25, 2009).

3. "Corporate Overview," Disney Corporate Information, http://corporate
.disney.go.com/corporate/overview.html (accessed February 28, 2008). See
also "Who Owns the Media?" Freepress.net, www.freepress.net/ownership/
chart.php (accessed February 28, 2008), and "Who Owns What," *Columbia
Journalism Review*, www.cjr.org/resources/?c=disney (accessed April 14,
2009).

4. Kimberly Potts, "iTunes Scores $1 Million B.O.," Movies.com, September 20, 2006, http://movies.go.com/moviesproxy/tipster?id=851020 (accessed
January 11, 2008).

5. The concentrated power of the corporate media has long been evident.
As the media conglomerates become more powerful, federal regulation will
likely be increasingly obstructed by private interests. The Federal Communications Commission has attempted more than once to eliminate some media
ownership rules designed to prevent monopolies, although the U.S. Court of
Appeals prevented one of the latest attempts. See Stephen Labaton, "Plan
Would Ease Limits on Media Owners," *New York Times*, October 18, 2007,
www.nytimes.com/2007/10/18/business/media/18broadcast.html (accessed
June 12, 2009).

6. Press release on Multiplatform Video Report by Solutions Research
Group, "Daily Hours Watching Video and TV to Match Sleep by 2013,"
Solutions Research Group, June 11, 2008, www.srgnet.com/pdf/TV%20Vid
eo%20Hours%20to%20Match%20Sleep%20Release%20(June%202008).pdf
(accessed June 18, 2009).

7. Cited in Don Hazen and Julie Winokur, eds., *We the Media* (New York:
New Press, 1997), 64.

8. Robert Bryce, "Click and Sell," *University of Texas at Austin News*,
August 15–22, 2005, www.utexas.edu/features/2005/advertising/index.html
(accessed June 16, 2009).

9. Brooks Barnes, "Disney Expert Uses Science to Draw Boy Viewers,"
New York Times, April 14, 2009, A1.

10. Barnes, "Disney Expert."

11. Brooks Barnes, "Disney Swoops into Action, Buying Marvel for $4
Billion," *New York Times*, September 1, 2009, www.nytimes.com/2009/09/01/
business/media/01disney.html (accessed September 1, 2009).

12. See Allen D. Kanner, "The Corporatized Child," *California Psychologist* 39, no. 1 (January/February 2006): 1–2, and Allen D. Kanner, "Globalization and the Commercialization of Childhood," *Tikkun* 20, no. 5 (September/
October 2005): 49–51. These articles are online at www.commercialfreechild
hood.org/articles (accessed May 20, 2009). See also Miriam H. Zoll, "Psychologists Challenge Ethics of Marketing to Children," American News Service,
April 5, 2000, www.mediachannel.org/originals/kidsell.shtml (accessed May
20, 2009).

13. Brooks Barnes, "Lab Watches Web Surfers to See Which Ads Work," *New York Times*, July 27, 2009, www.nytimes.com/2009/07/27/technology/27disney.html (accessed July 28, 2009).

14. Jeff Chester and Kathryn Montgomery, "No Escape: Marketing to Kids in the Digital Age," *Multinational Monitor* 30, no. 1 (July/August 2008), www.multinationalmonitor.org/mm2008/072008/chester.html (accessed July 10, 2009). Chester and Montgomery define the "marketing ecosystem" as comprising "cell phones, mobile music devices, instant messaging, video games, and virtual, three-dimensional worlds." They also identify "viral marketing," or word-of-mouth marketing, as an offshoot of the corporate recruitment of kids to help in product advertising to their peers and other social networks (also called "brand-generated marketing").

15. Pierre Bourdieu's analysis of the systemic corruption of television in France is equally informative when applied to the United States. See Pierre Bourdieu, *On Television*, trans. Priscilla Parkhust Ferguson (New York: New Press, 1998).

16. Cited in Joshua Karliner, "Earth Predators," *Dollars and Sense* (July/August 1998): 7.

17. Ted Turner cited in John Nichols and Robert W. McChesney, "FCC: Public Be Damned," *The Nation*, May 15, 2003, www.thenation.com/doc/20030602/nichols (accessed June 15, 2009).

18. Cited in Robert W. McChesney, *Corporate Media and the Threat to Democracy* (New York: Seven Stories Press, 1997), 18. There is an enormous amount of detailed information about the new global conglomerates and their effects on matters of democracy, censorship, free speech, social policy, national identity, and foreign policy. For example, see Herbert I. Schiller, *Culture Inc.: The Corporate Takeover of Public Expression* (New York: Oxford University Press, 1989); Edward S. Herman and Noam Chomsky, *Manufacturing Consent* (New York: Pantheon, 1988); Ben H. Bagdikian, *The Media Monopoly*, 4th ed. (Boston: Beacon Press, 1992); George Gerbner and Herbert I. Schiller, eds., *Triumph of the Image* (Boulder, CO: Westview Press, 1992); Douglas Kellner, *Television and the Crisis of Democracy* (Boulder, CO: Westview Press, 1990); Philip Schlesinger, *Media, State and Nation* (London: Sage, 1991); John Fiske, *Media Matters* (Minneapolis: University of Minnesota Press, 1994); Jeff Cohen and Norman Solomon, *Through the Media Looking Glass: Decoding Bias and Blather in the News* (Monroe, ME: Common Courage Press, 1995); Erik Barnouw et al., *Conglomerates and the Media* (New York: New Press, 1997); and C. Edwin Baker, *Media Concentration and Democracy: Why Ownership Matters* (Cambridge: Cambridge University Press, 2006).

19. Mark Crispin Miller, "What's Wrong with This Picture?" *The Nation*, December 20, 2001, www.thenation.com/doc/20020107/miller (accessed June 20, 2009).

20. Miller, "What's Wrong with This Picture?"

21. Toby Miller, *Technologies of Truth* (Minneapolis: University of Minnesota Press, 1998), 90.

22. Both quotations come from Susan Willis, "Problem with Pleasure," in *Inside the Mouse: Work and Play at Disney World*, ed. the Project on Disney (Durham, NC: Duke University Press, 1995), 5.

23. Lindor Reynolds, "Mad about Mickey: If You Still Believe in Magic, This Is the Happiest Place on Earth," *Winnipeg Free Press*, October 20, 2007, E1.

24. See Ernst Bloch, *The Utopian Function of Art and Literature*, trans. Jack Zipes and Frank Mecklenburg (Cambridge, MA: MIT Press, 1988), and Ernst Bloch, *The Principle of Hope*, Vol. 1, trans. Neville Plaice, Stephen Plaice, and Paul Knight, Studies in Contemporary German Social Thought (Cambridge, MA: MIT Press, 1986).

25. Ernst Bloch cited in Anson Rabinach, "Unclaimed Heritage: Ernst Bloch's *Heritage of Our Times* and the Theory of Fascism," *New German Critique* (spring 1977): 8.

26. As the documentary film *Mickey Mouse Monopoly* (2001, dir. Chyng Feng Sun) suggests, children's impressions of Disney are diverse, and even positive ones can be used very effectively to deepen critical perspectives of Disney films. In *Tinker Belles and Evil Queens: The Walt Disney Company from the Inside Out* (New York: New York University Press, 2000), Sean Griffin offers a balanced, yet cautious, perspective on audiences' ability to develop counternormative meanings from Disney culture in his discussion of queer appropriation, which he claims operates in far more subversive ways than the corporation would have intended, noting that Disney's apparently liberality is motivated by "economic pressures . . . to recognize a 'gay market' for its product" (xviii). For discussion of research based on audience impressions of Disney, see Janet Wasko, *Understanding Disney: The Manufacture of Fantasy* (Cambridge, MA: Polity, 2001), especially ch. 7, "Disney and the World," 183–218, and Janet Wasko, Mark Phillips, and Eileen R. Meehan, *Dazzled by Disney? The Global Disney Audiences Project* (London: Leicester University Press, 2001).

27. Francis Mulhern, "The Politics of Cultural Studies," *Monthly Review* 47, no. 3 (July 1995): 38.

28. We are invoking Meaghan Morris's argument in which she identifies the chief error of cultural studies to be the narcissistic identity made "between the knowing subject of cultural studies, and a collective subject, 'the people.'" The "people" in this discourse "have no necessary defining characteristics—except an indomitable capacity to 'negotiate' readings, generate new interpretations, and remake the materials of culture. . . . So against the hegemonic force of the dominant classes, 'the people' in fact represent the most creative energies

and functions of critical reading. In the end they are not simply the cultural student's object of study, [but] his native informants. The people are also the textually delegated, allegorical emblem of the critic's own activity." See Meaghan Morris, "Banality in Cultural Studies," *Discourse* 10, no. 2 (spring/summer 1988): 17.

29. Wasko, *Understanding Disney*, 218.

30. Douglas Brode, for example, in *Multiculturalism and the Mouse: Race and Sex in Disney Entertainment* (Austin: University of Texas Press, 2005), offers an alternative reading of Disney's films based on his argument that they demonstrate an antiestablishment, rather than a conservative, agenda. But his disparagement of critical readings of Disney for their "elitism" is not actually backed up by a populism grounded in audience research. Instead, Brode, as a Disney apologist, supports his claims with carefully constructed and selective readings of the films. There are several problems with Brode's argument: (1) he collapses his own analysis of the meaning of Disney films with selective biographical data about Walt Disney's intentions; (2) he ignores the important category of class—for instance, the fact that early consumers of Disney were middle-class and white—in his assessment of race and gender; (3) he arbitrarily divorces considerations of gender from those of race; (4) he claims that the very fact of Disney's representation of racial minorities, implied homosexuals, or women (regardless of whether the characters are construed as positive or negative or the politics of representation is actually suppressed) makes Disney's politics laudatory for promoting multicultural diversity; (5) he concludes with a circular argument that legitimates Disney's alleged broad-based, inoffensive politics by pointing out its universal appeal; and (6) he makes the assumption, without providing any evidence, that contemporary audiences are less racist, sexist, and homophobic than their predecessors (as a result of Disney's positive influence).

31. A classic example of this type of critique can be found in David Buckingham, "Dissin' Disney: Critical Perspectives on Children's Media Culture," *Media, Culture, and Society* 19 (1997): 290.

32. Edward W. Said, *The World, the Text, and the Critic* (Cambridge, MA: Harvard University Press, 1983), 169.

33. On another political register, expanding democratic public culture means working hard to get organized labor and progressive social movements to join together to forge new partnerships and pool some of their intellectual and material resources in order to create alternative public spheres in which democratic identities, relations, and values can flourish and offer multiple sites of resistance to a culture industry such as Disney in which the call for innocence, happiness, and unity appears to be "transformed into a prohibition on thinking itself." Theodor W. Adorno, *Critical Models: Interventions and Catchwords*, trans. Henry W. Pickford (New York: Columbia University Press, 1998), 290.

CHAPTER ONE

1. Walt Disney cited in Jennifer J. Laabs, "Disney Helps Keep Kids in School," *Personnel Journal* (November 1992): 58.

2. Nicholas Sammond, *Babes in Tomorrowland: Walt Disney and the Making of the American Child, 1930–1960* (Durham, NC: Duke University Press, 2005), 3.

3. Michael D. Eisner, "Planetized Entertainment," *New Perspectives Quarterly* 12, no. 4 (fall 1995): 8.

4. Michael D. Eisner, "Letter to Shareholders," in *The Walt Disney Company 1997 Annual Report* (Burbank, CA: Walt Disney Company, 1997), 3.

5. Robert Iger, "Letter to Shareholders, Part II," in *The Walt Disney Company 2008 Annual Report*, Disney Investor Relations, http://corporate.disney .go.com/investors/annual_reports/2008/introduction/letterToShareholdersII .html (accessed May 14, 2009).

6. Robert Iger, "Consumer Products, Part I," in *The Walt Disney Company 2007 Annual Report*, Disney Investor Relations, http://corporate.disney .go.com/investors/annual_reports/2007/cp/part1.html (accessed May 14, 2009).

7. Robert Iger, "Consumer Products, Part III," in *The Walt Disney Company 2007 Annual Report*, Disney Investor Relations, http://corporate.disney .go.com/investors/annual_reports/2007/cp/part3.html (accessed May 14, 2009).

8. Iger, "Consumer Products, Part I."

9. Iger, "Consumer Products, Part I."

10. "Disney's 2007 Holiday Best Sellers Top Consumer Wish Lists," Portfolio.com, January 9, 2008, www.portfolio.com/resources/company-profiles/ DIS/press/2008/01/09/disneys-2007-holiday-best-sellers-top-consumer-wish lists (accessed January 10, 2009).

11. Michael Santoli, "The Magic's Back: Disney's Bright Future," Smartmoney.com, February 26, 2008, www.smartmoney.com/barrons/index .cfm?story=20080226-Walt-Disney-DIS&nav=RSS20 (accessed March 15, 2008).

12. Stuart Hall, "The Centrality of Culture: Notes on the Cultural Revolutions of Our Time," in *Media and Cultural Regulation*, ed. Kenneth Thompson (Thousand Oaks, CA: Sage, 1997), 209.

13. On the influence of corporate media, see Robert W. McChesney, *Corporate Media and the Threat to Democracy* (New York: Seven Stories Press, 1997), and Erik Barnouw et al., *Conglomerates and the Media* (New York: New Press, 1997).

14. For an excellent analysis of the relationship between education and social justice, see R. W. Connell, *Schools and Social Justice* (Philadelphia: Temple University Press, 1993).

15. See "School Shooting," Wikipedia.org, http://en.wikipedia.org/wiki/School_shooting (accessed June 3, 2008). Fear for children's innocence is expressed in Peter Applebome, "No Room for Children in a World of Little Adults," *New York Times*, May 10, 1998, 1, 3.

16. See Henry A. Giroux, *Youth in a Suspect Society: Democracy or Disposability?* (New York: Palgrave Macmillan, 2009).

17. The shameful state of many of the children in America can be seen in some of the statistics that suggest a profound failure on the part of one of the richest democracies in the world: over 12.9 million children (21.9 percent) live in poverty, and 9.3 million in 2005 were without health insurance; 5.6 million young people between the ages of sixteen and twenty-four are out of work, and the joblessness rate among youth has surged by 16 percent since 2000. While the United States ranks first among all nations in military technology, military exports, defense expenditures, and the number of millionaires and billionaires, it is ranked eighteenth in the gap between rich and poor children, twelfth in the percentage of children in poverty, seventeenth in the efforts to lift children out of poverty, and twenty-third in infant morality. For more information, see Neil G. Bennett and Hsien-Hen Lu, *Childhood Poverty in the States: Level and Trends from 1979 to 1998*, National Center for Children in Poverty, August 2000, www.nccp.org/publications/pdf/text_385.pdf (accessed June 10, 2009).

18. Ann Powers, "Who Are These People, Anyway?" *New York Times*, April 29, 1998, E1, E8.

19. On the shifting attitude toward youth, see Lawrence Grossberg, "Why Does Neo-Liberalism Hate Kids? The War on Youth and the Culture of Politics," *Review of Education, Pedagogy, and Cultural Studies* 23, no. 2 (2001): 111–36; Henry A. Giroux, *The Abandoned Generation: Democracy beyond the Culture of Fear* (New York: Palgrave Macmillan, 2003); and Lawrence Grossberg, *Caught in the Crossfire: Kids, Politics, and America's Future* (Boulder, CO: Paradigm, 2005).

20. Thomas Hine, "Goths in Tomorrowland," in *The Rise and Fall of the American Teenager* (New York: Bard, 1999), 274–75.

21. Hine, "Goths in Tomorrowland," 276.

22. Hine, "Goths in Tomorrowland," 295.

23. See Giroux, *Youth in a Suspect Society*, especially ch. 2, "Locked Up: Education and the Youth Crime Complex," 69–108.

24. This figure is based on the Euromonitor International 2006 report, *Tweens: A Force to Be Reckoned With: Changing Consumption Habits of 8–12 Year-Olds to 2010*, summarized in "Tweens: Empowered and with Money to Burn," Euromonitor.com, March 10, 2006, www.euromonitor.com/Tweens_empowered_and_with_money_to_burn (accessed June 18, 2007).

25. Samantha Critchell, "Disney Targets Tween Shoppers," *Washington Post*, June 20, 2007, www.washingtonpost.com/wp-dyn/content/article/2007/06/20/AR2007062001741.html (accessed June 15, 2007).

26. See Harry C. Boyte, "Citizenship Education and the Public World," *Civic Arts Review* (fall 1992): 4–9.

27. This point is taken up in Powers, "Who Are These People, Anyway?" 8.

28. Lawrence Grossberg, "Toward a Genealogy of the State of Cultural Studies," in *Disciplinarity and Dissent in Cultural Studies*, ed. Cary Nelson and Dilip Parameshwar Gaonkar (New York: Routledge, 1996), 142.

29. Chris Rojek, "Disney Culture," *Leisure Studies* 12 (1993): 133.

30. According to Lawrence Grossberg, in the first place, neoliberalism "describes a political-economic project" whose "supporters are bound together by their fundamental opposition to Keynesian demand-side fiscal policy and to government regulation of business. Second, many neoliberals support laissez-faire and define the free economy as the absence of any regulation or control. . . . Neoliberals tend to believe that, since the free market is the most rational and democratic system of choice, every domain of human life should be open to the forces of the marketplace. At the very least, that means that the government should stop providing services that would be better delivered by opening them up to the marketplace. Third, neoliberals believe that economic freedom is the necessary precondition for political freedom (democracy); they often act as if democracy were nothing but economic freedom or the freedom to choose. Finally neoliberals are radical individualists. Any appeal to larger groups (e.g., gender, racial, ethnic, or class groups) as if they functioned as agents or had rights, or to society itself, is not only meaningless but also a step toward socialism and totalitarianism." Grossberg, *Caught in the Crossfire*, 112. While the literature on neoliberalism is vast, some important examples include Alain Touraine, *Beyond Neoliberalism* (London: Polity, 2001); Lisa Duggan, *The Twilight of Equality* (Boston: Beacon Press, 2003); David Harvey, *A Brief History of Neoliberalism* (New York: Oxford University Press, 2005); Wendy Brown, *Edgework: Critical Essays on Knowledge and Politics* (Princeton, NJ: Princeton University Press, 2005); Alfredo Saad-Filho and Deborah Johnston, eds., *Neoliberalism: A Critical Reader* (London: Pluto Press, 2005); Neil Smith, *The Endgame of Globalization* (New York: Routledge, 2005); Aihwa Ong, *Neoliberalism as Exception: Mutations in Citizenship and Sovereignty* (Durham, NC: Duke University Press, 2006); Randy Martin, *An Empire of Indifference: American War and the Financial Logic of Risk Management* (Durham, NC: Duke University Press, 2007); and Henry A. Giroux, *Against the Terror of Neoliberalism: Politics beyond the Age of Greed* (Boulder, CO: Paradigm, 2008).

31. Alexander Lynch, "U.S.: The Media Lobby," AlterNet, March 11, 2005, www.corpwatch.org/article.php?id=11947&printsafe=1 (accessed June 13, 2009).

32. Lynch, "U.S.: The Media Lobby."

33. Cited in Lynch, "U.S.: The Media Lobby."

34. Reed Irvine, "As ABC's Story on Disney's Pedophile Problem Gets the Spike," BNet, December 28, 1998, http://findarticles.com/p/articles/mi_m 1571/is_48_14/ai_53475813/?tag=content;col1 (accessed June 14, 2009). The issue of pedophiles working at Disney theme parks was originally raised in a book by Peter Schweizer and Rochelle Schweizer titled *Disney: The Mouse Betrayed: Greed, Corruption and Children at Risk* (Washington, DC: Regnery, 1998), which is also a scorching critique of Disney as a bastion of family entertainment turned hawker of pornography, violent song lyrics, and anti-Christian messages.

35. Quoted in Sandra L. Borden and Michael S. Pritchard, "Conflict of Interest in Journalism," in *Conflict of Interest in the Professions*, ed. Michael Davis and Andrew Stark (Oxford: Oxford University Press, 2001), 87.

36. See Gail Shister, "Decision to Kill '20/20' Piece on Disney Upsets *ABC News* Staffers," *Philadelphia Inquirer*, October 15, 1998, D6.

37. Iger, "Letter to Shareholders, Part II." See also Brooks Barnes, "Slowing Economy Posing Test for Disney," *New York Times*, November 13, 2007, www .nytimes.com/2007/11/13/business/media/13disney.html?_r=1&oref=slogin (accessed November 14, 2009).

38. See, for instance, Ariel Dorfman and Armand Mattelart, *How to Read Donald Duck: Imperialist Ideology in the Disney Comic* (New York: International General Editions, 1975); Matt Roth, "A Short History of Disney-Fascism," *Jump Cut* 40 (1996): 15–20; Carl Hiassen, *Team Rodent: How Disney Devours the World* (New York: Ballantine, 1998); and Schweizer and Schweizer, *Disney: The Mouse Betrayed*.

39. Scott Bukatman, "There's Always . . . *Tomorrowland*: Disney and the Hypercinematic Experience," *October* 57 (1991): 58.

40. Douglas Brode, for instance, reinterprets Disney's portrayals of racial and sexual difference, especially in the early films, as a "scathing indictment of the status quo" that contributed to today's culture of tolerance based on Disney's alleged "distillation of the human condition." See Douglas Brode, *Multiculturalism and the Mouse: Race and Sex in Disney Entertainment* (Austin: University of Texas Press, 2005), 18, 257. There is little doubt that Disney tries not to offend its audiences and therefore adapts to more progressive views, but Brode's readings are too laudatory. He fails to account for the way in which privilege is shored up rather than undermined by paternalism, while even positive representations of the exotic "other" remain exploitative discourses that serve the interests of hegemonic American identity and ideals. See also Douglas Brode, *From Walt to Woodstock: How Disney Created the Counterculture* (Austin: University of Texas Press, 2004).

41. Robert Iger, "Studio Entertainment, Part IV," in *The Walt Disney Company 2007 Annual Report*, Disney Investor Relations, http://corporate.disney.go.com/investors/annual_reports/2007/se/part4.html (accessed June 4, 2009).

42. Frank Ahrens, "Disney's Theme Weddings Come True for Gay Couples," *Washington Post*, April 7, 2007, www.washingtonpost.com/wp-dyn/content/article/2007/04/06/AR2007040602286.html (accessed June 10, 2009). For an early critique of Disney's alleged progressive policies toward gays and lesbians, see Stuart Gill, "Never-Never Land," *Out*, March 1998, 70–113.

43. Sean Griffin, *Tinker Belles and Evils Queens: The Walt Disney Company from the Inside Out* (New York: New York University Press, 2000), xvii, xviii.

44. For an excellent commentary on this issue, see Herbert I. Schiller, "Corporate Sponsorship," *Art Journal* (fall 1991): 56–59.

45. Eisner, "Planetized Entertainment," 9.

46. Eisner, "Planetized Entertainment," 9.

47. Benjamin Barber, "The Making of McWorld," *New Perspectives Quarterly* 12, no. 4 (fall 1995): 16.

48. Kenneth Burke, *A Rhetoric of Motives* (Berkeley: University of California Press, 1962), 26.

49. Eisner, "Planetized Entertainment," 9.

50. Eisner cited in Alan Bryman, *Disney and His Worlds* (New York: Routledge, 1995), 57. Eisner's own autobiography presents him as the ideal chief executive of a family-oriented company while conveniently leaving out Old Walt's anti-Semitism and his red-baiting of Disney cartoonists in order to break their union, as well as the firing of the popular progressive talk-radio host Jim Hightower once Disney bought Cap Cities. See Eisner with Tony Schwartz, *Work in Progress* (New York: Random House, 1998). Geraldine Fabrikant, in a review of the book, captures the flavor of Eisner's self-serving discourse. She writes, "The autobiography of Michael D. Eisner, the Chairman of Walt Disney, is a true Disney production: a PG-rated adventure with broad family appeal where the hero, by dint of hard work, sound judgment and—yes—brilliance, triumphs over adversity. It's 'The Lion King' in corporate America." Geraldine Fabrikant, "Top Mouse," *New York Times Book Review*, November 8, 1998, 28.

51. Bryman, *Disney and His Worlds*, 57.

52. For a concise yet devastating critique of what Eisner left out of his rendering of Disney history, see Mark Crispin Miller, "Michael Eisner, Launderer Extraordinaire," *Slate*, October 14, 1998, www.slate.com/id/2000012/entry/1002118 (accessed July 14, 2009).

53. Mike Wallace, *Mickey Mouse History* (Philadelphia: Temple University Press, 1996), 170.

54. Gary Cross, *Kid's Stuff: Toys and the Changing World of American Childhood* (Cambridge, MA: Harvard University Press, 1997), 105.

55. Ernest Larsen, "Compulsory Play," *The Nation*, March 16, 1998, 32.

56. "How Marketers Target Kids," Media Awareness Network, www.media-awareness.ca/english/parents/marketing/marketers_target_kids.cfm (accessed June 3, 2008); Margaret Magnarelli, "Big Spenders," *Parents*, March 2004, 146, 244–47.

57. Hiaasen, *Team Rodent*, 6–7.

58. Iger, "Letter to Shareholders, Part II."

59. Press release, "The Walt Disney Company Takes Control of Disney Stores in North America," Reuters, May 1, 2008, www.reuters.com/article/pressRelease/idUS76578+01-May-2008+BW20080501 (accessed May 10, 2008).

60. Kristina Cooke, "Children's Place to Exit Disney Chain," *Business Spectator*, March 21, 2008, www.businessspectator.com.au/bs.nsf/Article/Childrens-Place-to-exit-Disney-chain-CWVTJ?OpenDocument (accessed May 10, 2008).

61. Rojek, "Disney Culture," 121.

62. Philip Corrigan and Derek Sayer, *The Great Arch* (London: Basil Blackwell, 1985), 4.

63. Figures cited in Steven Watts, *The Magic Kingdom: Walt Disney and the American Way of Life* (New York: Houghton Mifflin, 1998), 387, and Michael Billing, "Sod Baudrillard! Or Ideology in Disney World," in *After Postmodernism*, ed. Herbert Simons and Michael Billing (Thousand Oaks, CA: Sage, 1994), 150.

64. Themed Entertainment Association/Economics Research Associates, *2008 Attraction Attendance Report*, Themed Entertainment Association, 2009, www.teaconnect.org/etea/TEAERA2008.pdf (accessed July 12, 2009).

65. Walt Disney cited in Leonard Mosley, *Disney's World: A Biography* (New York: Stein and Day, 1985), 221.

66. Both quotations are from Watts, *The Magic Kingdom*, 392, 393.

67. Watts, *The Magic Kingdom*, 392, 393.

68. On the issue of control in the parks, see Michael Sorkin, "See You in Disneyland," in *Variations on a Theme Park*, ed. Michael Sorkin (New York: Hill and Wang, 1992), 205–32.

69. Watts, *The Magic Kingdom*, 441.

70. Stephen F. Mills, "Disney and the Promotion of Synthetic Worlds," *American Studies International* 28, no. 2 (October 1990): 73.

71. Hiassen, *Team Rodent*, 27.

72. See Richard Foglesong, *Married to the Mouse: Walt Disney World and Orlando* (New Haven, CT: Yale University Press, 2001).

73. Michael Harrington, "To the Disney Station," *Harper's*, January 1979, 39.

74. The phrase "Taylorized fun," is take from Sorkin, "See You in Disneyland," 223.

75. Wayne Ellwood, "Service with a Smile: Wayne Ellwood Talks to a Disney Trade-Union Activist about Working in the Fun Factory," *New Internationalist* 308 (December 1998): 17.

76. Watts, *The Magic Kingdom*, 391.

77. Eric Smoodin, "Introduction: How to Read Walt Disney," in *Disney Discourse: Producing the Magic Kingdom*, ed. Eric Smoodin (New York: Routledge, 1994), 4–5.

78. All of these quotations are from Elayne Rapping, "A Bad Ride at Disney World," *The Progressive*, November 1995, http://findarticles.com/p/articles/mi_m1295/is_n11_v59/ai_18008842 (accessed May 15, 2007).

79. Bryman, *Disney and His Worlds*, 87–88.

80. Cited in Wallace, *Mickey Mouse History*, 136–37.

81. Michael D. Eisner, "Critics of Disney's America on the Wrong Track," *USA Today*, July 12, 1994, 10A.

82. Bryman, *Disney and His Worlds*, 141.

83. A great deal of material exists that points to Disney's omissions in constructing history. See, for example, Stephen Fjellman, *Vinyl Leaves: Walt Disney World and America* (Boulder, CO: Westview Press, 1992); Rojek, "Disney Culture"; Jon Wiener, "Tall Tales and True," *The Nation*, January 31, 1994, 133–35; Wallace, *Mickey Mouse History*; and Bryman, *Disney and His Worlds*.

84. Bukatman, "There's Always . . . *Tomorrowland*," 56.

85. Wallace, *Mickey Mouse History*, 138.

86. Wallace, *Mickey Mouse History*, 137.

87. Associated Press, "Disney Exhibit Teaches Kids Financial Lessons," MSNBC.com, May 19, 2009, www.msnbc.msn.com/id/30830451/ns/business personal_finance (accessed June 10, 2009).

88. Jane Kuenz, "It's a Small World After All: Disney and the Pleasures of Identification," *South Atlantic Quarterly* 92, no. 1 (winter 1993): 78.

89. Rapping, "A Bad Ride at Disney World," 37.

90. Richard Schickel's *The Disney Version* (1968; rpt. New York: Simon & Schuster, 1985), is a classic and important critique of Disney.

91. Cited in Watts, *The Magic Kingdom*, 471.

92. See, for example, Jon Wiener's chilling tale of how Disney has attempted to censor books dealing with the legacy of Walt Disney and of the chilling effect such pressure has had on authors who refuse to grant the Walt Disney Company such power. Jon Wiener, "Murdered Ink: Media Conglomerates Are Censoring Authors," *The Nation*, May 31, 1993, 743–50.

93. Jeff Cohen and Norman Solomon, "In Disneyland, Journalism Means Saying You're Sorry," *Extra!* (November/December 1995): 20.

94. Cohen and Solomon, "In Disneyland," 20.

95. Hightower cited in Norman Solomon, "Three Men and a Mouse," *Z Magazine*, January 1998, 63–64.

96. "ABC Shut Down Blogger Who Criticized Violent Rhetoric on One of Its Radio Stations," Media Matters for America, January 9, 2007, http://media matters.org/print/research/200701090004 (accessed June 15, 2009).

97. Jacques Steinberg, "Television Cul-de-Sac Mystery: Why Was Reality Show Killed?" *New York Times*, January 21, 2006, www.nytimes.com/2006/01/21/arts/television/21welc.html?pagewanted=all (accessed February 12, 2007).

98. Steinberg, "Television Cul-de-Sac Mystery."

99. Steinberg, "Television Cul-de-Sac Mystery."

100. Figures are cited in Nathan Gardels, "Resisting the Colonels of Disney," *New Perspectives Quarterly* 12, no. 4 (fall 1995): 6.

101. Liane Bonin, "The Tragic Kingdom," *Detour Magazine*, April 1998, 71.

102. Wallace, *Mickey Mouse History*, 134.

103. Mark Crispin Miller and Janine Jacquet Biden, "The National Entertainment State," *The Nation*, June 3, 1996, 23–26.

104. Paul L. Blocklyn, "Making Magic: The Disney Approach to People Management," *Personnel* 65, no. 12 (December 1989): 29. For an inside look at Disney's work culture, see David Koenig, *Mouse Tales: A Behind-the-Ears Look at Disneyland* (New York: Bonaventure Press, 1995).

105. Blocklyn, "Making Magic," 32.

106. This information is based on a memo from the Walt Disney Company given to Henry A. Giroux by a person working in the Career and Life Education Office at Penn State.

107. Robert Iger, "Letter to Shareholders, Part VII," in *The Walt Disney Company 2007 Annual Report*, Disney Investor Relations, http://corporate.disney.go.com/investors/annual_reports/2007/lts/part7.html (accessed June 12, 2009).

108. Aldous Huxley, *Brave New World* (1932; rpt. Toronto: Vintage Canada, 2007), 42.

109. Alison Gardy, "They're Doing It for Mickey," *California Magazine* 14, no. 1 (January 1989): 23.

110. Cited in Bryman, *Disney and His Worlds*, 108.

111. Gardy, "They're Doing It for Mickey," 24.

112. John Van Maanen, "The Smile Factory: Work at Disneyland," in *Reframing Organizational Culture*, ed. Peter J. Frost et al. (Newbury Park: Sage, 1991), 67.

113. Cited in Van Maanen, "The Smile Factory," 65.

114. Van Maanen, "The Smile Factory," 73.

115. Bonin, "The Tragic Kingdom," 71.

116. Van Maanen, "The Smile Factory," 69.

117. Van Maanen, "The Smile Factory," 76.

118. See Watts, *The Magic Kingdom*, 203–27.

119. Marc Eliot, *Walt Disney, Hollywood's Dark Prince* (New York: Birch Lane Press, 1993), 89.

120. Robert Holguin, "Disney Labor Protest Ends in 32 Arrests," *ABC News*, August 15, 2008, http://abclocal.go.com/kabc/story?section=news/local/orange_county&id=6329575 (accessed July 8, 2009).

121. Holguin, "Disney Labor Protest Ends in 32 Arrests."

122. Adam Townsend, "800 Demonstrators March on Disney over Labor Dispute," *Orange County Register*, July 14, 2009, http://ocresort.freedomblogging.com/2009/07/14/one-thousand-demonstrators-march-on-disney-over-labor-dispute/11653 (accessed July 8, 2009).

123. Andrew Ross, *The Celebration Chronicles: Life, Liberty and the Pursuit of Property Value in Disney's New Town* (New York: Ballantine, 1999), 24, 134.

124. Associated Press, "Disney Sues Anaheim over Low-Cost Housing Plan," *USA Today*, February 27, 2007, www.usatoday.com/travel/news/2007-02-27-disney-sues-anaheim-low-cost-housing_x.htm (accessed May 10, 2008).

125. Theodor Adorno and Max Horkheimer, *Dialectic of the Enlightenment* (1944; rpt. New York: Herder and Herder, 1972), 144.

126. Denise Levin, "It's a Dangerous, Litigious World, Disney Suit Says," *Los Angeles Daily Journal*, January 7, 1999, 1, 8.

127. Stuart Pfeiffer, "Trial Nears over Alleged Wild Disney Ride," *Orange County Register*, December 30, 1998, 1–2. See also Elaine Gale, "Lawsuit Blames Injuries on Park Ride," *Los Angeles Times*, December 10, 1998, 1–2.

128. Levin, "It's a Dangerous, Litigious World, Disney Suit Says," 1.

129. Zipora Jacob et al., *Plaintiff v. The Walt Disney Company et al., Defendants*, Case No. BC 153319, Superior Court of the State of California for the County of Los Angeles, December 9, 1998. Filed by Barry Novack, Attorney for the Plaintiff, November 25, 1998, 5.

130. Marisha Goldhamer, "Disney Accidents Since 1990," *Orange County Register*, June 5, 2002, www.highbeam.com/doc/1G1-86731506.html (accessed May 2, 2009).

131. Sarah Tully, "Disney Settles with Family," *Orange County Register*, January 5, 2007, www.ocregister.com/ocregister/homepage/abox/article_1465741.php (accessed May 2, 2009).

132. Chris Knap et al., "State: Disney Ride Unsafe," *Orange County Register*, December 20, 2000, B1.

133. Jessica Garrison, Meg James, and Kimi Yoshino, "Disneyland Waited 5 Minutes to Call 911," *Los Angeles Times*, October 19, 2001, http://articles .latimes.com/2000/oct/19/local/me-38930?pg=1 (accessed May 2, 2009).

134. Kimi Yoshino, "Disney Admits Errors on Ride," *Los Angeles Times*, November 26, 2003, B1.

135. Associated Press, "Poor Maintenance Blamed for Coaster Crash," CNN.com, November 26, 2003, www.cnn.com/2003/US/West/11/26/disney land.accident.ap/index.html (accessed May 2, 2009).

136. Theodor W. Adorno, *Critical Models: Interventions and Catchwords*, trans. Henry W. Pickford (New York: Columbia University Press, 1998), 193.

CHAPTER TWO

1. Benjamin R. Barber, "More Democracy! More Revolution!" *The Nation*, October 26, 1998, 12.

2. See Henry A. Giroux, *The University in Chains: Confronting the Military-Industrial-Academic Complex* (Boulder, CO: Paradigm, 2007).

3. See, for example, Henry A. Giroux, *Politics after Hope: Obama and the Crisis of Youth, Race, and Democracy* (Boulder, CO: Paradigm, 2010). See also Sam Dillon, "Dangling Money: Obama Pushes Education Shift," *New York Times* (August 17, 2009), A1.

4. The term *national entertainment state* comes from Mark Crispin Miller, "Free the Media," *The Nation*, June 3, 1996, 9.

5. Raymond Williams, *Communications* (New York: Barnes and Nobles, 1967), 15.

6. Victoria Rideout, *Parents, Children and Media: A Kaiser Family Foundation Survey*, Kaiser Family Foundation, June 2007, 7. Available online at www.kff.org/entmedia/upload/7638.pdf (accessed June 22, 2009).

7. Frederick J. Zimmerman, Dimitri A. Christakis, and Andrew N. Meltzoff, "Television and DVD/Video Viewing in Children Younger Than 2 Years," *Archives of Pediatrics and Adolescent Medicine* 161 (2007): 473–79.

8. Joel Schwarz, "Baby DVDs, Videos May Hinder, Not Help, Infants' Language Development," *University of Washington News*, August 7, 2007, http://uwnews.washington.edu/ni/article.asp?articleID=35898 (accessed June 24, 2009).

9. See Frederick J. Zimmerman, Dimitri A. Christakis, and Andrew N. Meltzoff, "Associations between Media Viewing and Language Development

in Children under Age 2 Years," *Journal of Pediatrics* 151, no. 4 (October 2007): 364–68.

10. A transcript of this letter from Robert A. Iger to Mark A. Emmert, president of the University of Washington, dated August 13, 2007, is available online. See Meg Marco, "Walt Disney Demands Retraction from University of Washington over Baby Einstein Video Press Release," The Consumerist, August 13, 2007, http://consumerist.com/consumer/take-it-back/walt-disney-demands-retraction-from-university-of-washington-over-baby-einstein-video-press-release-289008.php (accessed September 10, 2008).

11. Victoria J. Rideout, Elizabeth A. Vandewater, and Ellen A. Wartella, *Zero to Six: Electronic Media in the Lives of Infants, Toddlers and Preschoolers*, Kaiser Family Foundation, fall 2003, 5. Available online at www.kff.org/entmedia/upload/Zero-to-Six-Electronic-Media-in-the-Lives-of-Infants-Toddlers-and-Preschoolers-PDF.pdf (accessed July 20, 2009).

12. "About Baby Einstein," Disney Baby Einstein website, www.babyeinstein.com/en/our_story/about_us (accessed July 24, 2009).

13. Letter from Mark A. Emmert to Robert Iger, dated August 16, 2007, is available online. See Joel Schwarz, "UW President Rejects Disney Complaints," *University of Washington News*, August 16, 2007, http://uwnews.org/article.asp?articleID=36148 (accessed July 10, 2009).

14. For an excellent critique of how parental fears are mobilized as part of a larger effort to professionalize parenting, see Frank Furedi, *Paranoid Parenting*, 2nd ed. (New York: Continuum, 2008).

15. Disney news release, "Disney Creates One-Stop Online Resource for Parents," Walt Disney Interactive Media Group Newsroom, March 13, 2007, http://corporate.disney.go.com/wdig/press_releases/2007/2007_0313_familycom.html (accessed June 20, 2009).

16. Powered press release, "Disney Family.com and Sony Electronics Launch Virtual Classroom for Moms," RedOrbit, May 16, 2007, www.redorbit.com/news/entertainment/937334/disney_familycom_and_sony_electronics_launch_virtual_classroom_for_moms/index.html (accessed May 20, 2009).

17. Powered press release, "Disney Family.com and Sony Electronics Launch Virtual Classroom for Moms."

18. Kenneth R. Ginsburg, "The Importance of Play in Promoting Healthy Child Development and Maintaining Strong Parent-Child Bonds," *Pediatrics* 119, no. 1 (January 2007): 185. Available online at www.commercialfreechildhood.org/pdf/aapplay.pdf (accessed July 10, 2009). See also Judith Warner, *Perfect Madness: Motherhood in the Age of Anxiety* (New York: Riverhead, 2005).

19. Disney news release, "The Walt Disney Company Acquires Club Penguin," Disney News Releases, August 1, 2007, http://corporate.disney.go.com/news/corporate/2007/2007_0801_clubpenguin.html (accessed June 10, 2008).

20. Sara M. Grimes, "Saturday Morning Cartoons Go MMOG," *Media International Australia* 126 (February 2008): 120–31. Available online at www.commercialfreechildhood.org/pdf/satammmog.pdf (accessed July 20, 2009).

21. Brooks Barnes, "Web Playgrounds of the Very Young," *New York Times*, December 31, 2007, www.nytimes.com/2007/12/31/business/31virtual.html (accessed January 10, 2008).

22. Disney news release, "Disney Interactive Studios Announces Disney Fairies: Tinker Bell and the Lost Treasure for Nintendo DS," *Financial Post*, June 2, 2009, www.financialpost.com/markets/news-releases/story.html?id=1654467 (accessed June 10, 2009).

23. Paul M. Fischer et al., "Brand Logo Recognition by Children Aged 3 to 6 Years: Mickey Mouse and Old Joe the Camel," *Journal of the American Medical Association* 266, no. 22 (1991): 3145–48; American Psychological Association news release, "Television Advertising Leads to Unhealthy Habits in Children, Says APA Task Force," APA Online, February 23, 2004, www.apa.org/releases/childrenads.html (accessed June 20, 2008).

24. Ginsburg, "The Importance of Play," 183. Additional factors affecting this loss of time include (1) pressure on parents "to produce superachieving children," which leads them to overschedule their kids' time in structured, "enrichment" activities; and (2) the restructuring of public schools to focus on academic study, which has led to decreased time for recess periods, physical education, and creative-arts programming.

25. Susan Linn, "Too Much and Too Many: How Commercialism and Screen Technology Combine to Rob Children of Creative Play," *Exchange* (March/April 2009): 46. Available online at www.commercialfreechildhood.org/pdf/susanexchange.pdf (accessed January 12, 2009).

26. Susan Linn, "Baby Einstein and the Bush Administration: There's More Than Meets the Eye," CommonDreams.org, January 25, 2007, www.commondreams.org/views07/0125-24.htm (accessed January 12, 2009).

27. Linn, "Too Much," 47.

28. Diane E. Levin and Barbara Rosenquest, "The Increasing Role of Electronic Toys in the Lives of Infants and Toddlers: Should We Be Concerned?" *Contemporary Issues in Early Childhood* 2, no. 2 (2001): 242–47.

29. Jennifer Cypher and Eric Higgs, "Colonizing the Imagination: Disney's Wilderness Lodge," in *Critical Studies: From Virgin Land to Disney World, Nature and Its Discontents in the USA of Yesterday and Today*, ed. Bernd Herzogenrath (Amsterdam: Rodopi, 2001), 405.

30. Josh Golin, "The Commercialization of Narnia," Campaign for a Commercial-Free Childhood, December 2005, www.commercialfreechildhood.org/articles/featured/commercializationofnarnia.htm (accessed January 15, 2009).

31. Linn, "Too Much," 48.

32. Cited in Donna Leinsing, "Building a Community of Excellence," *National Forum: Phi Kappa Phi Journal* 77, no. 1 (winter 1997): 31.

33. Calvin Reid, "Disney Comics Goes to School," *Publishers Weekly,* May 7, 2007, www.publishersweekly.com/article/CA6439438.html (accessed May 25, 2007).

34. For more information on these programs, see Disney.com.

35. Alex Dobuzinskis, "City, Schools Rely on Disney for Local Help Alvord: We'd Hate to Lose Good Burbank Connection," *Los Angeles Daily News*, February 12, 2004, www.thefreelibrary.com/_/print/PrintArticle .aspx?id=113255641 (accessed May 26, 2007).

36. Jennifer J. Laabs, "Disney Helps Keep Kids in School," *Personnel Journal* (November 1992): 66.

37. Michael Pollan, "Town-Building Is No Mickey Mouse Operation," *New York Times Magazine*, December 4, 1997, 58.

38. Tom Vanderbilt, "Mickey Mouse Goes to Town(s)," *The Nation*, August 28, 1995, 197.

39. Cited in "Disney Tries to Create the Perfect Community . . . Blending Old and New in Celebration, Fla.," *CQ Researcher*, March 21, 1997, 254.

40. Hugh Bartling, "The Magic Kingdom Syndrome: Trials and Tribulations of Life in Disney's Celebration," *Contemporary Justice Review* 7, no. 4 (December 2004): 375.

41. Mike Davis, *City of Quartz* (London: Verso, 1990), 224.

42. Cited in Russ Rymer, "Back to the Future: Disney Reinvents the Company Town," *Harper's*, October 1996, 68.

43. Pollan, "Town-Building," 59.

44. Andrew Ross, *The Celebration Chronicles: Life, Liberty and the Pursuit of Property Value in Disney's New Town* (New York: Ballantine, 1999), 263. Ross gives an account of his experiences living in the newly minted Celebration for a twelve-month period in 1997 and 1998. According to Ross, three problems plagued Celebration in its first years of existence: shoddy housing construction, failing retail businesses, and parental disagreement regarding the school's pedagogical practices. See also Douglas Frantz and Catherine Collins, *Celebration, USA: Living in Disney's Brave New Town* (New York: Henry Holt, 1999), another memoir that discusses these issues from the perspective of a family living in Celebration in 1997.

45. Ross, *Celebration Chronicles*, 44.

46. Bartling, "Magic Kingdom Syndrome," 382.

47. Theresa Vargas, "Utopia at a Discount," *Washington Post*, July 21, 2009, www.washingtonpost.com/wp-dyn/content/article/2009/07/20/ AR2009072003342.html.

48. Ross, *Celebration Chronicles*, 322.

49. Quoted in Pollan, "Town-Building," 78.

50. Juliet Schor, "Tackling Turbo Consumption: An Interview with Juliet Schor," *Soundings* 34 (fall 2006): 45–46.

51. Quoted in Pollan, "Town-Building," 59.

52. Vanderbilt, "Mickey Mouse Goes to Town(s)," 199.

53. Quoted in Rymer, "Back to the Future," 67.

54. Quoted in "Disney Tries to Create the Perfect Community," 255.

55. Frank Furedi, *Culture of Fear* (London: Cassell, 1997), 1.

56. Leslie Postal, "Celebration School Schedule Gets Boost: Disney and District Officials Work Out a Payment Plan to Avoid Postponing Construction," *Orlando Sentinel*, April 14, 1996, 1.

57. This description is from a packet given to new families moving to Celebration and to visitors.

58. Pippin Ross, "Celebrating Education," *Disney Magazine* (fall 1997): 84.

59. For an excellent analysis of the relationship between cognitive science, especially the work of Howard Gardner and the demands of capitalism, see James Paul Gee, Glynda Hull, and Colin Lankshear, *The New Work Order* (Boulder, CO: Westview Press, 1996), especially ch. 3, "Alignments: Education and the New Capitalism," 49–72.

60. William Glasser, *Schools without Failure* (New York: Harper & Row, 1969), 204.

61. Ronald Aronson, "The Meaning of Politics," *Dissent* (spring 1998): 119.

62. William Glasser, *The Control Theory Manager* (New York: HarperCollins, 1994), 3.

63. See, for example, William Glasser, *Control Theory in the Classroom* (New York: Harper & Row, 1986); William Glasser, *The Quality School: Managing Students without Coercion* (New York: HarperCollins, 1990); and William Glasser, *The Quality School Teacher* (New York: HarperCollins, 1993).

64. Ross, *Celebration Chronicles*, 184.

65. Cited in Steven Friedman, "Taking Action against Disney," *Rethinking Schools* (summer 1997): 18.

66. Ross, *Celebration Chronicles*, 167.

67. Ross, *Celebration Chronicles*, 314.

68. This comment appeared in a fawning piece in *Disney Magazine*. See Ross, "Celebrating Education," 88.

69. Cited in Caroline E. Mayer, "At the Mickey House Club," *Washington Post National Week Edition*, September 1, 1996, 17.

70. Cited in Pollan, "Town-Building," 76.

71. Cited in Pollan, "Town-Building," 76.

72. Steve Stecklow, "Disney's Model School: No Cause to Celebrate," *Wall Street Journal*, June 3, 1997, B10.

73. Ross, *Celebration Chronicles*, 103.

74. Bartling, "Magic Kingdom Syndrome," 387.

75. Ross, *Celebration Chronicles*, 154.

76. Ross, *Celebration Chronicles*, 161.

77. Cited in Leslie Postal, "Disney's Experiment in Education Takes Off," *Orlando Sentinel*, August 13, 1996, A1.

78. Jenny Diski, "Celebrating Conformity: Disney's Mickey Mouse Utopia," *London Review of Books*, August 15, 2000, http://books.guardian.co.uk/lrb/articles/0,6109,354685,00.html.

79. Ross, *Celebration Chronicles*, 126–30.

80. Kevin Shortsleeve, "The Wonderful World of the Depression: Disney, Despotism, and the 1930s. Or, Why Disney Scares Us," *The Lion and the Unicorn* 28 (2004): 21.

81. Elayne Rapping, "A Bad Ride at Disney World," *The Progressive*, November 1995, www.encyclopedia.com/doc/1G1-18008842.html (accessed June 20, 2007).

82. Rapping, "A Bad Ride at Disney World."

83. *New York Times*, "Premiere of 'High School Musical 2' Breaks Ratings Record," August 18, 2007, www.nytimes.com/2007/08/18/arts/television/18cnd-disney.html?_r=1&ref=arts&oref=slogin (accessed August 30, 2007).

84. Rick Kissel and Michael Schneider, "'High School Musical 2 Aces Test," *Variety*, August 18, 2007, www.variety.com/article/VR1117970479.html?categoryid=14&cs=1 (accessed August 30, 2007).

85. Kissel and Schneider, "'High School Musical 2 Aces Test."

86. Virginia Heffernan, "Life as High School, This Time on Vacation," *New York Times*, August 17, 2007, www.nytimes.com/2007/08/17/arts/television/17musi.html (accessed August 30, 2007).

87. David Bianculli, "Disney Makes It Cool to Go Back to 'School,'" *NY Daily News*, August 16, 2007, www.nydailynews.com/entertainment/tv/2007/08/16/2007-08-16_disney_makes_it_cool_to_go_back_to_school.html (accessed August 30, 2007).

88. David Itzkoff, "Move Over Mickey: A New Franchise at Disney," *New York Times*, August 20, 2007, www.nytimes.com/2007/08/20/business/media/20disney.html (accessed August 30, 2007).

89. Kelefa Sanneh, "3 Girls for the Price of One (if You Could Get a Ticket)," *New York Times*, December 31, 2007, www.nytimes.com/2007/12/31/arts/music/31hann.html?_r=1&oref=slogin (accessed January 10, 2008).

90. Sanneh, "3 Girls for the Price of One."

91. "Hannah Montana/Miley Cyrus: Best of Both Worlds Concert Tour," BoxOfficeMojo.com, www.boxofficemojo.com/movies/?page=weekend&id=hannahmontanaconcert.htm (accessed March 9, 2008).

92. Mike Budd, "Introduction: Private Disney, Public Disney," in *Rethinking Disney: Private Control, Public Dimensions*, ed. Mike Budd and Max H. Kirsch (Middletown, CT: Wesleyan University Press, 2005), 1.

93. Steve Maich and Lianne George have identified a phenomenon called the "you sell" as part of an overall marketing trend away from bolstering the qualities of the product for sale toward affirming the consumer's narcissistic self-image and sense of entitlement. See Steve Maich and Lianne George, *The Ego Boom: Why the World Really Does Revolve around You* (Toronto: Key Porter, 2009).

94. Brooks Barnes, "Disney Expert Uses Science to Draw Boy Viewers," *New York Times*, April 14, 2009, A1.

95. Ethan Smith and Lauren A. E. Schuker, "Disney Nabs Marvel Heroes," *Wall Street Journal*, September 1, 2009, A1.

96. Brooks Barnes, "After Mickey's Makeover, Less Mr. Nice Guy," *New York Times*, November 5, 2009, www.nytimes.com/2009/11/05/business/media/05mickey.html (accessed November 7, 2009).

97. Jonathan Rutherford, "Cultures of Capitalism," *Soundings* 38 (spring 2008), www.lwbooks.co.uk/journals/soundings/cultures_capitalism/cultures_capitalism5.html (accessed November 24, 2009).

98. Sanneh, "3 Girls for the Price of One."

99. Zygmunt Bauman, *Liquid Times: Living in an Age of Uncertainty* (London: Polity, 2007), 107, 109.

100. Ernest Bloch, cited in Anson Rabinach, "Unclaimed Heritage: Ernst Bloch's *Heritage of Our Times* and the Theory of Fascism," *New German Critique* (spring 1977): 8.

101. See Bauman, *Liquid Times*.

CHAPTER THREE

1. Norman M. Klein, *Seven Minutes: The Life and Death of the American Animated Cartoon* (1993; rpt. London: Verso, 1998).

2. For a critical engagement of commercialization, popular culture, and children's culture, see Marsha Kinder, *Playing with Power in Movies, Television, and Video Games* (Berkeley: University of California Press, 1991); David Buckingham and Julian Sefton-Green, *Cultural Studies Goes to School* (London: Taylor and Francis, 1994); Douglas Kellner, *Media Culture* (New York: Routledge, 1995); Shirley Steinberg and Joe Kincheloe, *Kinderculture: The Corporate Construction of Childhood* (Boulder, CO: Westview Press, 1997); Jane Kenway and Elizabeth Bullen, *Consuming Children: Education-Entertainment-Advertising* (Philadelphia: Open University Press, 2001); Daniel

Thomas Cook, *The Commodification of Childhood: The Children's Clothing Industry and the Rise of the Child Consumer* (Durham, NC: Duke University Press, 2004); Benjamin R. Barber, *Consumed: How Markets Corrupt Children, Infantilize Adults, and Swallow Citizens Whole* (New York: W. W. Norton, 2007); and Deron Boyles, ed., *The Corporate Assault on Youth* (New York: Peter Lang, 2008).

3. Cited in Michiko Kakutani, "This Mouse Once Roared," *New York Times Magazine*, January 4, 1998, 8. Compare Kakutani's analysis with Matt Roth, "A Short History of Disney-Fascism," *Jump Cut* 40 (1996): 15–20.

4. Robert Iger, "Letter to Shareholders, Part II," in *The Walt Disney Company 2008 Annual Report*, Disney Investor Relations, http://corporate.disney .go.com/investors/annual_reports/2008/introduction/letterToShareholdersII .html (accessed June 10, 2009).

5. There is an ever-growing list of authors who have been pressured by Disney either through rejection of requests to use copyrighted materials or through Disney's reputation for influencing publishers not to publish certain works. Examples can be found in Jon Wiener, "In the Belly of the Mouse: The Dyspeptic Disney Archives," *Lingua Franca* (July/August 1994): 69–72. Also, Jon Wiener, "Murdered Ink," *The Nation*, May 31, 1993, 743–50. One typical example occurred in a book in which one of Henry A. Giroux's essays on Disney appears. While in the process of editing a book critical of Disney, Laura Sells, Lynda Haas, and Elizabeth Bell requested permission from Disney executives to use the archives. In response, the editors received a letter from one of Disney's legal assistants asking to approve the book. The editors declined, and Disney forbade the use of its name in the title of the book and threatened to sue if the Disney name was used. Indiana University Press argued that it did not have the resources to fight Disney, and the title of the book was changed from *Doing Disney* to *From Mouse to Mermaid*. In another instance, Routledge publishers decided to omit an essay by David Kunzle on the imperialist messages in Disney's foreign comics in a book entitled *Disney Discourse: Producing the Magic Kingdom*. Anticipating that Disney would not provide permission for illustrations from the Disney archives, Routledge decided it could not publish the essay. Discouraged, Kunzle told Jon Wiener, "I've given up. I'm not doing any more work on Disney. I don't think any university press would take the risk. The problem is not the likelihood of Disney winning in court, it's the threat of having to bear the cost of fighting them." Kunzle cited in Wiener, "In the Belly of the Mouse," 72.

6. This figure comes from Michael Meyer et al., "Of Mice and Men," *Newsweek*, September 5, 1994, 41.

7. The mutually determining relationship of culture and economic power as a dynamic hegemonic process is captured by Sharon Zukin, *Landscapes of Power: From Detroit to Disney World* (Berkeley: University of California

Press, 1991), 221. She writes, "The domestication of fantasy in visual consumption is inseparable from centralized structures of economic power. Just as the earlier power of the state illuminated public space—the streets—by artificial lamplight, so the economic power of CBS, Sony, and the Disney Company illuminates private space at home by electronic images. With the means of production so concentrated and the means of consumption so diffused, communication of these images becomes a way of controlling both knowledge and imagination, a form of corporate social control over technology and symbolic expressions of power."

8. For a listing of various public service programs that Disney has initiated, see Jennifer J. Laabs, "Disney Helps Keep Kids in School," *Personnel Journal* (November 1992): 58–68.

9. Disney executives, quoted in Mark Walsh, "Disney Holds Up School as Model for Next Century," *Education Week*, June 22, 1994, 1.

10. Tom Vanderbilt, "Mickey Mouse Goes to Town(s)," *The Nation*, August 28, 1995, 199.

11. Jean Baudrillard, *Simulations* (New York: Semiotext[e], 1983), 25. Also see Jean Baudrillard, "Consumer Society," in *Jean Baudrillard: Selected Works*, ed. Mark Poster (Stanford, CA: Stanford University Press, 1988), 29–56.

12. Alan Bryman, *Disney and His Worlds* (New York: Routledge, 1995), 26.

13. Eric Smoodin, "Introduction: How to Read Walt Disney," in *Disney Discourse: Producing the Magic Kingdom*, ed. Eric Smoodin (New York: Routledge, 1994), 18.

14. Jon Wiener, "Tall Tales and True," *The Nation*, January 31, 1994, 134.

15. Several of Disney's animated films of the 1990s were among the decade's top-grossing films. In 1994, *The Lion King* ranked first, at $253.5 million; *Aladdin* ranked second, at $217.4 million; and *Beauty and the Beast* ranked seventh, grossing $145.9 million. See Thomas King, "Creative but Unpolished Top Executive for Hire," *Wall Street Journal*, August 26, 1994, B1.

16. Elizabeth Bell, Lynda Haas, and Laura Sells, "Walt's in the Movies," in *From Mouse to Mermaid*, ed. Elizabeth Bell, Lynda Haas, and Laura Sells (Bloomington: Indiana University Press, 1995), 3.

17. The celebrations of Walt Disney are too numerous to mention in detail, but an early example is Bob Thomas, *Walt Disney: An American Original* (New York: Simon and Schuster, 1976). Thomas's book followed on the heels of a scathing attack on Disney in Richard Schickel, *The Disney Version* (New York: Simon and Schuster, 1968). A more recent version of the no-holds-barred critique of Disney is Carl Hiassen, *Team Rodent: How Disney Devours the World* (New York: Ballantine Publishing, 1998). The more moderate position is Steven Watts, *The Magic Kingdom: Walt Disney and the American Way*

of Life (New York: Houghton Mifflin, 1997). Schickel's book remains one of the best critiques of Disney.

18. Barbara Foley, "Subversion and Oppositionality in the Academy," in *Pedagogy Is Politics: Literary Theory and Critical Teaching*, ed. Maria-Regina Kecht (Urbana: University of Illinois Press, 1992), 79. See also Roger I. Simon, "Forms of Insurgency in the Production of Popular Memories," in *Between Borders: Pedagogy and the Politics of Cultural Studies*, ed. Henry A. Giroux and Peter McLaren (New York: Routledge, 1994).

19. A number of authors address Disney's imagined landscape as a place of economic and cultural power. See, for example, Zukin, *Landscapes of Power*; Michael Sorkin, "Disney World: The Power of Facade/the Facade of Power," in *Variations on a Theme Park*, ed. Michael Sorkin (New York: Noonday Press, 1992); Stephen M. Fjellman, *Vinyl Leaves: Walt Disney World and America* (Boulder, CO: Westview Press, 1992); Eric Smoodin, ed., *Disney Discourse: Producing the Magic Kingdom* (New York: Routledge, 1994); Janet Wasko, *Understanding Disney: The Manufacture of Fantasy* (Cambridge, MA: Polity, 2001); and Mike Budd and Max H. Kirsch, eds., *Rethinking Disney: Private Control, Public Dimensions* (Middletown, CT: Wesleyan University Press, 2005).

20. In his brilliant book, Norman Klein argues that Disney actually constructed his expanded cartoons as a form of animated consumer memory. As Klein puts it, "The atmospheric lighting of Disney epic cartoons is very similar to the reverie of shopping, to shopping arcades, even to the permanent dusk of a room illuminated by television. It takes us more to the expanded shopping mall than a planned suburb, to a civilization based on consumer memories more than urban (or suburban) locations. . . . Disney showed us how to stop thinking of a city as residential or commercial, but rather as airbrushed streets in our mind's eye, a shopper's nonscape. If we can make a city remind us of animated consumer memory, it removes the alienation of changing cities, and replaces it with a cloud of imaginary store windows." See Klein, *Seven Minutes*, 144.

21. The phrase *marketplace of culture* comes from Richard de Cordova, "The Mickey in Macy's Window: Childhood Consumerism and Disney Animation," in Smoodin, *Disney Discourse*, 209. It is worth noting that Disney was one of the first companies to tie in the selling of toys with the consumption of movies, with challenging the assumption that toy consumption was limited to seasonal sales.

22. Cited in Karen Schoemer, "An Endless Stream of Magic and Moola," *Newsweek*, September 5, 1994, 47.

23. Richard Corliss, "The Mouse that Roars," *Time*, June 20, 1994, 59.

24. For a list of the highest-grossing animated films, see "Animation, 1980–Present," BoxOfficeMojo.com, www.boxofficemojo.com/genres/chart/?id=animation.htm (accessed August 1, 2008).

25. For an amazing summation of the merchandizing avalanche that accompanied the film version of *The Lion King*, see Sallie Hofmeister, "In the Realm of Marketing, the 'Lion King' Rules," *New York Times*, July 12, 1994, D1, D17.

26. Jessica J. Reiff, an analyst at Oppenheimer and Company, cited in Hofmeister, "In the Realm of Marketing," D1.

27. Moira McCormick, "'Hunchback' Soundtrack Tie-Ins Abound," *Billboard*, May 25, 1996, 10.

28. Cited in Robert W. McChesney, *Corporate Media and the Threat to Democracy* (New York: Seven Stories Press, 1997), 20–21.

29. Tom McNichol, "Pushing 'Pocahontas,'" *USA Weekend*, June 9–11, 1995, 4.

30. Douglas A. McIntyre, "Disney: Wall St. Misses the Theme Park Point," 24/7 Wall St., May 8, 2007, www.247wallst.com/2007/05/disney_wall_st_ .html (accessed May 10, 2008).

31. Vincent E. Faherty, "Is the Mouse Sensitive? A Study of Race, Gender, and Social Vulnerability in Disney Animated Films," *Studies in Media and Information Literacy Education* 1, no. 3 (August 2001), http://utpjournals.metapress .com/content/08r60826151511l8/fulltext.pdf (accessed June 11, 2008).

32. Jennifer Viegas, "Study: Disney Films, TV Darken Elderly," Discovery Channel News, June 11, 2007, http://dsc.discovery.com/news/2007/06/11/ disney_hum.html?category=human&guid=20070611120030 (accessed June 13, 2007).

33. Kathi Maio, "Disney's Dolls: The Skin Colour of the Female Characters in Disney's Recent Animated Films," *New Internationalist* 308 (December 1998), www.newint.org/issue308/dolls.html (accessed May 12, 2007).

34. Faherty, "Is the Mouse Sensitive?"

35. Rosina Lippi-Green, *English with an Accent: Language, Ideology, and Discrimination in the United States* (New York: Routledge, 1997), 80, 101.

36. Wasko, *Understanding Disney*, 188.

37. Tony Bennett touches on this issue through an explication of a reading formation. He argues, "The concept of reading formation is an attempt to think context as a set of discursive and inter-textual determinations, operating on material and institutional supports, which bear in upon a text not just externally, from the outside in, but internally, shaping it—in the historically concrete forms in which it is available as a text-to-be-read—from the inside out." See Tony Bennett, "Texts in History: The Determinations of Readings and Their Texts," in *Post-structuralism and the Question of History*, ed. Derek Atridge, Geoff Bennington, and Robert Young (Cambridge, MA: Cambridge University Press, 1987), 72.

38. Critiques of Disney's portrayal of girls and women can be found in Elizabeth Bell, Lynda Haas, and Laura Sells, eds., *From Mouse to Mermaid*

(Bloomington: Indiana University Press, 1995); Susan White, "Split Skins: Female Agency and Bodily Mutilation in *The Little Mermaid*," in *Film Theory Goes to the Movies*, ed. Jim Collins, Hilary Radner, and Ava Preacher Collins (New York: Routledge, 1993), 182–95.

39. Bonnie J. Leadbeater and Gloria Lodato Wilson, "Flipping Their Fins for a Place to Stand: 19th- and 20th-Century Mermaids," *Youth and Society* 27, no. 4 (June 1993): 466–86.

40. Maio, "Disney's Dolls."

41. Susan Jefford develops this reading of *Beauty and the Beast* in *Hard Bodies: Hollywood Masculinity in the Reagan Era* (New Brunswick, NJ: Rutgers University Press, 1994), 150.

42. Maio, "Disney's Dolls."

43. Janet Maslin, "Disney Turns to a Warrior of the East in 'Mulan,'" *New York Times*, June 19, 1998, B10.

44. Henry A. Giroux would like to thank Valerie Janesick for this insight.

45. Cited in June Casagrande, "The Disney Agenda," *Creative Loafing*, March 17–23, 1994, 6–7.

46. Upon its release in 1946, *Song of the South* was condemned by the NAACP for its racist representations.

47. For a historical context that provides insight into the development of Frontierland, see Fjellman, *Vinyl Leaves*.

48. These racist episodes are highlighted in Wiener, "Tall Tales and True," 133–35.

49. Yousef Salem cited in Richard Scheinin, "Angry over 'Aladdin,'" *Washington Post*, January 10, 1993, G5.

50. Howard Green, a Disney spokesperson, dismissed the charges of racism as irrelevant, claiming that such criticisms were coming from a small minority and that "most people were happy" with the film. Quoted in Scheinin, "Angry over 'Aladdin,'" G1.

51. I have taken this criticism from Jack Shaheen, "Animated Racism," *Cineaste* 20, no. 1 (1993): 49.

52. See Susan Miller and Greg Rode for a rhetorical analysis of *The Jungle Book* and *Song of the South* in their chapter, "The Movie You See, the Movie You Don't: How Disney Do's that Old Time Derision," in Bell, Haas, and Sells, *From Mouse to Mermaid*, 86–104.

53. Edward Said, *Culture and Imperialism* (New York: Knopf, 1993).

54. Maio, "Disney's Dolls."

55. Susan Willis brilliantly explores this theme in "Fantasia: Walt Disney's Los Angeles Suite," *Diacritics* 17 (summer 1987): 83–96.

56. James B. Stewart, *Disney War* (New York: Simon and Schuster, 2005), 479–80.

57. Laura M. Holson, "Disney Agrees to Acquire Pixar in a $7.4 Billion Deal," *New York Times*, January 25, 2006, www.nytimes.com/2006/01/25/business/25disney.html?_r=2&oref=slogin (accessed January 31, 2008).

58. See the discussion of creative play in chapter 2, which draws from Susan Linn, "Too Much and Too Many: How Commercialism and Screen Technology Combine to Rob Children of Creative Play," *Exchange* (March/April 2009): 46. Available online at www.commercialfreechildhood.org/pdf/susanexchange.pdf (accessed August 10, 2009).

59. Lee Artz, "Monarchs, Monsters, and Multiculturalism: Disney's Menu for Global Hierarchy," in *Rethinking Disney*, ed. Mike Budd and Max H. Kirsch (Middletown, CT: Wesleyan University Press, 2005), 83.

60. Manohla Dargis, "'Cars' Is a Drive down a Lonely Highway," *New York Times*, June 9, 2006, http://movies.nytimes.com/2006/06/09/movies/09cars.html?scp=5&sq=cars&st=cse (accessed July 12, 2007).

61. Annalee R. Ward, *Mouse Morality: The Rhetoric of Disney Animated Film* (Austin: University of Texas Press, 2002).

62. Eleanor Byrne and Martin McQuillan, *Deconstructing Disney* (London: Pluto, 1999), 126–32, 170–73.

63. Alan Ackerman, "The Spirit of Toys: Resurrection and Redemption in *Toy Story* and *Toy Story 2*," *University of Toronto Quarterly* 74, no. 4 (fall 2005): 911.

64. In order to maintain the close identification between the viewers and the anthropomorphic toys, *Toy Story* must resist the kind of destructive nihilism exhibited by Sid and his monstrous hybrid creations, despite the fact that Sid's creative engagement with the toys as objects exhibits more originality and agency in his deviation from the scripted play suggested by the toy manufacturers.

65. Artz, "Monarchs, Monsters, and Multiculturalism," 88, 91.

66. Karl Marx, "The Fetishism of the Commodity and Its Secret," in *Capital*, Vol. 1, trans. Ben Fowkes (London: Penguin, 1976), 163.

67. Laurie Frankel, "Finding Nemo," *Film and History* 34, no. 1 (2004): 75.

68. Frankel, "Finding Nemo," 76.

69. David S. Whitley, *The Idea of Nature in Disney Animation* (Aldershot, UK: Ashgate, 2008), 136.

70. Elizabeth Jackson, "Acquiring Nemo," *Radio National Business Report* (Australia), November 29, 2003, www.abc.net.au/rn/talks/8.30/busrpt/stories/s1000651.htm (accessed June 15, 2008); Mark Corcoran, "Vanuatu—Saving Nemo," *ABC News* (Australia), November 9, 2004, www.abc.net.au/foreign/content/2004/s1239666.htm (accessed June 15, 2008).

71. Frankel, "Finding Nemo," 75.

72. For example, *Ratatouille* received a 96 percent score on Metacritic.com, which placed it seventh (between *Dr. Strangelove* and *The Manchurian Candidate*) on the site's list of best-reviewed films of all time.

73. "Ratatouille Breaks French Record," Starpulse.com, August 11, 2007, www.starpulse.com/news/index.php/2007/08/11/ratatouille_breaks_french_ record (accessed August 12, 2008).

74. "'Ratatouille' Comes Out: A Lecture for Friends of Remy at UCLA," *Los Angeles Times Daily Dish*, March 4, 2009, http://latimesblogs.latimes.com/ dailydish/2009/03/queering-ratato.html (accessed August 12, 2008).

75. Sean Griffin, *Tinker Belles and Evil Queens: The Walt Disney Company from the Inside Out* (New York: New York University Press, 2000).

76. David Denby, "The Wanderers," *The New Yorker*, June 8, 2009, www .newyorker.com/arts/critics/cinema/2009/06/08/090608crci_cinema_denby (accessed June 19, 2009).

77. Quoted in Louis Hau, "How to Build a Disney Franchise," *Forbes*, February 5, 2008, www.commercialexploitation.org/news/howto.htm (accessed May 10, 2008).

78. Dana Stevens, "Princess MasterCard: There's Something Rotten about *Enchanted*," *Slate*, November 29, 2007, www.slate.com/id/2178849 (accessed June 24, 2009).

79. Linn, "Too Much and Too Many, 47.

80. Brooks Barnes, "Her Prince Has Come. Critics, Too," *New York Times*, May 29, 2009, www.nytimes.com/2009/05/31/fashion/31disney .html?pagewanted=1 (accessed June 10, 2009).

81. Quoted in John Anderson, "Away Gabriella! Now She's the Emo Girl," *New York Times*, August 7, 2009, www.nytimes.com/2009/08/09/movies/ 09ande.html?_r=2 (accessed August 12, 2009).

82. Deborah Ross, "Escape from Wonderland: Disney and the Female Imagination," *Marvel and Tales: Journal of Fairy-Tale Studies* 18, no. 1 (2004): 63.

83. George Gerbner et al., "Growing Up with Television: The Cultivation Perspective," in *Media Effects: Advances in Theory and Research*, ed. Jennings Bryant and Dolf Zillmann (Hillsdale, NJ: Erlbaum, 1995), 17.

84. David Buckingham, "Conclusion: Re-Reading Audiences," in *Reading Audiences: Young People and the Media*, ed. David Buckingham (Manchester, UK: Manchester University Press, 1993), 211.

85. Cited in Zukin, *Landscapes of Power*, 222. While this quotation refers to Disney's view of its theme parks, it is an ideological view of history that strongly shapes all of Disney's cultural productions. For commentary on how this view affects Disney's rendering of adult films, see Henry A. Giroux, *Dis-*

turbing Pleasures: Learning Popular Culture (New York: Routledge, 1994), especially 25–45.

86. Fjellman, *Vinyl Leaves*, 400.

87. Rustom Bharacuha, "Around Ayodhya: Aberrations, Enigmas, and Moments of Violence," *Third Text* 24 (fall 1993): 51.

88. Bennett, "Texts in History," 80.

89. See, for instance, Andrew Hart, ed., *Teaching the Media: International Perspectives* (Hillsdale, NJ: Erlbaum, 1998).

90. Artz, "Monarchs, Monsters, and Multiculturalism," 95.

91. Smoodin, "How to Read Walt Disney," 4–5.

92. George Monbiot, "Of Mice and Money Men," *Guardian*, February 17, 2004, www.guardian.co.uk/world/2004/feb/17/usa.shopping/print (accessed March 12, 2009).

93. Mark Crispin Miller, "Free the Media," *The Nation*, June 3, 1996, 9–15. For an update on the national entertainment state, see "The National Entertainment State, 2006," in the June 20, 2006, issue of *The Nation*.

94. For an example of such an analysis, see Henry A. Giroux, *Youth in a Suspect Society: Democracy or Disposability?* (New York: Palgrave Macmillan, 2009). For excellent theoretical work on consumerism and neoliberalism, see Zygmunt Bauman, *Consuming Life* (London: Polity, 2007), and Zygmunt Bauman, *Does Ethics Have a Chance in a World of Consumers* (Cambridge, MA: Harvard University Press, 2008). See also Jeremy Seabrook, *Consuming Cultures: Globalization and Local Lives* (New York: New Internationalist, 2006); Mike Davis, *Planet of Slums* (London: Verso, 2007); and Mike Davis and Daniel Bertrand Monk, *Evil Paradises: Dreamworlds of Neoliberalism* (New York: New Press, 2008). For an excellent history analyzing the politics of mass consumption in postwar America, see Lizabeth Cohen, *A Consumer's Republic: The Politics of Mass Consumption in Postwar America* (London: Vintage, 2003). For an equally impressive history of the commodification of childhood in the clothing industry, see Cook, *The Commodification of Childhood*. See also the now-classic Jackson Lears, *A Cultural History of Advertising in America* (New York: Basic Books, 1994). Some of the books that address the commercialization of young people while drawing on the theoretical legacy of now-classic theories of reification, consumption, and simulacra include Kenway and Bullen, *Consuming Children*; Steinberg and Kincheloe, *Kinderculture*; Henry A. Giroux, *The Abandoned Generation: Democracy beyond the Culture of Fear* (New York: Palgrave Macmillan, 2003); Lawrence Grossberg, *Caught in the Crossfire: Kids, Politics, and America's Future* (Boulder, CO: Paradigm, 2005); and Barber, *Consumed*.

95. Inderpal Grewal and Caren Kaplan, "Introduction: Transnational Feminist Practices and Questions of Postmodernity," in *Scattered Hegemonies*, ed.

Inderpal Grewal and Caren Kaplan (Minneapolis: University of Minnesota Press, 1994).

96. For other examples of how communities rallied to resist Disney's encroachment, see Stacy Warren, "Saying No to Disney: Disney's Demise in Four American Cities," in *Rethinking Disney: Private Control, Public Dimensions*, ed. Mike Budd and Max H. Kirsch (Middletown, CT: Wesleyan University Press, 2005), 231–60.

97. Scott Powers, "Disney Settles Labor Complaint over 2005 Job Cuts," *Orlando Sentinel*, March 2, 2007, www.wdwradio.com/forums/walt-disney-world-wdw-news/11247-disney-settles-labor-complaint-over-05-job-cuts.html (accessed July 22, 2009).

CHAPTER FOUR

1. Robert E. Stripling and H. A. Smith, "The Testimony of Walter E. Disney before the House Committee on Un-American Activities," in *Walt Disney: Conversations*, ed. Kathy Merlock Jackson (Jackson: University of Mississippi Press, 2006), 40.

2. Stripling and Smith, "Testimony," 36.

3. Stripling and Smith, "Testimony," 40.

4. Kevin Shortsleeve, "The Wonderful World of the Depression: Disney, Despotism, and the 1930s. Or, Why Disney Scares Us," *The Lion and the Unicorn* 28 (2004): 13. For more information on current Disney labor relations, see Jane Kuenz, "Working at the Rat," in *Inside the Mouse: Work and Play at Disney World*, ed. the Project on Disney (Durham, NC: Duke University Press, 1995), 98–109.

5. Stripling and Smith, "Testimony," 38, 40–41.

6. See Henry A. Giroux, *Hearts of Darkness: Torturing Children in the War on Terror* (Boulder, CO: Paradigm, 2010).

7. Disney, quoted in Richard Shale, *Donald Duck Joins Up: The Walt Disney Studio during World War II* (Ann Arbor: University of Michigan Research Press, 1982), 12.

8. Shale, *Donald Duck Joins Up*, 16.

9. This statement can be found on the dust jacket of the Walt Disney Treasures DVD collection, *Walt Disney on the Front Lines: The War Years*, produced and released by Disney Studio in 2004.

10. Shale, *Donald Duck Joins Up*, xv.

11. Shale, *Donald Duck Joins Up*, xv, 22.

12. John Grierson, quoted in Shale, *Donald Duck Joins Up*, 16.

13. Shale, *Donald Duck Joins Up*, 43–44.

14. Shale, *Donald Duck Joins Up*, 41–49.

15. Dale Adams, "Saludos Amigos: Hollywood and FDR's Good Neighbor Policy," *Quarterly Review of Film and Video* 24 (2007): 289.

16. The films, produced for adult audiences and occasionally verging on the psychedelic, are indeed a departure from traditional Disney fare, as explained by Julianne Burton-Carvajal, "'Surprise Package': Looking Southward with Disney," in *Disney Discourse: Producing the Magic Kingdom*, ed. Eric Smoodin (New York: Routledge, 1994), 131–47. Not only does the mix of cartoon and live action create an uncanny effect for the viewer, as Burton-Carvajal suggests, but *The Three Caballeros* is fascinating because it so irrepressibly, if unconsciously, captures, only to comically defuse, U.S. colonial desires toward the Latin American "other." On the complex role of gender in these films, see José Piedra, "Pato Donald's Gender Ducking," in Smoodin, *Disney Discourse*, 148–68.

17. Shale, *Donald Duck Joins Up*, 24.

18. Leonard Maltin, introduction to "From the Vault," Disc 1, Walt Disney Treasures DVD collection, *Walt Disney on the Front Lines: The War Years*.

19. Film historian Leonard Maltin makes this assertion in his introduction to "Victory through Air Power," Disc 2, Walt Disney Treasures DVD collection, *Walt Disney on the Front Lines: The War Years*.

20. On the growing militarization of American culture, see Henry A. Giroux, *The University in Chains: Confronting the Military-Industrial-Academic Complex* (Boulder, CO: Paradigm, 2007), and Henry A. Giroux, *Against the Terror of Neoliberalism: Politics beyond the Age of Greed* (Boulder, CO: Paradigm, 2008).

21. Mark Langer, "Disney's Atomic Fleet," *Animation World Magazine* 3, no. 1 (April 1998), www.awn.com/mag/issue3.1/3.1pages/3.1langerdisney.html (accessed January 15, 2007).

22. Langer, "Disney's Atomic Fleet."

23. Janet Wasko, *Understanding Disney: The Manufacture of Fantasy* (Cambridge, MA: Polity, 2001), 218.

24. Christiane Staninger, "Disney's Magic Carpet Ride: *Aladdin* and Women in Islam," in *The Emperor's Old Groove: Decolonizing Disney's Magic Kingdom*, ed. Brenda Ayres (New York: Peter Lang, 2003), 69.

25. Diane Sachko Macleod, "The Politics of Vision: Disney, *Aladdin*, and the Gulf War," in Ayres, *The Emperor's Old Groove*, 180.

26. Macleod, "The Politics of Vision."

27. Macleod, "The Politics of Vision," 182. See also Leslie Felperin Sharman, "New Aladdins for Old," *Sight and Sound* (November 1993): 12–15.

28. Susan Hines and Brenda Ayres, introduction to Ayres, *The Emperor's Old Groove*, 10.

29. Macleod, "The Politics of Vision," 185.

30. Jim Rutenberg, "Disney Is Blocking Distribution of Film that Criticizes Bush," *New York Times*, May 5, 2004, http://query.nytimes.com/gst/fullpage .html?res=9B01E2DB1E3DF936A35756C0A9629C8B63 (accessed January 14, 2007).

31. See Ted Hearn, "Cablers Are Ponying Up Presidentially," Multichannel News, July 26, 2004, www.multichannel.com/article/CA438589 .html?display=Top+Stories (accessed January 16, 2007).

32. Rutenberg, "Disney Is Blocking Distribution of Film."

33. Sharon Waxman and Laura M. Holson, "The Split between Disney and Miramax Gets a Little Wider," *New York Times*, June 7, 2004, http://query .nytimes.com/gst/fullpage.html?res=9401E3D71131F934A35755C0A9629C8 B63 (accessed January 18, 2007); and Laura M. Holson, "Hollywood Ending for Weinsteins and Disney?" *New York Times*, February 22, 2005, www.nytimes .com/2005/02/22/business/media/22movie.html (accessed January 19, 2007).

34. See David Bauder, "ABC Airs 9/11 Film with Changes," *Herald-Tribune*, September 11, 2006, www.heraldtribune.com/article/20060911/ FEATURES/60911005/-1/MULTIMEDIA0201 (accessed January 22, 2007). The BBC promotional trailer promoting the miniseries as the "official true story" is available online at www.youtube.com/watch?v=aHgbeJu1WGk (accessed January 22, 2007). For more on the controversy surrounding the sources for the miniseries, see Jesse McKinley, "9/11 Miniseries Is Criticized as Inaccurate and Biased," *New York Times*, September 5, 2006, www.nytimes. com/2006/09/06/us/06path.html?ex=1315195200&en=efca0d9281dd6d4c&ei =5088 (accessed January 22, 2007); "ABC Tells Fox that Path to 9/11 'Is Based Solely and Completely on the 9/11 Commission Report,'" ThinkProgress.org, September 6, 2006, http://thinkprogress.org/2006/09/06/abc-fox (accessed January 22, 2007); and "European 'Path to 9/11' Trailer Promotes 'Official True Story' Which Falsely Blames Clinton Officials," Rawstory.com, September 9, 2007, www.rawstory.com/news/2006/European_Path_to_911_trailer__0909. html (accessed January 22, 2007).

35. John F. Borowski, "ABC/Disney and Scholastic, Inc. Solicits Teacher to Peddle Lies with 'The Path to 9/11,'" CommonDreams.org, September 7, 2006, www.commondreams.org/views06/0907-32.htm (accessed January 22, 2007).

36. Govindi Murty, "Interview: Writer-Producer Cyrus Nowrasteh on His 'Into the West' and '9/11' Miniseries," *Libertas: A Forum for Conservative Thought on Film*, June 9, 2005, www.libertyfilmfestival.com/libertas/index .php?p=462 (accessed January 22, 2007).

37. On Nowrasteh's and Cunningham's connection to right-wing activists such as David Horowitz, see Max Blumenthal, "Discover the Secret Right-

Wing Network behind ABC's 9/11 Deception," *Huffington Post*, September 8, 2006, www.huffingtonpost.com/max-blumenthal/discover-the-secret-right_ b_29015.html (accessed January 24, 2007), and Max Blumenthal, "ABC 9/11 Docudrama's Right-Wing Roots," *The Nation*, September 11, 2006, www .thenation.com/doc/20060925/path_to_911 (accessed January 24, 2007).

38. "Top Bush Counterterrorism Official: ABC's Path to 9/11 is 'Shameful,' 'Straight Out of Disney and Fantasyland,'" ThinkProgress.org, September 6, 2006, http://thinkprogress.org/2006/09/06/bush-official-blasts-abc (accessed January 14, 2007).

39. "Tell ABC to Tell the Truth about 9/11," ThinkProgress.org, http:// thinkprogress.org/tellabc (accessed January 14, 2007).

40. Tom Shales, "ABC's Twisted 'Path to 9/11,'" *Washington Post*, September 9, 2006, www.washingtonpost.com/wp-dyn/content/article/2006/09/08/ AR2006090801949.html (accessed January 10, 2007).

41. Shales, "ABC's Twisted 'Path to 9/11.'"

42. See "Leading Historians Call for Cancellation of 'Fraudulent' ABC 9/11 Docudrama," Open Letter to ABC: Don't Airbrush 9/11, September 8, 2006, http://openlettertoabc.blogspot.com/2006/09/leading-historians-call-for.html (accessed January 15, 2007).

43. Harvey Keitel, "Showbiz Tonight Exclusive," September 7, 2006, video and transcript at www.crooksandliars.com/2006/09/07/harvey-keitel-speaks-out-on-path-to-911-it-turned-out-not-all-the-facts-were-correct (accessed January 10, 2007).

44. Scholastic press release, "Scholastic Replaces 'The Path to 9/11' Classroom Guide with New Discussion Materials Focusing on Critical Thinking and Media Literacy Skills," Scholastic, September 7, 2006, www.scholastic.com/ aboutscholastic/news/press_09072006_CP.htm (accessed January 15, 2007).

45. PR Newswire, "The Free Enterprise Action Fund: Disney CEO Shouldn't Put Personal Politics and Favorite Presidential Candidate over Shareholders," Reuters, February 26, 2008, www.reuters.com/article/pressRelease/ idUS176919+26-Feb-2008+PRN20080226 (accessed January 18, 2009).

46. Benjamin Toff, "Arts, Briefly; Ratings Ride Coattails," *New York Times*, September 13, 2006, http://query.nytimes.com/gst/fullpage.html?res=9 D02E7D71531F930A2575AC0A9609C8B63 (accessed January 18, 2007).

47. Michael Eisner once conveyed the corporate idea of synergy in the statement "The Disney stores promote the consumer products, which promote the theme parks, which promote the TV shows. The TV shows promote the company." Mike Budd defines Disney synergy as the process through which "every Disney product [exists as] both a commodity and an ad for every other Disney commodity," in *Rethinking Disney: Private Control, Public Dimensions*, ed. Mike Budd and Max H. Kirsch (Middletown, CT: Wesleyan University Press, 2005), 1. For another discussion of synergy, see Frank Roost, "Synergy City:

How Times Square and Celebration Are Integrated into Disney's Marketing Cycle," in Budd and Kirsch, *Rethinking Disney*, 261–98.

48. George W. Bush, "President's Address to the Nation," September 11, 2006, www.whitehouse.gov/news/releases/2006/09/20060911-3.html (accessed September 15, 2006).

49. Bush, "President's Address to the Nation."

50. Sara Ivry, "Disney Chief's Gift to College Draws Students' Ire, Briefly," *New York Times*, October 16, 2006, www.nytimes.com/2006/10/16/business/media/16iger.html (accessed December 20, 2007).

51. Ivry, "Disney Chief's Gift."

52. PR Newswire, "The Free Enterprise Action Fund."

53. Louis Marin, "Utopic Degeneration: Disneyland," in *Utopics: The Semiological Play of Textual Spaces*, trans. Robert A. Vollrath (1973; rpt. New York: Humanity Books, 1984), 240.

54. Marin, "Utopic Degeneration."

55. See Henry A. Giroux, *Against the New Authoritarianism: Politics after Abu Ghraib* (Winnipeg, Canada: Arbeiter Ring, 2005).

56. David Barstow, "Behind TV Analysts, Pentagon's Hidden Hand," *New York Times*, April 20, 2008, www.nytimes.com/2008/04/20/us/20generals.html (accessed July 22, 2009).

57. Steven Watts, *The Magic Kingdom: Walt Disney and the American Way of Life* (Boston: Houghton Mifflin, 1997), 390.

58. Disney memo cited in Watts, *The Magic Kingdom*, 349. See also Eric Smoodin, *Animating Culture: Hollywood Cartoons from the Sound Era* (New Brunswick, NJ: Rutgers University Press, 1993), especially ch. 5, "Disney Diplomacy: The Links between Culture, Commerce, and Government Policy," 136–85.

59. Herbert Mitgang, "Disney Link to the F.B.I. and Hoover Is Disclosed," *New York Times*, May 6, 1993, B1.

60. Watts, *The Magic Kingdom*, 349.

61. Eric Smoodin, "Introduction: How to Read Walt Disney," in Smoodin, *Disney Discourse*, 7–8.

62. Ty Burr, "Inventive 'Incredibles' May Be Pixar's Most Family-Friendly Film Yet," *Boston Globe*, November 5, 2004, www.boston.com/movies/display?display=movie&id=2593 (accessed June 15, 2007).

63. A. O. Scott, "Being Super in Suburbia Is No Picnic," *New York Times*, November 5, 2004, http://movies.nytimes.com/2004/11/05/movies/05incr.html (accessed June 15, 2007).

64. Jessica Winter, "Full Metal Racket," *Village Voice*, November 1, 2004, www.villagevoice.com/film/0444,winter2,58041,20.html.

65. Burr, "Inventive 'Incredibles.'"

66. Burr, "Inventive 'Incredibles.'"

67. Scott, "Being Super."

68. Scott, "Being Super."

69. Jeremy Heilman, "The Incredibles," MovieMartyr.com, November 8, 2004, www.moviemartyr.com/2004/incredibles.htm (accessed June 15, 2007).

70. David Morley and Kevin Robins, "Spaces of Identity: Communications Technologies and the Reconfiguration of Europe," *Screen* 30, no. 4 (1989): 31.

71. Shortsleeve, "Wonderful World," 3.

72. M. Keith Booker, *The Post-utopian Imagination: American Culture in the Long 1950s* (Westport, CT: Greenwood, 2002), 144.

73. David Hastings Dunn, "The Incredibles: An Ordinary Day Tale of a Superpower in the Post 9/11 World," *Millennium: Journal of International Studies* 34, no. 2 (2005): 560, 559.

74. Burr, "Inventive 'Incredibles'"; Heilman, "The Incredibles."

75. Heilman, "The Incredibles."

76. George Soros, "The U.S. Is Now in the Hands of a Group of Extremists," *Guardian*, January 26, 2004, www.commondreams.org/views04/0126-01 .htm (accessed June 19, 2007).

77. Hastings Dunn, "The Incredibles," 561.

78. On the history of America's self-perception as a moral exemplar, active crusader, and benevolent superpower, see Susan M. Matarese, *American Foreign Policy and the Utopian Imagination* (Amherst: University of Massachusetts Press, 2001), especially ch. 3, "Visions of World Redemption," 33–60.

79. Abigail Solomon-Godeau, *Photography at the Dock* (Minneapolis: University of Minnesota Press, 1991), xxii.

CHAPTER FIVE

1. Sonia Verma, "'Disneyland' Comes to Baghdad with Multi-million Pound Entertainment Park," *Times*, April 24, 2008, www.timesonline.co.uk/ tol/news/world/iraq/article3802051.ece (accessed May 10, 2008).

2. Michael Chossudovsky, "War Propaganda: Disneyland Goes to War-Torn Iraq," Centre for Research on Globalization, April 28, 2008, www.global research.ca/PrintArticle.php?articleId=8837 (accessed May 10, 2008).

3. Chossudovsky, "War Propaganda."

4. Verma, "'Disneyland.'"

5. Zygmunt Bauman, *Globalization: The Human Consequences* (New York: Columbia University Press, 1998).

6. Ariel Dorfman and Armand Mattelart, *How to Read Donald Duck: Imperialist Ideology in the Disney Comic* (New York: International General Editions, 1975).

7. Jonathan Weber, "The Ever-Expanding, Profit-Maximizing, Cultural-Imperialist, Wonderful World of Disney," *Wired*, February 2002, www.wired.com/wired/archive/10.02/disney_pr.html (accessed July 22, 2008).

8. Wayne Ellwood, "Inside the Disney Dream Machine," *New Internationalist* 308 (December 1998), www.newint.org/issue308/keynote.htm (accessed June 13, 2007).

9. Mark Phillips, "The Global Disney Audiences Project: Disney across Cultures," in *Dazzled by Disney? The Global Disney Audiences Project*, ed. Janet Wasko, Mark Phillips, and Eileen R. Meehan (London: Leicester University Press, 2001), 45.

10. Of course, Disney's decision to coproduce the film with a Chinese company also means that the film does not incur the restrictions and censorship imposed on "foreign" films by the Chinese government. Associated Press, "Disney Hopes to Strike 'Magic' in China," *China Daily*, May 17, 2007, www.chinadaily.com.cn/entertainment/2007-05/17/content_874524.htm (accessed June 20, 2009).

11. AFP, "Disney Says to Produce Anime 'Made in Japan,'" AFP, March 5, 2008, http://afp.google.com/article/ALeqM5hnULEhW5mU8ZBork 014LPKxW8VvQ (accessed June 24, 2009).

12. "Disney's Dance Contest 'My School Rocks' Kicks Off in Mumbai," IndianTelevision.com, November 16, 2006, www.indiantelevision.com/headlines/y2k6/nov/nov199.htm (accessed June 28, 2009).

13. Robert Iger, "Walt Disney International," in *The Walt Disney Company 2008 Annual Report*, Disney Investor Relations, http://corporate.disney.go.com/investors/annual_reports/2008/keyBusinesses/waltDisneyInternational.html (accessed July 4, 2009).

14. Annalee R. Ward, *Mouse Morality: The Rhetoric of Disney Animated Film* (Austin: University of Texas Press, 2002), 112. We should note, however, that *Mulan* was accepted by the Chinese government for distribution, thereby enabling Disney films to regain access to a market that had been closed to them for the preceding three years (following Disney's decision to distribute Martin Scorsese's *Kundun* [1996], a film that seriously offended the Chinese government for its sympathetic portrayals of the Dalai Lama and the Tibetan fight for independence). See Erik Eckholm, "Easing Tension, Disney Gains O.K. to Show 'Mulan' in China," *New York Times*, February 8, 1999, www.nytimes.com/1999/02/08/world/easing-tensions-disney-gains-ok-to-show-mulan-in-china.html (accessed July 10, 2009). It turned out that *Mulan* was not well received in China because audiences thought the Disney characters were too "foreign looking." See "Chinese Unimpressed with Disney's *Mulan*," *BBC News*, March 19, 1999, http://news.bbc.co.uk/2/hi/entertainment/299618.stm (accessed July 10, 2009).

15. Mike Davis and Daniel Bertrand Monk, introduction to *Evil Paradises* (New York: New Press, 2007), ix.

16. Weber, "The Ever-Expanding."

17. Weber, "The Ever-Expanding."

18. Janet Wasko, *Understanding Disney: The Manufacture of Fantasy* (Cambridge, MA: Polity, 2001), 184.

19. Phillips, "The Global Disney Audiences Project," 42.

20. Phillips, "The Global Disney Audiences Project," 42.

21. Janet Wasko and Eileen R. Meehan, "Dazzled by Disney? Ambiguity in Ubiquity," in Wasko, Phillips, and Meehan, *Dazzled by Disney?* 334.

22. Phillips, "The Global Disney Audiences Project," 48.

23. Wasko, *Understanding Disney*, 192.

24. Shunya Yoshimi develops a compelling argument that "Disneyland is a three-dimensional Disney film." See Shunya Yoshimi, "Japan: American in Japan/Japan in Disneyfication: The Disney Image and the Transformation of 'America' in Contemporary Japan," in Wasko, Phillips, and Meehan, *Dazzled by Disney?* 173–75.

25. Alan Bryman, *The Disneyization of Society* (London: Sage, 2004), 4.

26. Bryman, *The Disneyization of Society*, 158, 13.

27. Bryman, *The Disneyization of Society*, 4.

28. Brooks Barnes, "Disney's Retail Plan Is a Theme Park in Its Stores," *New York Times*, October 13, 2009, www.nytimes.com/2009/10/13/business/media/13disney.html (accessed October 13, 2009).

29. Bryman, *The Disneyization of Society*, 173.

30. Sharon Zukin, "Learning from Disney World," *The Cultures of Cities* (Malden, MA: Blackwell, 1995), 77.

31. Bryman, *The Disneyization of Society*, 169.

32. Jack Lyne, "Hong Kong Disneyland Tops Out Centerpiece Structure," *The Site Selection Online Insider*, October 10, 2004, www.siteselection.com/ssinsider/snapshot/sf041014.htm (accessed July 12, 2009).

33. Michael Hardt and Antonio Negri, *Empire* (Cambridge, MA: Harvard University Press, 2000), 331.

34. See, for example, Aviad E. Raz, *Riding the Black Ship: Japan and Tokyo Disneyland* (Cambridge, MA: Harvard University Asia Center and Harvard University Press, 1999).

35. Jeremy Seabrook, "Racketeers of Illusion," *New Internationalist* 308 (December 1998), www.newint.org/issue308/illusion.htm (accessed May 12, 2009).

36. Jeff Chester and Kathryn Montgomery, "No Escape: Marketing to Kids in the Digital Age," *Multinational Monitor* 30, no. 1 (July/August 2008), www.multinationalmonitor.org/mm2008/072008/chester.html (accessed July 22, 2009).

37. Hardt and Negri, *Empire*, 304.

38. Bryman, *The Disneyization of Society*, 173.

39. Hardt and Negri, *Empire*, 321–22.

40. Hardt and Negri, *Empire*, 314, 321.

41. Sheldon Wolin, *Democracy, Inc.: Managed Democracy and the Specter of Inverted Totalitarianism* (Princeton: Princeton University Press, 2008), 65.

42. See Henry A. Giroux, *Against the Terror of Neoliberalism: Politics beyond the Age of Greed* (Boulder, CO: Paradigm, 2008).

43. Seabrook, "Racketeers of Illusion."

44. *The Walt Disney Company 2008 Corporate Responsibility Report*, Disney Corporate Information, http://disney.go.com/crreport/workplaces/labor standards/influence.html (accessed June 15, 2009).

45. *The Walt Disney Company 2008 Corporate Responsibility Report* is online at http://disney.go.com/crreport/home.html (accessed June 2, 2009).

46. On various resistance strategies and movements involving globalization, see Arjun Appadurai, "Grassroots Globalization and the Research Imagination," *Public Culture* 12, no. 1 (2000): 1–19; Barry K. Gills, ed., *Globalization and the Politics of Resistance* (London: Macmillan, 2000); Jeremy Brecher, Tim Costello, and Brendan Smith, *Globalization from Below* (Boston: South End, 2000); Naomi Klein, "Farewell to the End of History: Organization and Vision in Anti-corporate Movements," *Socialist Register* (2002): 1–13; Jackie Smith and Hank Johnston, *Globalization and Resistance: Transnational Dimensions of Social Movements* (Lanham, MD: Rowman and Littlefield, 2002); Stanley Aronowitz and Heather Gautney, eds., *Implicating Empire: Globalization and Resistance in the 21st Century World Order* (New York: Basic Books, 2003); Louise Amoore, ed., *The Global Resistance Reader* (New York: Routledge, 2005); Richard Kahn and Douglas Kellner, "Oppositional Politics and the Internet: A Critical/Reconstructive Approach," in *Media and Cultural Studies: Key Works*, ed. Meenakshi Gigi Durham and Douglas Kellner (Malden, MA: Blackwell, 2006), 703–25; Richard Kahn and Douglas Kellner, "Resisting Globalization," in *The Blackwell Companion to Globalization*, ed. George Ritzer (Malden, MA: Blackwell, 2007), 662–74.

47. See Campaign for a Commercial-Free Childhood at www.commercial exploitation.org. The implications of the commercialization of childhood are discussed in more detail in chapter 2 of this book.

48. For China Labor Watch's letter to Disney, see "Take Action!" China Labor Watch, July 2, 2009, www.chinalaborwatch.org/20090702disney.htm (accessed July 10, 2009).

49. Wasko and Meehan, "Dazzled by Disney?" 341.

50. Peter Marcuse, "The Language of Globalization," *Monthly Review* 52, no. 3 (July/August 2000), www.monthlyreview.org/700marc.htm (accessed June 22, 2009).

51. For an account and analysis of the web of lies and legal illegalities perpetrated by the Bush regime, see Henry A. Giroux, *Hearts of Darkness: Torturing Children in the War on Terror* (Boulder, CO: Paradigm, 2010).

52. Il Viaggiatore, "Why Villains in Movies Have English Accents," BBC h2g2, January 15, 2003, www.bbc.co.uk/dna/h2g2/A891155 (accessed July 12, 2009).

53. Chinese censors ordered scenes involving Sao Feng to be cut from the film version released in China because the character was too reminiscent of a Fu Manchu–type villain typical of the Hollywood tradition of "vilifying and defacing the Chinese." Associated Press, "Censored 'Pirates' Is Low-Fat in China," *Seattle Times*, June 16, 2007, http://seattletimes.nwsource.com/html/nationworld/2003750371_chow16.html (accessed July 12, 2009). The gender politics of the film are no better than its racial politics. The few female characters are primarily defined in relation to their romantic attachments to men and ultimately assume "domesticated" roles in contrast to the adventure-seeking men. For example, the female lead's brief stint as pirate king ends with her symbolically "returning" the boots she wore to her husband, while the sea, personified as a female human, vents its fury in a maelstrom that symbolizes the self-defeating wrath of a scorned woman.

54. Figures from Jerry W. Markham, *A Financial History of Modern U.S. Corporate Scandals: From Enron to Reform* (Armonk, NY: M. E. Sharpe, 2005), 264.

55. Maurya Wickstrom, "*The Lion King*, Mimesis, and Disney's Magical Capitalism," in *Rethinking Disney: Private Control, Public Dimensions*, ed. Mike Budd and Max H. Kirsch (Middletown, CT: Wesleyan University Press, 2005), 115.

56. James B. Stewart, *Disney War* (New York: Simon and Schuster, 2005).

57. Russell Mokhiber and Robert Weissman, *Corporate Predators: The Hunt for Mega-profits and the Attack on Democracy* (Monroe, ME: Common Courage Press, 1999), 167.

58. David Leonhardt, "Eisner's 19 Years at Walt Disney," *New York Times*, December 1, 2003, www.nytimes.com/2003/12/01/us/eisner-s-19-years-at-walt-disney.html (accessed June 12, 2009).

59. Daniel Gross, "The Louse in the Mouse House: Why Disney's Michael Eisner Should Be Fired," *Slate*, August 6, 2002, http://slate.msn.com/id/2069052 (accessed June 18, 2009); Henry M. Caroselli, *Cult of the Mouse: Can We Stop Corporate Greed from Killing Innovation in America?* (Berkeley, CA: Ten Speed Press, 2004), 1. Eisner's connection to the Shrek character is speculative, but the film was made by DreamWorks CEO Jeffrey Katzenberg, a former Disney employee whom Eisner had alienated and forced to resign.

60. Wickstrom, "*The Lion King*," 117.

61. Caroselli, *Cult of the Mouse*, 25.

62. Quoted in Paul R. La Monica, "Eisner Out as Disney Chair," CNNMoney.com, March 4, 2004, http://money.cnn.com/2004/03/03/news/companies/disney/index.htm (accessed June 20, 2009).

63. Markham, *A Financial History*, 263–64.

64. Press release, "SEC Charges the Walt Disney Company for Failing to Disclose Relationships between Disney and Its Directors," U.S. Securities and Exchange Commission, December 20, 2004, www.sec.gov/news/press/2004 176.htm (accessed June 22, 2009).

65. Jonathan R. Macey, *Corporate Governance: Promises Kept, Promises Broken* (Princeton, NJ: Princeton University Press, 2008), 78.

66. Macey, *Corporate Governance*, 76.

67. Macey, *Corporate Governance*, 78–79.

68. Macey, *Corporate Governance*, 78.

69. Stewart, *Disney War*, 2.

70. Phillips, "The Global Disney Audiences Project," 48.

71. Daniel Gross, "The Haunted Mansion: How Michael Eisner Continues to Hang On at Disney," *Slate*, February 4, 2004, www.slate.com/id/2094923 (accessed July 14, 2009).

72. Zygmunt Bauman, *The Individualized Society* (London: Polity, 2001), 9.

73. Ruth Rosen, "Note to Nancy Pelosi: Challenge Market Fundamentalism," CommonDreams.org, January 30, 2007, www.commondreams.org/views07/0130-22.htm (accessed July 15, 2009).

74. Wickstrom, "*The Lion King*," 116.

75. Chris Hedges, "America Is in Need of a Moral Bailout," Truthdig.com, March 23, 2009, www.truthdig.com/report/print/20090323_america_is_in_need_of_a_moral_bailout (accessed March 26, 2009).

76. Betsy Schiffman, "Michael Eisner: Mouse in a Gilded Mansion," *Forbes*, April 26, 2001, www.forbes.com/2001/04/26/eisner.htm (accessed July 3, 2009).

77. Peter Dreier, "Bush's Class Warfare," *Huffington Post*, December 21, 2007, www.huffingtonpost.com/peter-dreier/bushs-class-warfare_b_77910.html (accessed July 15, 2009).

78. Dreier, "Bush's Class Warfare."

79. Bauman, *Globalization*, 70.

80. Dollars and Sense and United for a Fair Economy, *The Wealth Inequality Reader*, 2nd ed. (Chicago: Dollars and Sense, 2008).

81. Hedges, "America Is in Need of a Moral Bailout."

82. Robert Iger, "Letters to Shareholders: Part IV," in *The Walt Disney Company 2007 Annual Report*, Disney Investor Relations, http://corporate.disney.go.com/investors/annual_reports/2007/lts/part4.html (accessed July 20, 2009).

83. Peter Bart, "Extreme Makeover: Mouse Edition," *Variety,* February 22, 2008, www.variety.com/article/VR1117981322.html?categoryid=1&cs=1&nid =2562 (accessed July 22, 2009).

84. On the "you sell" as the new approach to advertising, see Steve Maich and Lianne George, *The Ego Boom: Why the World Really Does Revolve around You* (Toronto: Key Porter Books, 2009).

85. Iger quoted in Associated Press, "Disney Tackles a DVD Dilemma," *Taipei Times,* September 4, 2005, www.taipeitimes.com/News/bizfocus/archives/ 2005/09/04/2003270373/print (accessed August 2, 2009).

86. Brooks Barnes, "Disney Tolerates a Rap Parody of Its Critters. But Why?" *New York Times,* September 24, 2007http://query.nytimes.com/gst/ fullpage.html?res=9503EEDD1F3EF937A1575AC0A9619C8B63 (accessed September 28, 2007).

87. Alexander Wilson, "Managed Landscape: The Organization of Disney World," *Impulse* 12, no. 1 (1985): 25.

88. "Parks and Resorts: Part V," in *The Walt Disney Company 2008 Annual Report,* Disney Investor Relations, http://corporate.disney.go.com/investors/ annual_reports/2008/keyBusinesses/parksAndResortsV.html (accessed July 28, 2009).

89. Quoted in Reuters, "Update 2—Disney Says Business Resilient Despite Economy," Reuters, September 10, 2008, www.reuters.com/article/markets News/idUSLA43864820080910 (accessed July 22, 2009).

90. Elayne Rapping, "A Bad Ride at Disney World," *The Progressive,* November 1995, www.thefreelibrary.com/A+bad+ride+at+Disney+World-a 018008842 (accessed July 19, 2009).

91. Laura M. Holson, "Disney Bows to Feng Shui," *New York Times,* April 25, 2005, www.nytimes.com/2005/04/24/business/worldbusiness/24iht-disney .html (accessed July 15, 2009).

92. Stacy Warren, "Saying No to Disney: Disney's Demise in Four American Cities," in Budd and Kirsch, *Rethinking Disney,* 242.

93. Warren, "Saying No to Disney," 246, 231–32.

94. Quoted in Alan Riding, "Only the French Elite Scorn Mickey's Debut," *New York Times,* April 13, 1992, www.nytimes.com/1992/04/13/world/only-the-french-elite-scorn-mickey-s-debut.html?pagewanted=all (accessed July 25, 2009).

95. Riding, "Only the French Elite Scorn Mickey's Debut."

96. Susan Hines and Brenda Ayres, introduction to *The Emperor's Old Groove: Decolonizing Disney's Magic Kingdom,* ed. Brenda Ayres (New York: Peter Lang, 2003), 9.

97. Hines and Ayres, introduction to Ayres, *The Emperor's Old Groove.*

98. Andrew Lainsbury, *Once upon an American Dream: The Story of Euro Disneyland* (Lawrence: University Press of Kansas, 2000), 10.

99. Dianne Sachko Macleod, "The Politics of Vision: Disney, *Aladdin*, and the Gulf War," in Ayres, *The Emperor's Old Groove*, 188.

100. Daniel Workman, "Disneyland Resort Paris Lessons: American Management Adapts to Cultural Diversity in France," *Suite101.com*, February 11, 2008, http://internationaltrade.suite101.com/article.cfm/disneyland_resort_paris_lessons (accessed June 13, 2009).

101. "A Disney Dress Code Chafes in the Land of Haute Couture," *New York Times*, December 25, 1991, www.nytimes.com/1991/12/25/business/a-disney-dress-code-chafes-in-the-land-of-haute-couture.html?scp=6&sq=Euro%20disney%20employee&st=cse&pagewanted=all&pagewanted=print (accessed June 15, 2009).

102. Quoted in "'Work in Progress,' Michael Eisner Memoir, with Tony Schwartz, to be Released by Random House; in Stores Sept. 24," *Business Wire*, September 24, 1998, http://findarticles.com/p/articles/mi_m0EIN/is_1998_Sept_24/ai_53027025 (accessed June 10, 2009).

103. Ellwood, "Inside the Disney Dream Machine."

104. Louis Marin, "Utopic Degeneration: Disneyland," in *Utopics: The Semiological Play of Textual Spaces*, trans. Robert A. Vollrath (1973; rpt. New York: Humanity Books, 1984), 241.

105. Mitsuhiro Yoshimoto, "Images of Empire: Tokyo Disneyland and Japanese Cultural Imperialism," in *Disney Discourse: Producing the Magic Kingdom*, ed. Eric Smoodin (New York: Routledge, 1994), 189.

106. See Weber, "The Ever-Expanding."

107. Yoshimi, "Japan," 176–77.

108. Mary Yoko Brennan, "'Bwana Mickey': Constructing Cultural Consumption at Tokyo Disneyland," in *Re-made in Japan: Everyday Life and Consumer Taste in a Changing Society*, ed. Joseph J. Tobin (New Haven, CT: Yale University Press, 1992), 219.

109. Gary Cross and Gregory Smits, "Japan, the U.S., and the Globalization of Children's Consumer Culture," *Journal of Society History* 38, no. 4 (summer 2005): 877.

110. Cross and Smits, "Japan, the U.S.," 885.

111. Cross and Smits, "Japan, the U.S.," 877.

112. Cross and Smits, "Japan, the U.S.," 886.

113. Yoshimoto, "Images of Empire," 185.

114. Yoshimoto, "Images of Empire," 191.

115. Yoshimoto, "Images of Empire," 194–95.

116. Yoshimoto, "Images of Empire," 197.

117. Yoshimi, "Japan," 175–76.

118. Aviad E. Raz, "Domesticating Disney: Onstage Strategies of Adaptation in Tokyo Disneyland," *Journal of Popular Culture* 33, no. 4 (spring 2000): 77.

119. Raz, "Domesticating Disney," 77.

120. Raz, "Domesticating Disney," 95.

121. Weber, "The Ever-Expanding."

122. Weber, "The Ever-Expanding."

123. James T. Areddy and Peter Sanders, "Disney's Shanghai Park Plan Advances," *Wall Street Journal*, January 12, 2009, http://online.wsj.com/article/SB123152852355168823.html (accessed July 22, 2009).

124. Frederik Balfour and Bruce Einhorn, "Hong Kong Disneyland's Future Is in Danger," *Business Week*, March 17, 2009, www.businessweek.com/global biz/content/mar2009/gb20090317_923737.htm (accessed July 22, 2009).

125. Balfour and Einhorn, "Hong Kong Disneyland's Future."

126. Holson, "Disney Bows to Feng Shui."

127. Associated Press, "Disney Hopes to Strike 'Magic' in China."

128. "Disney Appeals to China's Youth," *BBC News*, September 23, 2004, http://news.bbc.co.uk/2/hi/business/3683894.stm (accessed July 22, 2009).

129. Bauman acknowledges this phrase was first coined by John Dunn. Zygmunt Bauman, *Consuming Life* (London: Polity, 2007), 140.

130. Andrew Ross, *The Celebration Chronicles: Life, Liberty and the Pursuit of Property Value in Disney's New Town* (New York: Ballantine, 1999), 316.

131. Rapping, "A Bad Ride at Disney World."

132. See SACOM, "Tianyu Toys Bring You . . . Winnie the Pooh: A Survey of Conditions at a Disney Supplier in China," EvB, October 2007, www.evb.ch/cm_data/Tianyu_Toys_DISNEY_Oct2007_SACOM.pdf (accessed November 22, 2008).

133. See Lisa Cartwright and Brian Goldfarb, "Cultural Contagion: On Disney's Health Education Films for Latin America," in Smoodin, *Disney Discourse*, 169–80.

134. See www.losdisneys.com/messageboard.html (accessed July 25, 2009).

135. See www.losdisneys.com/about.html (accessed July 25, 2009).

136. Mexica Movement press release, "International Boycott of the Walt Disney Company," Mexica Movement, July 7, 2006, www.mexica-movement.org/boycottdisney.htm (accessed November 15, 2008).

137. Mexica Movement press release, "International Boycott of the Walt Disney Company."

138. "Disney Rewrites Carib History," *New Internationalist* 379 (June 2005), www.newint.org/columns/currents/2005/06/01/disney (accessed June 15, 2008).

139. Tom Leonard, "Disney Accused of Bad Taste over Carib Cannibals in Pirate Movie," *Telegraph*, February 15, 2005, www.telegraph.co.uk/news/

worldnews/centralamericaandthecaribbean/1483583/Disney-accused-of-bad-taste-over-Carib-cannibals-in-pirate-movie.html (accessed June 15, 2008).

140. Quoted in Murray MacAdam, "Working for the Rat," *New Internationalist* 308 (December 1998), www.newint.org/issue308/rat.htm (accessed June 10, 2009).

141. Walt Disney Company, "Code of Conduct for Manufacturers," Disney Corporate Information, http://corporate.disney.go.com/responsibility/codeof conduct.html (accessed June 22, 2009).

142. MacAdam, "Working for the Rat."

143. NACLA, "Disney Union Busting in Haiti," *NACLA Report on the Americas* 32, no. 3 (September/October 1998): 43–44.

144. Walt Disney Company, "Corporate Responsibility: Frequently Asked Questions," Disney Corporate Information, http://corporate.disney.go.com/responsibility/faq.html (accessed July 22, 2009).

145. *The Walt Disney Company 2008 Corporate Responsibility Report.*

146. *The Walt Disney Company 2008 Corporate Responsibility Report.*

147. *The Walt Disney Company 2008 Corporate Responsibility Report.*

148. China Labor Watch, "Take Action!"

149. "Corporate Responsibility: Part I," in *The Walt Disney Company 2008 Annual Report*, Disney Investor Relations, http://corporate.disney.go.com/investors/annual_reports/2008/keyBusinesses/corporateResponsibility.html (accessed July 22, 2009).

150. "Disney," SACOM, 2005, http://sacom.hk/category/campaigns/disney (accessed July 20, 2009).

151. John Sexton, "Labor Group Pricks Mickey Mouse's Bad Conscience," China.org.cn, May 4, 2009, http://sacom.hk/archives/521 (accessed July 20, 2009).

152. SACOM, "Tianyu Toys," 4.

153. SACOM, "Tianyu Toys," 7.

154. SACOM, "Yonglida Toys Brings You . . . X-mas Gifts: A Survey of Conditions at a Disney Supplier in China," SACOM, November 2007, http://sacom.hk/wp-content/uploads/2008/07/yonglida-toys-disney-nov2007.pdf (accessed October 20, 2008).

155. SACOM, "Yonglida Toys, 5.

156. See *Final Report by the Project Kaleidoscope Working Group*, Disney Corporate Information, March 2008, http://corporate.disney.go.com/corporate/pdfs/project_kaleidoscope.pdf (accessed July 19, 2009).

157. Walt Disney Company, "Corporate Responsibility: Frequently Asked Questions."

158. SACOM, "Tianyu Toys," 7.

159. John Sexton, "Disney in Child Labor Storm," China.org.cn, May 17, 2009, www.china.org.cn/china/news/2009-05/17/content_17787852.htm (accessed August 5, 2009).

160. David Barboza, "Despite Law, Job Conditions Worsen in China," *New York Times*, June 23, 2009, www.nytimes.com/2009/06/23/business/global/23labor.html (accessed August 5, 2009).

161. China Labor Watch, "Take Action!"

162. Jennifer Anopolosky, "Open Letter to 'Friends,'" Disney Corporate Information, July 30, 2009, http://corporate.disney.go.com/files/Yiu-Wah-Factory.pdf (accessed August 5, 2009).

163. Nick Couldry, "Media and the Problem of Voice," unpublished paper, 2009.

164. Achille Mbembe, "Necropolitics," *Public Culture* 15, no. 1 (winter 2003): 11–12.

165. Some of the most brilliant work on racist exclusion can be found in David Theo Goldberg, *Racist Culture* (Malden, MA: Blackwell, 1993), and David Theo Goldberg, *The Threat of Race: Reflections on Racial Neoliberalism* (Malden, MA: Blackwell, 2009).

166. Wendy Brown, *Edgework: Critical Essays on Knowledge and Politics* (Princeton, NJ: Princeton University Press, 2005), 42.

167. Brown, *Edgework*, 42.

168. Angela Davis, "Locked Up: Racism in the Era of Neoliberalism," *ABC News* (Australia), March 18, 2008, www.abc.net.au/news/stories/2008/03/19/2193689.htm (accessed July 25, 2009).

169. Jean Comaroff, "Beyond Bare Life: AIDS, (Bio)Politics, and the Neoliberal Order," *Public Culture* 19, no. 1 (winter 2007): 207.

170. Nick Couldry, "In Place of a Common Culture, What?" *Review of Education, Pedagogy, and Cultural Studies* 26, no. 1 (2004): 15. On the issue of emergent publics, see Ian Angus, *Emergent Publics* (Winnipeg, Canada: Arbeiter Ring, 2001).

171. Comaroff, "Beyond Bare Life," 200.

172. Comaroff, "Beyond Bare Life," 214.

CONCLUSION

1. Cited in Lori Sharn, "Southern Baptists Denounce Disney, Urge Boycott," *USA Today*, June 19, 1997, 1A.

2. Chris Woodyard, "Disney to Extend Health Benefits to Gay Partners," *Los Angeles Times*, October 7, 1995, http://articles.latimes.com/1995-10-07/news/mn-54276_1_partner-benefits (accessed January 12, 2008).

3. Associated Press, "Southern Baptists End 8-Year Disney Boycott," *Fox News*, June 22, 2005, www.foxnews.com/story/0,2933,160382,00.html (accessed January 12, 2008).

4. Sean Griffin, *Tinker Belles and Evil Queens: The Walt Disney Company from the Inside Out* (New York: New York University Press, 2000), xii, 205, 214, 229.

5. For an analysis of the "national entertainment state," along with a chart that tracks the acquisitions of four major media conglomerates, including Disney, see Mark Crispin Miller and Janine Jacquet Biden, "The National Entertainment State," *The Nation*, June 3, 1996, 23–26. See also Mark Crispin Miller, "Free the Media," *The Nation*, June 3, 1996, 9–15.

6. Ovitz is quoted in Peter Bart, "Disney's Ovitz Problem Raises Issues for Showbiz Giants," *Daily Variety*, December 16, 1996, 1.

7. Robert Iger, "Letter to Shareholders, Part II," in *The Walt Disney Company 2008 Annual Report*, Disney Investor Relations, http://corporate.disney .go.com/investors/annual_reports/2008/introduction/letterToShareholdersII .html (accessed August 6, 2009).

8. Daniel Brook, "Mickey Mouse Operation: Forget Miley Cyrus, Check Out Disney's Chinese Underwear Ad," *Slate*, April 29, 2008, www.slate.com/ id/2190209 (accessed August 10, 2009).

9. Brooks Barnes, "Disney, by Design," *New York Times*, November 6, 2008,www.nytimes.com/2008/11/06/fashion/06disney.html?pagewanted=print (accessed August 15, 2009).

10. Barnes, "Disney, by Design."

11. Press release, "Television Advertising Leads to Unhealthy Habits in Children; Says APA Task Force," *APA Online*, February 23, 2004, www.apa .org/releases/childrenads.html (accessed June 29, 2009).

12. Anup Shah, "Children as Consumers," *Global Issues*, January 8, 2008, www.globalissues.org/TradeRelated/Consumption/Children.asp (accessed June 29, 2009).

13. James U. McNeal, *Kids as Customers: A Handbook of Marketing for Children* (New York: Lexington Books, 1992).

14. Christine Lagorio, "Resources: Marketing to Kids," *CBS News*, May 17, 2007, www.cbsnews.com/stories/2007/05/14/fyi/main2798401.shtml (accessed August 10, 2009). For further resources on marketing to children and teens, see Shirley Steinberg and Joe Kincheloe, *Kinderculture: The Corporate Construction of Childhood* (Boulder, CO: Westview Press, 1997); Jane Kenway and Elizabeth Bullen, *Consuming Children: Education-Entertainment-Advertising* (Philadelphia: Open University Press, 2001); Alissa Quart, *Branded: The Buying and Selling of Teenagers* (New York: Basic, 2004); Susan Linn, *Consuming Kids: The Hostile Takeover of Childhood* (New York: New Press, 2004), and Susan Linn, *Consuming Kids: Protecting Our Children from the Onslaught of*

Marketing and Advertising (New York: Anchor, 2005); Juliet B. Schor, *Born to Buy: The Commercialized Child and the New Consumer Culture* (New York: Scribner, 2005); Susan Gregory Thomas, *Buy, Buy Baby: How Consumer Culture Manipulates Parents and Harms Young Minds* (Boston: Houghton Mifflin, 2007); Benjamin Barber, *Consumed: How Markets Corrupt Children, Infantilize Adults, and Swallow Citizens Whole* (New York: W. W. Norton, 2007); Sharon Lamb, *Packaging Girlhood: Rescuing Our Daughters from Marketers' Schemes* (New York: St. Martin's Griffin, 2007); Deron Boyles, ed., *The Corporate Assault on Youth* (New York: Peter Lang, 2008); and Henry A. Giroux, *Youth in a Suspect Society: Democracy or Disposability?* (New York: Palgrave Macmillan, 2009), especially chapter 1, "Born to Consume: Youth and the Pedagogy of Commodification," 27–68.

15. With properties spread across a variety of markets, Disney can generate enormous profits from these latter outlets even if an animated film does not do well at the box office. For instance, the "animated films *Pocahantas* and *Hunchback of Notre Dame* were only marginal successes at the box office, with roughly $100 million in gross U.S. revenues, but both films will generate close to $500 million in profit for Disney, once it has exploited all other venues: TV shows on its ABC network and cable channels, amusement park rides, comic books, CD-ROMs, CDs, and merchandising." Robert W. McChesney, "Making Media Democratic," *Boston Review* 23, no. 3–4 (summer 1998): 4.

16. George R. Wright, *Selling Words: Free Speech in a Commercial Culture* (New York: New York University Press, 1997), 181.

17. Robert McChesney uses the phrase "commercial carpet bombing" and argues that "advertising should be strictly regulated or removed from all children's programming." See McChesney, "Making Media Democratic," 6–7.

18. Michael Jacobson and Laurie Ann Mazur cited in *We the Media*, eds. Don Hazen and Julie Winokur (New York: New Press, 1997), 40.

19. Wright, *Selling Words*, 182.

20. Gerald Grace, "Politics, Markets, and Democratic Schools: On the Transformation of School Leadership," in *Education: Culture, Economy, Society*, ed. A. H. Halsey et al. (New York: Oxford University Press, 1997), 315.

21. Quoted in Burton Bollag, "UNESCO Has Lofty Aims for Higher-Education Conference, but Critics Doubt Its Value," *Chronicle of Higher Education*, September 4, 1998, A76.

22. Press release, "Disney.com Break Records with 'Camp Rock' Online Streaming Event," Reuters, June 26, 2008, www.reuters.com/article/press Release/idUS126615+26-Jun-2008+BW20080626 (accessed August 4, 2009).

23. This story is based on Henry A. Giroux's own experience: "My three boys were watching television news clips of the Disney parade in New York City and were in awe that Disney could hold an extravaganza capable of tying up 30 city blocks while pulling out every stop in the glitzy grab bag of pomp

and spectacle. Of course, they couldn't wait to see the film, buy the spinoff toys, and be the first on their block to wear a Hercules pin. 'Pin? What pin I asked?' I hadn't watched the promotional ad carefully enough, which indicated that pins were sold with tickets to a special showing of the film *Hercules* before its general release date."

24. Michael D. Eisner, with Tony Schwartz, *Work in Progress* (New York: Random House, 1998), 414.

25. For excellent critical analysis of how toys limit the imaginations of children, see Stephen Kline, *Out of the Garden: Toys and Children's Culture in the Age of TV Marketing* (London: Verso, 1993), and Diane E. Levin and Barbara Rosenquest, "The Increasing Role of Electronic Toys in the Lives of Infants and Toddlers: Should We Be Concerned?" *Contemporary Issues in Early Childhood* 2, no. 2 (2001): 242–47. For an analysis of how marketing is spreading to different populations of youth in a variety of sites, see Larry Amstrong, "Is Madison Avenue Taking 'Get 'em While They're Young' Too Far?" *Business Week*, June 30, 1997, 62–67. For a critique of the commercialization of public schools, see Alex Molnar, *Giving Kids the Business: The Commercialization of America's Schools* (Boulder, CO: Westview Press, 1996), and Alex Molnar and Faith Boninger, *Adrift: Schools in a Total Marketing Environment* (The Tenth Annual Report on Schoolhouse Commercialism Trends: 2006–2007) (Tempe: Arizona State University, 2007), http://epsl.asu.edu/ceru/Annual%20reports/EPSL-0710-244-CERU.pdf (accessed July 28, 2009).

26. John Dewey, *Democracy and Education* (New York: Free Press, 1916).

27. Molnar, *Giving Kids the Business*, 17.

28. Andre Schiffrin, the director of the New Press, brilliantly illustrates how the takeover of the book-publishing industry by conglomerates is eliminating books that cannot be made into films or television series or achieve instant blockbuster status. The result has been that important literary works, scholarly books, books that are critical of corporate power, and others that do not fit into the for-profit formula driving the big publishing houses simply do not get published. This is no small matter, considering that independent and university publishers constitute only about 1 percent of the total sales in book publishing. See Andre Schiffrin, "Public-Interest Publishing in a World of Conglomerates," *Chronicle of Higher Education*, September 4, 1998, B4–B5.

29. Benjamin Barber, "The Making of McWorld," *New Perspectives Quarterly* 12, no. 4 (fall 1995): 13–17.

30. Robert W. McChesney, *Corporate Media and the Threat to Democracy* (New York: Seven Stories Press, 1997), 7.

31. McChesney, "Making Media Democratic," 4.

32. See Miller, "Free the Media," 9–15; see also John Keane, *The Media and Democracy* (London: Polity, 1991); Noam Chomsky, *Manufacturing*

Consent (New York: Pantheon, 1988); George Gerbner, Hamid Mowlana, and Herbert I. Schiller, *What Conglomerate Control of Media Means for America and the World* (Boulder, CO: Westview Press, 1996); Charles Derber, *Corporation Nation* (New York: St. Martin's, 1998); and C. Edwin Baker, *Media Concentration and Democracy: Why Ownership Matters* (Cambridge: Cambridge University Press, 2006).

33. Robert McChesney argues that this is not a call to abolish the commercial media but to make sure that it is not the dominant sector of the culture industry. Moreover, if the dominant sector is to be nonprofit, noncommercial, and accountable to the public, the commercial media should have a 1 percent tax levied on them to subsidize the noncommercial sector. He also calls for the leasing of spectrum space. See McChesney, *Corporate Media and the Threat to Democracy*, 67.

34. Makani Themba, "Holding the CEOs Accountable," in Hazen and Winokur, *We the Media*, 88.

35. Eyal Press, "Barbie's Betrayal: The Toy Industry's Broken Workers," *The Nation*, December 30, 1996, 12.

36. For a similar critique, see Eric Smoodin, ed., *Disney Discourse: Producing the Magic Kingdom* (New York: Routledge, 1994), and Norma Pecora, *The Business of Children's Entertainment* (New York: Guilford, 1998).

37. Robert McChesney argues that labor could subsidize nonprofit and noncommercial media without micromanaging them. For such media to flourish, they must remain independent. He writes, "We need a system of real public broadcasting, with no advertising, that accepts no grants from corporations or private bodies, and that serves the entire population, not merely those who are disaffected from the dominant commercial system and have to contribute during pledge drives." McChesney, "Making Media Democratic," 4–5.

Index

ABC, 26, 141
abuse, 106
Academy Awards, 136
accents, 110
accountability, 79, 153
acquisition, 32
activism, 130
actors, 39
addiction, 21
administration: liberal, 58; policy, 71; space, 160
admissions, 188
adult: environment, 92; films, 97; society, 23
adulthood, 89, 93
adventure, 74
advertising, xi; affirmation used in, 180; billboard, 208; dreams, 15–16; industry, 31; Internet, 4, 211
aesthetics, 101, 184
African Americans, 123
agency: collective, 162; critical, 52; individual, xii; sense of, 55; women's, 108
agenda, 6, 131, 225n30
Aladdin, 99, 109

alienation, 10, 87
allegory, 151
allusion, 182
alter ego, 84
altruism, 149
America. *See* U.S.
analysis, 129, 200
anarchy, 68
anger, 106
animation, 66; forms of, 91; hand-drawn, 112; tradition of, 186; unique capacity of, 137
animatronics, 36
anonymity, 26
antagonist, 172
anti-Semitism, 230n50
appropriation, 192
arcades, 244n20
archetype, 113
architecture, 70, 96
archives, 242n5
Ariel, 104–5, 208
artists, 219
asexuality, 82
assimilation, 192
attention deficit disorders, 66

received by, 97; normal, 17;
recruitment of, 223n14
China, 13
China Labor Watch. *See* CLW
choice, 30; ambiance of, 164; false,
    105
Christian Right, 45
citizenship: consumption model of,
    77; democratic, 13; replacing, 24
class, 18
cliché, 78, 107
Clinton, Bill, 141
Club Penguin, 62–63
CLW (China Labor Watch), 198
CNN, 26
Code of Conduct, 195
coercion, 146, 195
collaboration, 119
collectibles, 114
colonialism, 107; indoctrination into,
    192; stereotyping, 139
color, 111, 125
comedy, 137
comics, 66, 267n15
commodification, 100, 115
communication, 47
community: activism, 130; global,
    xii; lack of, 67; upscale, 95
competition, 24
computer-generated imagery. *See*
    CGI
computers, 69
concerts, 84
conformity, 70
conglomerate: media, 173; takeover,
    268n28
consciousness, 215
conservatism, 94; ideological, 125;
    staunch, 37
conspiracy, 193
construction, 92
consultants, 210

consumption: act of, 57; citizenship
    modeled on, 77; diffused,
    242–43n7; environment for, 41;
    extolling, 160; habits of, xii, 88;
    hyper, 13; image, 126; passive, 14
content, 65
context, 143
contracts, 197
contradictions, 32; free from, 190;
    message, 98
contributions, 77
control, 46; environmental, 39, 147;
    hierarchical, 52; media, 146
convention, 171
conversation, 68
copyright, 45, 93; hidden, 71; strict,
    242n5
corporations: accountability, 79;
    agenda, 6; ambivalence to, 163;
    benevolent, 13; consortium
    of, 100; cues from, 147;
    downsizing at, 31; ideology of,
    131; imperative of, 114; media,
    xii; multinational, 25, 166;
    regulating, 169; scrutiny of, 156;
    society swayed by, 90; utopia
    by, 38; voting at, 200. *See also*
    megacorporations
correctness, 142
corruption: consistent, 153–54;
    moral, 81
courtship, 122
creativity, 112
criticism: Disney, 93; Eisner
    handling, 140
critique, 57, 76
cross-promotion, 19, 83
cruise ships, 8, 120
culture: Americanization of, 159;
    appropriation of, 192; Arab, 109;
    ascendancy of, 155; battle over,
    15; children's, x, 19, 126; Disney,

Mickey Mouse Goes to Haiti, 194
Mickey Mouse Monopoly, 76, 217
middle-class: family, 81;
    imagination, 68; liberal, 73;
    position, 108; privileged, 111;
    taste, 44; values, 27
militarization, 135
miniseries, 141
minorities, 246n50
monopolies: global, 167; media, 12,
    59; preventing, 222n5
Monsters, Inc., 112
morality, 145; considerations of, 20;
    corruption of, 81; difficulties of,
    93; nostrums of, 44
motto, 49
MoveOn, 217
Mulan, 99
music, 80
musicals, 80
myth, 216

narcissism, 86, 224n26
narratives: alternative, 129; cliché in,
    107; commonsense, 11; counter,
    55, 199; extended, 144; rigid,
    105; transforming, 202
Native Americans, 109
Nazi, 135–36
NBC, 26
negotiation, 160
neoliberalism, 25, 199
networks: distribution, 5; global, 115
nostalgia: appropriating, 43; aura of,
    206; celebration with, 55; Disney
    invoking by, 9; generating, 65;
    imitating, 96; machine, 40;
    trademark, 123

Obama, Barack, 58
obedience, 50
obesity, 66

objectification, 85
optimism, 35
organization, 47
Orientalism, 111
Our Friend the Atom, 138
outsourcing, 31, 131
Ovitz, Michael, 175
ownership, 27

parents: concerns of, 27; responsible,
    42; today's, 61
parody, 79, 150
partnerships, 215
The Path to 9/11, 143
patriarchy, 107
patriotism, 31, 44
pedagogy, 1, 12; concerns of,
    159; entertainment related to,
    128; forces of, 219; forging of,
    125; sites of, 35; theme parks
    employing, 21
pedophilia, 229n34
peers, 83
Penelope, 124
perception, 2
persona, 33
perspective, 130
Peter Pan, 8
philosophy, 49, 181
Pinocchio, 113
*Pirates of the Caribbean: At World's
    End*, 170–72
Pixar, ix, 13
pixie dust, 47, 169
play: creative, 64; game, 203;
    scripted, 247n64
pleasure, 10, 127
Pocahontas, 99, 208
policy: administering, 71; Keynesian,
    228n30; labor, 50
politics: cultural, 6; me-centered,
    75; modes of, 203; partisan, 134;

About the Authors

Henry A. Giroux left the United States in 2004 to assume the Global Television Network Chair in English and Cultural Studies at McMaster University. His most recent books include *Take Back Higher Education*, coauthored with Susan Searls Giroux (2004); *The University in Chains: Confronting the Military-Industrial-Academic Complex* (2007); *Youth in a Suspect Society: Democracy or Disposability?* (2009); *Politics after Hope: Obama and the Crisis of Youth, Race, and Democracy* (2010); and *Hearts of Darkness: Torturing Children in the War on Terror* (2010).

Grace Pollock completed her doctoral degree in English and cultural studies at McMaster University in 2006, followed by a two-year postdoctoral fellowship at the University of Western Ontario. She is currently pursuing a masters' degree in social work at Wilfrid Laurier University, guided by the hope of building connections between critical theory and everyday cultural practices in a larger community setting. Her ongoing research interests include social policy development, cultural and media studies, and historical formations of the public sphere.